TOWARD A BETTER WORLD

TOWARD A BETTER WORLD

ADVENTURES OF A "MISSIONARY" ENGINEER

John R. Snell

WinePress Publishing
MUKILTEO, WA 98275

Toward a Better World
Adventures of a "Missionary" Engineer
© 1997, text by John R. Snell

Published by WinePress Publishing
PO Box 1406
Mukilteo, WA 98275

Cover by **DENHAM**DESIGN, Everett, WA

Printed in the United States of America.

Library of Congress Catalog Card Number: 97-60466
ISBN 1-57921-017-1

Dedicated to Florence, my life partner.

Contents

Selected Stories

Foreword

John R. Snell is a giant among men. Not just that his imposing physical stature commands attention—John Snell inspires people! He gives his best to the Master. He dedicates himself to the needs of people everywhere. In this, his book, John communicates his deepest thoughts and convictions to motivate the reader to the highest potential in life.

John tells an exciting story. His story. We deepen and enrich ourselves by reading the exploits of this multi-faceted entrepreneurial adventurer. As a child in Suzhou, China, he became interested in developing countries. That led quite naturally to thirty-five years of overseas work and university teaching. Ten years after he received his doctorate from Harvard (1938), he formed the Snell Environmental Group which continues on today. This was a natural development for a man deeply concerned about the environment and man's relationship to God as a steward of God's resources. He founded and continues to administer Bootstrap International, a philanthropic foundation that develops and supports farming and aquacultural projects in Belize, Central America.

John accepted environmental engineering challenges everywhere—in Michigan, New England, Venezuela, China, and Southeast Asia. His firm (a worldwide organization with 150 engineers) completed major projects in over twenty states and twenty-five foreign countries. Miles and miles of expressways. More than 100 bridges. Wastewater treatment plants. Treatment and soil utilization processes for solid waste. All were designed and developed with deep respect for the environment.

And although he made, lost, and regained fortunes in real estate and business, he always remained on the cutting edge of environmental engineering. Meanwhile, he is also recognized for having flown some five million miles to and from more than 100 countries.

John's and my common interest in community and worldwide service, the focus of Rotary International of which we are both members, brought us into a common bond. His invitation to share his Bootstrap International work was a recognition I did not take lightly. He is a visionary friend, and I have learned much from him.

During the past several years I have experienced John's reflective side. We have shared our thoughts and tales of foreign adventures. John has a story to tell. But he has more than a story—a sermon—his lifetime experiences. This octogenarian's mission drove him to dig deeply into his mind and into the past. In this book, he shares his life with the reader.

John does not hesitate to recognize his wife Florence as the love of his life, his confidant. She is the rudder that helped him maintain his course; she deserves all his acclamations.

Whatever vain thoughts may have crept into the manuscript are overshadowed by positive unselfish reflections that will leave indelible imprints on the discretionary reader. His story is not only a personal message for his family and friends, but also a lesson for all his readers.

The most important facet of his life, one that binds all his accomplishments into a meaningful legacy, is John's unswerving pursuit of Christian moral principles. He is a man of God. His reliance on the guidance of God's Holy Spirit has resulted in the development of programs that today serve his fellow human beings at home and abroad.

I pray that every reader will be challenged by John's story. It is a privilege and an honor to write this foreword. To God be the glory!

Dr. Dirk W. Vander Steen
1367 Bent Tree Dr.
Hudsonville, MI 49426

Introduction

Most people will agree that there are a lot more books written than should be. One might well ask if this is not one that belongs in this category? After all the author is not a celebrity and not even a writer. Why then was the decision made to spend the better part of two years researching the detail of one's life going back to 1912, and laying out of eighty-four years of my life adventure? Would this book be interesting and perhaps helpful to others and if so who?

I am grateful to the constant encouragement and urging of friends and especially to my mentor, Dr. Dirk Vander Steen. Dirk's friend Greta Rey, was an invaluable help to me professionally and with the final editing. I'm also deeply grateful to Cliff Kellemeyn for his professional help in final editing and publishing. It was Florence, my life partner of fifty-seven years, whose encouragement saw me through the hard times.

This book, the adventures of a long and busy life, is written especially for today's youth. The leaders of tomorrow are now being forged and need all the help they can get if they are going to rise to the challenge of building a new and better world.

If my life's story tells anything, it shows that an ordinary person with the right inspiration and encouragement can accomplish extraordinary things. Hard work and discipline can sometimes serve in the place of brains, strength, and talent. Even for the mind, schooled in today's secular thinking, there are many lessons of life and living buried in these adventures. To my secular friends I say keep an open mind to my experiences and what may be applicable and useful to yourself and others, and to the future leaders of the world. Think too of the alternative for one's life without considering the help of a wisdom beyond our own! Can we adequately solve the basic, more complex problems of mankind using only our flawed thinking?

One should not apologize for what they have written or how they have written it but after over forty years in the consulting field where one owned the firm and did much of the selling, one gets into the habit of describing accomplishments in a positive way and leaves off some of the humility which may not close the sale. Please overlook this long time habit as you find it.

For those who worry about retirement or getting older, I close with one very reassuring thought—look forward to life as it unfolds for the best is yet to come. It is quite possible that the last decade may be your very best. I feel strongly that what I will be led to do in the next ten years may be a greater contribution to mankind than that made in the eighty four years already past. Included with the contents is a list of twenty-four specific adventure stories, each with a title to help recall them, and a point of reference by chapter and page number. May you find the book entertaining and helpful and perhaps when you have finished you will pass it on to a friend.

Sincerely,
John R. Snell

CHAPTER ONE

Early Days in China

*D*estiny may be too powerful a word. Let us call it *appropriateness.*

It could be said that appropriately the author of this story, a civil and environmental engineer, was born on the banks of the Grand Canal of China at Suzhou on December 9, 1912. I say appropriately, for a major portion of my professional work was in designing and building waterways and systems and facilities for handling wastewater and other environmental situations.

The Grand Canal of China, about two thousand miles long and hand dug about two thousand years ago is, they say, the only manmade waterway in the world that can be seen from the moon. The Great Wall of China, they say, is the only other manmade structure that can also be seen from the moon. The great wall is a structure relating to war, whereas the Grand Canal was constructed for peace and prosperity.

Two coincidences of my early life stand out. First, my mother and father had met and dedicated their lives to each other at two Student Volunteer Movement national meetings. (The Student Volunteer Movement was a large Christian conference of potential missionaries held every four years.) As a young Methodist couple with missionary zeal they went to make their home and had their family in Suzhou, where my father, a surgeon, was medical director of a large hospital. My wife-to-be's parents also attended like conferences together, and also became life long missionaries in China. Some thirty years later, my wife-to-be and I had similar experiences at two Student Volunteer meetings, which were also the turning points in our lives.

Another coincidence also involved the two of us. I was the third child to be born to my parents but the first boy. In China much more importance is placed on male children; hence, upon my arrival my father was given the full esteem of the Chinese accorded a father in raising a family. The period of 1911-12 was essentially a period of revolution in China. Its old imperial form of government was giving way to its beginning form of democracy, and the Republic of China had a national assembly. Another missionary family, the Lacy Moffetts living not too far from Suzhou, had five boys and no girls. During this period of the revolution and fighting, when Sun Yat-Sen created the Chinese Republic, the Moffetts were forced to seek refuge in Suzhou for a few months. There, exactly a year and a day before I came, was born to them their first girl, Florence. Exactly twenty-eight years later Florence and I were married.

In 1912 Suzhou was a city of about 500,000 located about fifty miles inland from Shanghai, the largest city in China. Only a few years before my birth a railway had been built north from Shanghai, but before that transportation was mainly by slow boat along the Grand Canal and its tributaries. Suzhou was often referred to as the Venice of China because of all the canals within the city. It was a walled city about three miles square with a canal moat both inside and outside the city wall. There were both land and water gates to the wall, and these were guarded and closed at a certain hour each night for general security of the city. The cobblestone streets were very narrow and dirty and bounded by either residence or shop walls on each side. Suzhou had no water supply or sewer system as we know them today. The canals served in both capacities. They also carried heavy transportation and disposed of storm water, which also served the useful purpose of being a means of flushing.

Fortunately for their public health the Chinese boiled most of their drinking water. For centuries the Chinese had practiced recycling both forms of the raw, undiluted human fecal matter by fertilizing their rice and vegetable fields from open boats.

In 1912 there were almost no electric lights in the cities, homes, and stores, which were lit instead by kerosene lamps. Cooking was also quite primitive with almost everyone using rice straw or now and then charcoal.

Although Suzhou was at the same latitude as New Orleans and very hot in the summer months, it did snow some and was cold and damp in the winter. There was no such thing as central heat; in fact, any form of heating in homes was almost nonexistent. To keep warm during the winter season, more and more layers of clothes were put on in the fall as it got colder and taken off in the spring as the weather warmed.

Modern medicine and sanitation were generally unavailable to the Chinese people, and knowledge of modern science and technology virtually unknown. Before the arrival of the missionaries there was little chance that things would have improved soon. Suzhou was more fortunate than most Chinese cities in that several church denominations had built and placed their efforts in various parts of the city. The Southern Methodists, who supported the work of my parents, also had established over several decades a nearby university of growing reputation.

Until I was about five years of age our family lived in a home without any of the modern conveniences. When I became five years old we moved into to a very modern home complete with clean hot and cold running water, flush toilets, electric lights, and central heat, including a coal-fired cookstove. Our home was part of a larger project to build in Suzhou the largest and most modern hospital in that part of China, with two hundred and fifty beds and a very large outpatient department. When Dad had started his work at Suzhou, the hospital was housed in one older residence with almost no up-to-date facilities and largely untrained personnel.

My mother described the event of my birth in her diary: "He was a laughing, dancing baby, and full of fun!" During the first two or three years of our lives we children—eventually to be seven altogether—were cared for by a Chinese nanny known as an amah. This arrangement gave my mother time to do many of the other things expected of her, including work with the women's groups in the church, the Sunday school, and care of the home education of us kids. It also had one distinct advantage for us kids: we each learned spoken Chinese, easily as children, and without an accent. The family also had two other servants, a cook and a coolie, or gardener. Even with a Chinese cook we ate American-style food except for perhaps one Chinese meal a week.

Everyone seemed to worry for me that I did not have any boys my own age to play with. That was not my worry, for I found many things to occupy my time but did not always keep out of trouble. By the time I was ready for school my mother had settled on the Calvert School Correspondence method as the best way for children like us to get an education. Most of the time she was the one to teach us.

In retrospect I can say that I learned a lot about most things, but the two things I did not especially like were reading and spelling. Needless to say, weakness in these two areas stayed with me the rest of my life. Science and math were interesting and easy for me, which helped me later to take up engineering.

From an early age I liked mechanical and scientific things. We had a Chinese carpenter who had a small shop within our walled yard. I watched him by the hour, and he took a special interest in me. He taught me to do the simpler things until I got quite good in woodworking. I even made a beautiful model sailboat and a small paddlewheel boat large enough for me to use in the canals.

My father and I together loved to hunt ducks. Also, now and then, we went some ten miles away on a houseboat to the Suzhou hills to hunt deer. I being the only boy in the family was allowed to go with my dad starting at age five. I was given a .22 rifle and a 20-gauge shotgun at an early age and did a lot of hunting on my own when my dad was unable to go.

Dad asked me to go with him whenever he went to make inspection trips to the southern part of the city where he had built a much-needed modern dairy with about thirty milk cows brought in from overseas. This dairy supplied clean milk for some of the urgent needs of the city and was the only one in Suzhou.

About 1920 my father also saw the great need of a modern

brick-and-tile factory in that part of China, raised the capital, and imported the technology for such a venture. It supplied the brick and tile not only for the new hospital but for many of the new buildings going up in Shanghai and elsewhere.

Naturally, seeing all these things going on under my father's general supervision created a lot of interest within me and taught me a great deal, which I am sure helped to mold my future. Although Dad always seemed to want me to get interested in medicine and follow in his footsteps, he never pushed me in that direction.

During the construction of the new hospital I would take delight in accompanying my dad on his routine inspections and learned a lot about all phases of the building of the structures as well as of a deep artesian well, an ammonia ice plant, and the direct-current electric plant which were part of the hospital project. I even persuaded Dad to let me sift a couple of hundred cubic yards of mortar sand for the project at ten cents per yard. The large project also inspired me to construct on my own, at age ten, a rather large chicken house complete with a tile roof.

A couple of years later, about twenty-five of the small direct-current electric fans the hospital had purchased burned out and instead of being thrown away were given to me to see what I could do with them. This started a long and interesting project for me where I also learned a lot about electricity. By exchanging parts and improvising this and that I was able to have at my disposal a dozen working fans or motors which I put to every conceivable use, including fans and lighting in my tree house.

About this time in my young life a civil war was going on in China, and the new hospital designed for two hundred fifty patients had to take in four hundred to five hundred patients, mostly wounded soldiers. I used to help out by developing X ray film needed to help locate the bullets. On Sun Yat-Sen's death on March 12, 1925, Chiang Kai-shek took over. It took two years to consolidate power from the many warlords.

I frequently stood on a low stool and watched my dad operate. One day I was watching when a patient who had been several days en route to the hospital was cut open, and there was an unexpected spurt of pus onto the floor. This turned my stomach and proved to be more than I was able to handle. I didn't want to embarrass my father to have his number one son faint on his operating room floor. Just in time I got the answer to my dilemma. I quietly got down off the stool. Although my shoestrings did not need tying, I tied them, and this gave a chance for the blood to run back into my head. I did not faint after all.

I remember another time when my dad needed his one and only platinum electric cautery to operate on a cancer, but it had come apart and needed to be welded. I had been playing around with homemade arc lights made from the carbon cores of large A batteries. After some experimentation I was able to weld the cautery so it would work properly for the operation the next day. But the strong ultraviolet light being emitted from the arc so affected my eyes, to which I had not provided the benefit of dark glasses, that I was sure I was going to go blind that night. Fortunately, they were almost well the next day.

These were the early days of the crystal set radios, and with one we could pick up Shanghai if we used our headphones and long high antenna. With the help of some diagrams I was able to build the first simple tube set in Suzhou, with which we were able to use a loudspeaker and hear Shanghai programs more easily, including news and modern music..

Twice a year my folks placed a big order to Montgomery Ward in the United States. One usually arrived just before Christmas with its many happy surprises. Tools for a very enjoyable workshop were one of the gifts that affected my life, as I would spend days there making about anything one could imagine.

Having a walled-in yard, I was able to have pets without the danger of their running away. Among the pets was a friendly monkey I had a lot of fun with. However, he would take great delight in hiding on a low branch that extended over the main walkway leading to the house. When a stranger came in, the monkey would reach down and grab the stranger's hat.

We also had a pet deer, brought to us by a Chinese friend, and my sister Dorothy raised him on a bottle until he could eat grass. The deer and our English pointer, Jip, were the best of friends and would play together, but when the dog went out hunting he forgot all about his friend the deer at home.

Jip was like a brother to me. We could communicate almost like humans. I would take him hunting whenever I went out. One of my favorite places was the rice fields around the Ink Pagoda, about a mile from us. It was a boarded-up pagoda with rickety old wooden steps leading up to the top, about six stories high. The pigeon hunting there was excellent, but it was a very scary place for an eight-to-ten-year-old going all by himself at all times of day, especially since it was boarded up and I knew that I was not supposed to enter. It was kind of my secret place to go with some special excitement.

There were, however, some side effects of this venture. Often I dreamed about it, and as dreams might evolve, they got worse and worse, and I would end up hearing and almost seeing a monster or ghost in the top of the pagoda every time I entered. It got to be such a recurrent bad dream or nightmare over ten years, that the only way I could stop it was to train myself so that every time I sensed the nightmare coming on in my sleep I was able to physically pinch myself and wake up before the worst of the dream would start.

The plan worked.

Now and then Dad and I took a houseboat overnight to the Suzhou hills, hunted deer all day, and returned the following night. Sometimes we would stay out two or even three days. These were great times together, and we would think nothing of hiking up and down those steep hillsides twenty to thirty miles in a day. However, my favorite hunting was for duck. We would find a good place outside the east side of the city and prepare for the ducks to come in and feed on their favorite paddy fields right at dusk. The distinct sound of the whir of their wings always sent chills up and down my spine. The key was to pick just the right instant to fire and the right distance to lead the fast-moving target with the sights. Until then the dog had been quivering but waiting patiently. When the duck fell into the paddy field, his turn came and he was always able to find and bring the duck in. He seemed to appreciate our thanks to him for his efforts.

Summer was Dad's busiest time at the hospital, for it was then that the diseases of China were at their peak. Cholera was the most dreaded and deadly. I shall never forget when the father of one of my American friends came down with it and in forty-eight hours was dead. Malaria also was a dreaded but much more common disease, for it was transmitted by the anopheles mosquito. With it came frequent chills and high fever, and the only treatment for it was quinine, but this was at times slow to act and not too effective. As a result, there were deaths. Each of us kids would get malaria from time to time despite the fact that we used mosquito nets at night. It was always a scary thing to have one of the family come down with those sudden severe chills, and especially when the high fever brought on delirium before it could be brought under control. Smallpox and diphtheria were also common in Suzhou.

One of my earliest memories was at age five. I had come down with a bad case of mastoiditis, an infection of the inner ear. In those days, long before wonder drugs like penicillin, one had to be operated on promptly to have the infection imbedded in the bone cut out or one would not live too long, for the infection would often spread to the brain. Normally a surgeon does not operate on his own child or even a relative. But in my case there was no other option, so Dad did the job. Dad was a very efficient man, and he figured while I was on the operating table already under ether, he would remove my appendix too, because I would likely have it done anyway at a later time, and this would save time and expense.

I remember well when the Rockefeller Foundation sent a Dr. Mellony to China to make a special study of a very bad but quite common disease called schistosoma, which had as an intermediate host a small snail living in the canals. I was delighted to be selected by Dr. Mellony to collect for his experiments a good supply of these snails.

Many of the missionaries got away from the sweltering heat of Suzhou to a summer resort, Mokanshan, in a mountainous area about a long day and night's travel by houseboat from Suzhou. Dad couldn't get away, and Mother felt it was better to keep the family together in the Suzhou heat than to have the family separated. As a result we only got up to the resort once, when I was six years old. I remember the summer as having been pleasant but felt that the family made the right decision to stay together and find ways to lessen the effects of the super Suzhou summer heat. We made a small home swimming place from a fifteen-foot diameter fish pool. Now and then we boated in the canals or sailed in the big Taiho Lake ten miles away. Outdoor silent movies at the University and homemade ice cream all helped.

Every seven years the mission board gave its missionaries a furlough year to return to the United States. The time was not only for rest and vacation but for professional updating and visits to churches to raise money. The furlough I remember was when I was ten, and it made a lasting impression on me. My mother's older sister Aunt Anna and her husband Uncle Jim, a minister, made available to us his father's spacious house in National City, a suburb of San Diego, California. My uncle's father, who had just passed on, had been a retired sea captain. My uncle also made available his father's car, which was an old Marion open touring car.

The large house had beautiful lawns and an acre of orange and lemon trees. I told my uncle that I would take care of the orchard and the lawns, and for my services he paid me ten dollars per month. I spent hours on some of the super big trees. And I used to like to sit up in the tree and eat oranges and lemons. In fact, I sucked so many lemons up against my teeth that it eroded the enamel, adversely affecting my teeth the rest of my life.

Unfortunately, Dad had to be away at various medical centers much of that year, but twice he took the older children off on trips. The first was a delightful but short camping trip, a warmup for the real trip which was a two-week camping trip to Yosemite National Park. Our family never forgot the glories and pleasures of that trip. I also remember well my uncle taking me sea fishing on several occasions when he and my aunt visited from Tennessee. While in National City I came down with my second bad inner ear infection, which ended with a specialist from San Diego performing another mastoidectomy. But at least my dad did not have to operate on me as he had when I was only five.

The three-week boat trips from China to the United States and back were memorable occasions, not only for the luxury of the ships but our experiencing the vastness of the Pacific Ocean and watching the porpoises and flying fish. Even the experience of rough weather and sea sickness made their indelible impression. As we came near China's Yangtze River, the deep blue of the ocean gave way to the turbid yellow of the river, and when we saw the junks we knew we were close to home. All that was left was a two-hour train trip and we were back in Suzhou. Despite the fun and adventure of our furlough trip we were excited to be home again.

When we kids were ready for the eighth grade we were enrolled at the Shanghai American School, which was a boarding school. When my time came to go I was twelve, going on thirteen. My two older sisters had preceded me, so I knew what to expect. They were to be five very happy and meaningful years of my life, ones when I made many lifetime friends and grew in ways not possible as a young child living at home virtually without male playmates near my own age.

In retrospect I would not have traded those first twelve years of being brought up in Suzhou for an equal time of being reared in a wealthy part of America. It was a time when Suzhou's old-culture (although changing) environment joined with my heritage to form the deep clear springs from which my whole life grew—the stuff from which my destiny was born and nurtured.

CHAPTER TWO

Shanghai American School

A lumni of the Shanghai American School (SAS) have a loyalty to their alma mater as great as any that exists toward any high school in the United States. The SAS campus, constructed about 1922 in the French Concession of Shanghai on the western outskirts of the city, taught about 250 day students and 250 boarding students in kindergarten through high school. The majority of the students in this private school were children of American or British missionaries and business people. (In the early 1900s China was forced to grant areas of Shanghai and other major cities to foreign countries. Each country controlled and had jurisdiction over its "concession.")

Graduates had little problem being admitted to the better colleges and universities in the United States, for our teachers were well qualified. The principal, Dr. Elam J. Anderson, administered the school well, and though strict, was respected by the students. He taught a required course called music appreciation, which I enjoyed and from which I acquired my lifelong love of good music, including classical.

About every other week the school put on a good black-and-white silent film. On Sunday evenings boys and girls could date by walking together around a large grass quadrangle surrounded by the three main buildings. Week nights there were formal study halls, and lights were off at ten.

The academic program was balanced with a good athletic program. We high school students competed very favorably against the area's Chinese colleges in everything except American football. Here our only competitors were the United States Marines, and we gave them some good games. Soccer, basketball, and track were other major sports, with tennis and baseball also popular.

When I came to SAS at age twelve in the eighth grade I was about five feet six inches tall and weighed under one hundred pounds. Through my junior year my classmates looked at me as a runt, but a tough little runt. At the end of that year I started to grow like a weed, and by the time I started my senior year was six feet three inches tall and weighed 135 pounds. Still very light, I was now able to enter into sports and make letters for soccer and American football. My height helped me to get into the position of left end. I will never forget one game especially. We did not wear helmets in those days. I made a hard tackle, leading too much with my head rather than my shoulders. I stopped my man, all right, but was, to say the least, confused. For two plays I lined up on the wrong team before it was noticed and I was taken out of the game. In track and field I got a start in distance running and high jump, and in soccer I played fullback on the first team.

SAS also had a strong chess team which successfully competed with the area colleges. My father had trained me in chess when I was very young, and now I was captain and number one player on our team. Tournaments were sponsored by the Shanghai Chess Club, and meets were often refereed by the Shanghai champion. One day my game ended way ahead of the other six games, and the champ suggested in a very friendly way that he and I have a game. He offered to start off by giving me his queen, which is a tremendous handicap. I took up his offer to play but declined any handicap. I guess I was lucky that day, for I beat him, much to his embarrassment.

SAS provided an environment in which to make lifelong friends. My two older sisters, Lura and Dorothy, and I traveled home to Suzhou for a weekend every four to five weeks, for the Christmas and Easter holidays, and for the summer vacation. Frequently we included a close friend or two as our guests, and at other times planned ahead for a deer hunt in the Suzhou hills. My senior year we hosted my whole class on a three-day outing to the hills on Chinese houseboats.

Two of these fellows and I did a lot of things together: John Caldwell and Lincoln Brownell. During the spring of our senior year the three of us decided to make the fifty-four mile hike from Shanghai to Suzhou in one day. To our knowledge no one had ever done this, but youth rises to a challenge. A month ahead we began practice walking so as to get in shape.

We started out one morning at five from the Shanghai railroad station, to which we had taken a taxi. We walked along the tracks until ten in the evening when we reached the Suzhou station, got in a rickshaw, and went to my home. That is, Lincoln and I did. About two thirds of the way John had gotten leg cramps and had to take the train the rest of the way. All of our leg muscles were very sore for a month.

Although I don't remember any teenage problems with my parents, I must come clean and admit that the seeds of problems were within me and did come out with the school authorities. One April Fools Day Lincoln Brownell and I thought we needed some excitement and decided to ring the school's main fire bell, which was in the middle of the grass quadrangle about two hundred feet from the nearest building. To merely ring the alarm and run, even after dark, was too risky. Instead, we tied a long stout string to the bell and laid it along the grass to the corner of the administration building, where the boys' dormitory occupied the third floor. After ringing the bell loudly and clearly we quickly walked up the three flights of stairs, slipped off our clothes, and jumped into bed. After no more than three minutes the principal made a dormitory inspection in which he found both of us innocently tucked in bed. The next day the whole student body was sternly lectured on the gravity of the act and told that, if caught, the culprit or culprits would certainly be expelled. Lincoln and I were on opposite sides of what was best to do. Fortunately, my view—to remain quiet—prevailed.

The night before graduation, Scott Crawford and I decided it would be a lot of fun to paint our class year in bright red four-foot-high numerals on the four sides of the white cupola that topped the administration building. In this case everyone else thought it was rather fun too, except for the administrators, and they were too occupied with the details of graduation to spend time finding the culprits. Hence the big red numerals remained. The following year Chinese professional painters were employed to paint the administration building. Thinking that the red numerals were part of the building's decoration, they repainted them too, but in a professional way.

Normally I would have spent that summer at home and then taken a ship across the Pacific to the United States to go to college, but my good friends the Brownells were planning for their whole family to return to the United States by way of Europe and invited me to go with them. The price for me, to be paid by the mission board, would be the same as going directly across the Pacific. If I were to go third class on the ship and on the trains in Europe and watch my other costs, my expenses would be covered. The Brownells would be going second class. We were to take the *President Fillmore* from Shanghai to Europe, trains across Europe, and the Canadian Pacific's *Duchess of Bedford* across the Atlantic to Montreal. The Brownells had relatives to meet them in Montreal with cars and a truck for their baggage to take them to their home in Burlington, Vermont. From there I would hitchhike to Nashville, Tennessee, to enter Vanderbilt University. After a final week at home my dad came to Shanghai with me and saw me off on the *Fillmore* on June 25, 1930.

The voyage took us to the Pacific rim countries and included Hong Kong, Manila, Singapore, and Colombo (pleasant colonial places in those days), to the Near East and up the Red Sea. We visited Cairo, the pyramids, Alexandria, and proceeded to Naples, Italy. We were captivated by then-active Mount Vesuvius, Pompeii, and Rome, where in an audience with the pope I only pretended to kiss his ring. We next went by train to Milan, through the Swiss Alps to Geneva and on to Paris, then by channel boat to London.

At this point my finances were running very low. I just missed getting on a work-my-way basis on the *Leviathan* so took third-class passage on the *Duchess of Bedford* to cross the Atlantic. The Brownells' second-class ticket allowed them to proceed all the way to Montreal, whereas I learned that my third-class ticket put me off in Quebec, about 150 miles short of Montreal. I disembarked in Quebec at about six in the evening and needed to meet them at their ship in Montreal by ten the next morning. I had heard so much about hitchhiking in America I decided to try it. I lucked out, was on the road all night, and in Montreal on time to meet them. After a couple of days' rest in Burlington, I hitchhiked to Cleveland, Ohio, to spend a day with my sister Lura, who was a student at Oberlin College, before I hitchhiked the final leg of the journey to Nashville.

Thus ended what were perhaps the most memorable and educational two and a half months of my young life, certainly equivalent to a year in college. And now I was ready for the real thing.

CHAPTER THREE

Vanderbilt

I planned to follow in my dad's footsteps and take up medicine when I entered Vanderbilt University in 1930.

With only twelve hundred students, Vanderbilt had an excellent reputation. My mother and father had met there in Nashville when she was at student in Peabody College and he in Vanderbilt Medical School. My sister Dorothy was already there studying nursing. Vanderbilt gave us missionary kids an automatic 50 percent tuition scholarship. My favorites, Uncle Jim and Aunt Anna, lived in Nashville as did two cousins, so except for the badly polluted air from soft coal burning, Nashville seemed almost perfect.

I stayed with my uncle for about a week until I was registered and settled in Kissam Hall, the main men's dormitory. Although I had received a letter of acceptance from Vanderbilt while I was passing through London, I still had to talk my situation over with the registrar. Unfortunately, the fine print in Vanderbilt's admission rules stated that to enter the premedical program the student had to have three years of Latin. I had not cared for Latin at Shanghai American School and had taken extra math for the third year instead. Of course, I had not known that this earlier choice would affect my planned admission to Vanderbilt's pre-med program.

The registrar suggested that I could stay out and make up that missing year of Latin, which was distasteful to me. His second suggestion was excellent: to register in engineering for the first term and then, if I wished, transfer to pre-med at the end of the first term and no questions would be asked by the university.

Knowing nothing about engineering, I registered in that field. Within three months I learned a lot of what engineering was all about and simultaneously had a good chance to see what medicine offered. I talked it over with my uncle, my professors, friends, and advisor and corresponded with Dad. Then I came to know that I was supposed to become an engineer, not a doctor, and elected civil as the type of engineering I would study.

It did not take me long to find out that studying engineering at Vanderbilt was a lot tougher and more time consuming than anything I had done in high school. My weaknesses from grade school—reading and spelling—caught up with me, and among my A's and B's I came up with an E in freshman English. I realized I had to spend extra time in these studies and consequently did much better from there on.

We were exceedingly fortunate in the engineering school, for not only did it have its own math division but our exceptional teacher inspired almost everyone in his class by his positive approach. Vanderbilt's policy was that those who were not going to make good engineers should be weeded out in the fist two years. They used math and a statics course (the first course in structures) to separate the sheep from the goats. Only about 50 percent of the students passed statics. I found both of these courses easy and very interesting. As a result, my confidence in the decision to become an engineer grew, and with that confidence I worked even harder.

Since I was not what academic people would term really bright, it is fortunate that early in my college career I learned that hard work and a lot of study went a long way toward making up for brilliance. I came out to be second in my class of about fifty in engineering.

The private proverb I lived by was, "Never let your lessons interfere with your education." In other words, if I was 100% caught up in studying, it was fine to take time off for other interests or educational fun. After my first term in the dormitory I found a much less expensive and more efficient way by taking a spare room in a home belonging to a little old lady who made it available to me for firing her furnace. I also found how inexpensive corn flakes and diluted canned milk were for breakfast and often for lunch. I would then eat supper in the cafeteria and toward the end of the year had a part-time job there as well. I often was invited to my uncle's home or one of my cousin's for Sunday dinner and made the most of such occasions.

My parents' furlough was to be from summer 1931 to summer 1932, and they decided to make Nashville their headquarters. Dorothy and I were already there, and Martha, the next younger one, was to start college in a year. We leased a very nice home on Gale Lane on the southern edge of town, really in the country.

Lura graduated from Oberlin and joined Dorothy and me, and the three of us drove to San Francisco in a new Chevy we had been authorized to buy. When the family arrived from China, Dad bought a good used Chrysler, and we stared out on a planned trip to see national parks and other places of great interest, using both cars for our family of nine. After a swing north through Oregon and Washington, we spent the better part of a month camping in Yellowstone National Park.

Unfortunately, while in Oregon my sister Martha grew ill, so she and Mother went to Nashville by train and left the rest of us to our camping. This suited Mother fine, for she never cared for camping.

The next ten months were memorable while the whole Snell family lived together on Gale Lane. Our being in the country enabled us to have both a horse and a cow. The horse was essentially Dorothy's, and she loved it. I remember trying it out a couple of times, but that was enough. A horse has a way of sensing whether its rider likes it or perhaps is a little afraid of it. I'm not sure which conclusion our horse came to about me. But I will never forget one day when he ran me under some trees in our yard where the branches were unusually low, and I saw he had the full intent of brushing me off onto the ground. Needless to say, that was the last time I took the horse for a ride.

Now the cow was a different matter. She had to be milked early in the morning and again in the evening. The task of milking fell to me, but I was not what you would call an early-morning person, in part because sometimes I had to study late in the evening. I came up with the idea of using the strategy of Huckleberry Finn on my nine-year-old brother Fred, who was small for his age. He rose to my challenge that he was too small for a task such as this but he wanted to do it so much that he begged me to teach him. So we both were very happy, and I limited my milking time to evenings.

Dad spent much of his time studying at the medical center at Vanderbilt but was home with the family well over half of the time. He got to know many good surgeons, including one specializing in plastic surgery. The time was right for this doctor friend to take me in hand and operate on both of my ears, which had been slightly malformed since birth but could be properly corrected only after I was fully grown. I never realized until after the surgery and I became (by comparison) a nice looking fellow that this was one of the reasons I had been quite shy. Although people had never really made fun of my "lop" ears, I certainly had a great feeling about myself after they were corrected and no longer a hindrance.

At the end of the ten months the family split up and we went our own ways. I had to attend six weeks of summer surveying camp in the Spartan Mountains. Lura and Dorothy kept the rented house going with the financial aid of boarders until the year's lease was up. The rest of the family drove the old Chrysler back across the continent. Dad felt that he needed to get back to his work at Suzhou Hospital as soon as possible.

At summer's end my three sisters and I decided to lease a large inexpensive apartment and keep house together. In this way I had to cook for a week once every four weeks. This was good for me although a bit hard on my sisters.

After summer camp I was fortunate to land a six-week job with the United States Corps of Engineers maintaining navigation signals on the Tennessee River. By my junior year I was past the basic preparatory courses and took up the more interesting professional courses, enjoying them very much. During the next two years President Roosevelt's National Recovery Act (NRA) program went into effect, and jobs were created for workers and students alike. One of the jobs on the campus was to form a surveying team and map the whole campus in detail. I was lucky to be the chief of the team and earned fifty cents an hour while everyone else earned thirty-five cents. The job was excellent experience and helped to buy groceries as well.

Although Vanderbilt's student politics and intramural athletics revolved around the fraternity groups, the major intramural sports being soccer and basketball, our nonfraternity group took the cups for both sports and also got some of our people on the student council. In addition to playing on the two winning intramural teams, I enjoyed regular workouts with the varsity track and field team, although I never won any events for them.

An engineering classmate, Bob Taylor, and I in 1932 purchased a 1928 Chevy, which had been hit head-on by a train, for twenty-five dollars. It took us most of the term—when we took the machine shops course and worked a lot of extra time—to tear apart the car almost to the last nut and bolt, straighten out the bent parts, and put it back together. The wood-framed body was completely shot, but we put in the back and front seats and put boards up just high enough to keep people from falling out. It needed no horn, for we had fixed a bypass around the muffler directly to the open air, and this could be opened up by pulling a wire. That year the Ford V-8s came out. We had little trouble out-accelerating them from a stoplight; the four-cylinder engine took us up to eighty miles per hour in a hurry.

That spring the Tennessee State Fair put on a much advertised race for all cars valued under fifty dollars, and I was elected to race ours. As the race was about to get underway the judge called all the drivers over to him and said, "Men, this is going to be one hell of a race! Run, jump in your cars, and drive once around the track in reverse gear." The one-mile dirt track was wet and very slippery. We were supposed to race around the track in a clockwise direction, so I jumped in our car, turned it around, and took off. The other forty-five or so cars (two didn't even have any reverse gear) just took off and started around the track in the wrong direction. Since the judge had not made clear his point of direction around the track, he felt that the only thing he could do was to turn me around the second time and have me follow the others around the track counterclockwise. My double delay turned out to give me a real advantage; it gave the rest of the racers time to become somewhat unclogged, which made it much easier for me to pass one at a time in a safe manner. By the time I had reached the final straightaway I had passed the last car and was the clear winner. I went in to collect my first prize, which everyone thought would be about one hundred dollars. We were shocked to find it was only five dollars. The worst of it was that to win we had raced the engine at top speed for almost two full minutes, and the car was never the same again.

After the race we had one very close call with the car before we decided to get rid of it. Late one afternoon I took eight of us out for a drive to show everyone that there was no problem going eighty on a straight concrete country road. As fate would have it, a car pulled out of a side road and did not hear our horn in time. The driver could not stop until his car completely blocked both lanes of the highway and stalled there. With only two wheel brakes, it was impossible for me to slow to less than fifty miles per hour. By the time we reached the stalled car in the middle of the road, I was able to pull our car over onto the right dirt shoulder, and we missed him by only a few inches. I learned my lesson from that experience and never took such chances again.

During Christmas vacation of my sophomore year I drove a group of six China-born missionary kids from Nashville to Buffalo to attend a Student Volunteer conference (a church-related organization concerned mainly with missionary work). The group included both Florence and her brother Bobby and three others. I had gone from eighth grade through high school at Shanghai American School with Florence and Bobby. It was on this trip that I first grew to have a deep feeling for Florence, but for another four years it was mainly a one-way feeling. During those four years at Vanderbilt I was so busy, I really didn't have any time for girls. It was study or work, with no money for dates. Besides, I was still very shy.

Once I borrowed a 1931 Ford roadster and visited Florence at Queens College in Charlotte, North Carolina. That trip had one close call and one stroke of bad luck. I was doing about seventy on a wet asphalt road going through the Smoky Mountains when I came over a sharp hill and saw about one hundred cattle all over the road. This was well before antilock breaks, and one of my brakes did lock, causing a bad skid. I went down into the ditch, came back out, spun around, and could then reach out and touch the nearest cow. I had just missed hitting any. When I reached Queens College I found Florence. We hadn't sat and talked in the car more than fifteen minutes when the night watchman came up and said that school hadn't started and it was against the rules for me to be there. I had to turn around and drive all the way home to Nashville. I should have learned earlier in life not to be so shy.

A group of us would make an occasional trip to a friend's home on the Cumberland River to swim and go water skiing. And now and then other friends near Percy Warner Park invited our group out to hike and have a picnic. It was on one of these picnics to the park, on a beautiful spring day, that I was walking alone with a girl in our group who seemed to have a real attraction to me and I to her when I had my first and only kiss in my four years in college.

I often made time to attend youth fellowship at the Methodist church and now and then go roller skating. I took my sister Dorothy to a "Vandy" gym dance, for she enjoyed it a lot and was trying to teach me to dance. I accepted a bet for ten dollars on January 1, 1933, that I wouldn't dare to swim in the Cumberland River. Even though the air temperature was below 20 degrees and the water about 35 degrees, I jumped in, swam around, and won my bet.

The summer of 1933, at the bottom of the Great Depression, jobs were impossible to find. I had just finished my third year of civil engineering at Vanderbilt. As survey chief in the NRA project to map the campus I had made fifty cents per hour. With the boarding house job for room and board, and with my fifty dollars per month mission scholarship I had been able to get by for all my expenses and was perhaps a couple of hundred dollars ahead. Now the only job around was to scrape plaster off salvaged bricks for a dollar a day. That was not enough to make staying in Nashville for the summer worthwhile. I figured that perhaps this was the summer for a very inexpensive break, even an outdoor vacation. One of my best friends from the Shanghai American School, Bernard Billings, and I had been writing each other for some time. Why not take the summer and work our way to Alaska on a ship, then go down the Yukon River in a canoe, which was the height of adventure?

Bernard was taking aeronautical engineering at the University of Washington. The first thing was for me to get out there; then we would try to work our way on a ship to Alaska. I had become an expert at hitchhiking and made my way to the west coast from Nashville for less than five dollars. I averaged 450 miles a day. To save money I carried a couple of blankets and slept out at night. I remember two nights that were too cold. I approached the police department to see if they would put me up overnight for free in their jail. In one case it was fine, but after the experience of the second place I vowed never to try it again. Fleas, bedbugs, and filth, plus being locked in all night, were not for me.

After a disappointing time over eight days trying to get a work-for-free job on a ship to Alaska we decided to hitchhike to Bernard's uncle's place in Missoula and then figure out where to camp out in Montana for the summer. Just as we got to Missoula several families were planning a Fourth of July weekend hike to the highest peak in the Mission Mountains, just over 10,000 feet. We accepted their invitation to join them. There were about twenty in the party.

We drove about one hundred miles and backpacked into a good overnight camping place about twelve miles from the road. It was a very wild and wooded terrain, and we saw evidence of many wild animals, including the big brown bear. The next morning the plan was to go to the summit and return on the same day. We took only lunches and light jackets. It was an interesting but very easy hike up a trail well known to those who had been there before. With women and kids along, stopping and resting, and eating lunch, it was almost four in the afternoon when we were about to descend the easy but somewhat long return trail.

I thought I would like to have a little more fun and excitement on the return trip to the camp and asked if anyone would be interested in joining me in taking a much shorter way back by just heading off in a rather direct but uncharted direction down the mountain and through the wooded part. There were no volunteers. I really wanted to go that way so much that I said I was going by myself and would see them back at the camp.

As I bade my new friends good-bye and headed off in the direction I estimated the camp to be, I realized that my decision to venture into the wilds alone was perhaps poor judgment and born of inexperience. I knew I was breaking a cardinal rule of the mountains: Never go off by yourself. I was twenty, weighed about 150 pounds, and was six feet four inches tall—all skin and bones and muscle. All I had brought with me was a light suede zipper jacket and hiking boots, my light pants, a pocket knife, and a small compass.

The first half mile took almost no time at all and was all downhill on an easy grade. I could see well, too, for I was above timberline and ran into frequent large patches of snow.

Suddenly the terrain changed. I had come into a part of the mountain I had been unable to see before. The slopes got steeper and steeper, and there was no way out of this area other than to go ahead or to turn back and climb out of the rather poor position in which I was finding myself. The steep slopes rapidly worsened into cliffs, and I wondered whether there was, in fact, a safe way down to the wooded, less steep area a quarter of a mile ahead. If I could just make it there, all would be well.

At this point I came upon a narrow, very steep snowbank sloped at perhaps a sixty-degree angle and three hundred feet long. I remembered a way to get down a snowbank like this: Push a stout stick into the snow and let it control your speed as you slowly slide down the embankment. Although it may have been a good idea in principle, I used very poor judgment in employing the method. I had not slid thirty feet before I lost all control and found myself sliding at about sixty miles an hour. Ahead I saw a six-foot boulder, and I raised my arms instinctively to protect my head as I hit. After bouncing up into the air over the boulder I slid uncontrolled another 150 feet to the end of the snowbank and over some large sharp rocks, where I came to a stop on the edge of a sheer cliff that dropped over a hundred feet.

What a mess I had gotten myself into! But the fact was, despite this fall, I was still alive. For that I was very grateful, and the first thing I did was to thank God.

My pants were badly torn, and my hip and leg were deeply cut and bleeding. I thought that otherwise I was in good shape until I tried to get up and found my left arm was broken at the elbow and I could not use it at all. I surveyed the situation in detail and figured I had really made not only one major wrong decision in coming by myself but also another in trying to slide down the steep snowbank in an unsafe manner.

The big question before me was how I could best get back to our camp in the condition I was in. I should not, at this point, make any more wrong moves. The right answer would be to call for help from my teammates. I did this for perhaps a half hour, listening between the calls, but to no avail. The position of the sun showed me that in two hours or less it would set and then there might be another hour of daylight. A long cold night would follow, and I was dressed in only a thin suede jacket and sitting on sharp rocks at the edge of a sheer cliff. If I could just make it down to the more normal mountain terrain which was several hundred feet below me, I had an excellent chance of going all the way to the camp on my own and in good time.

At this point I put my number two option, which was about to become my number one option, to the test. Was there a way down, and would it lead into a further trap or get me down onto safe ground? After perhaps ten minutes of studying this chess move I thought I could see a reasonable way and decided to make a try for it. I soon found out exactly what I could and could not do without the use of one arm and proceeded to move foot by foot downward with this limitation. The details of this next half hour are rather hazy in my mind, but I made the three-hundred-foot descent and was now on what I looked upon as safe terrain where I could move along with normal speed. Again I was extremely grateful and thanked God for helping me through this seemingly impossible descent. After marking directions by the distant peaks and estimating distances I set out on the trip with renewed confidence and a joyful heart. It took me less than an hour and a half to reach the camp. The sun had not set. Our party of twenty hikers was not yet back and did not return for over an hour. My only experience on the way was that I encountered a very large black bear. I realized that he was the native there and I was not, so I gave him a wide berth and all due respect.

By the time the group reached the camp my arm was swollen up to twice its size, and I looked something like Popeye. By morning, after having slept on the ground, I felt there was no way I could get up, for every bone in my body was sore. But with the help of a sling for my arm and someone to carry my backpack for me I was able to walk the twelve miles to the cars without too much trouble.

The next day Bernard's uncle took me to a doctor friend who x-rayed the arm, and it was decided that as soon as the swelling went down I should have it operated on. So at the end of the week they drilled two holes by the break and wired the two bone parts together with a piece of silver wire. After all these years the wire is still there, even though the plan had been to remove it once the break healed.

The summer was really just getting under way, and although we had two setbacks in our original plan to canoe down the Yukon River in Alaska, there were still opportunities for little-or-no-cost fun and adventure in the great outdoors, even with my broken arm in a cast. After a little research we settled on a very wild area with lots of elk, bison, and bear and, of course, good fishing. It was on the eastern edge of Yellowstone National Park along the upper reaches of the Lamar River.

Our two backpacks included everything we might need on a camping trip in the wild for a month, which was the time I was supposed to keep the cast on my arm. We hitchhiked the 250 miles to the place where we would start the hike in from the highway. After backpacking about fifteen miles we were very lucky to run into an old rundown log cabin which, we could see, had been used now and then by park rangers. It had rough beds, a stove, and a fireplace, and was a real protection from the cold, which most nights dropped to below freezing. Compared with sleeping out in the open the cabin seemed like a palace, and it made our stay much more enjoyable.

During our month's stay we never saw another person, but we did see wild animals everywhere. All told, we saw over eighty elk, one hundred fifty bison, and twenty bears, to say nothing of hundreds of smaller animals. The river had so many trout that it was a lot of trouble taking the fish off the barbed hooks. We would each catch about fifty a day but did not want to keep any more than we ate so let the rest go. By filing the barbs off our hooks we made the fishing a lot more fun. It was a little harder pulling the fish in, but we did no damage to the fish during the process of catching and letting them go again.

At about the middle of our stay we saw a big forest fire in the distance and thought that it might be a good idea to hike over to it. Bernard could get a job fighting the fire, and even with my broken arm I could be a paid timekeeper. After walking from early morning until late afternoon it seemed we were getting no closer to the fire, and we knew our plan to help fight the forest fire was not practical. We could have walked another two days and still not have been there. So after an early supper we decided to return to our headquarters at the cabin, traveling under the light of a full moon. Although we had kept track of the trails in the woods, there was more of a chance of getting lost at night, especially since we could not see some of our distant reference points, but we managed to make it back before daylight. We had only a half hour of excitement when we saw ahead on the trail a very large bison, but we respected each other's territory and gave each other no problems.

While hitchhiking back to Missoula we decided to try a different mode of travel from Livingston to Butte to Missoula—riding the freight trains. In 1933 this was a whole new world. Hundreds of people out of work, as well as the regulars known as bums, were doing the same thing. They stayed in places referred to as jungles. There fires usually were going and people would share the basic needs of life along with lots and lots of stories. After the newness of the experience had worn off we decided that hitchhiking was faster, more fun, and a cut above riding the freight trains.

The next two weeks I spent to real advantage in Missoula with Bernard's uncle and aunt. His uncle, being a chiropractor, knew what I needed after my cast was removed to get back the full motion and use of my arm. At first, to move it more than a few inches was impossible and very painful to try, but Dr. Billings helped me to accomplish the goal with a minimum of pain. After some weeks of this treatment I bade my friends good-bye and four days later was back in Nashville ready to start my senior year at Vanderbilt.

I look back on the month of camping and fishing in the wild along the Lamar River as one of the happiest times of my life. I have often thought of going back to see if the fishing is still the best I have ever experienced but have never found the time. But what I learned that summer about mountain climbing and about taking needless risks in the wild are lessons that paid off for me several times later in my life's adventures.

CHAPTER FOUR

My Return to China

In June 1934 I had just graduated as a civil engineer from Vanderbilt University. Now I needed to apply civil engineering for the good of China. I must go there as an adult to see the needs.

I had an open mind as to what I would do for a year. The United States was still in the middle of its worst depression ever, but in China the economy was excellent with many good jobs available. Civil engineers were plentiful, but sanitary engineers could not be found anywhere. Only a few places like Shanghai had modern facilities such as running water and sewers. Even Suzhou with its 500,000 inhabitants had no such improvements. I had many job offers, but the one which most appealed to me was teaching civil engineering at a fine Southern Presbyterian-supported school, Hangzhou University. This would give me a chance to help the Chinese engineering students for the year and time to decide what kind of graduate work I should take when I went back to the States.

We had a good faculty at Hangzhou University but were short one member in the engineering school. I wound up with nineteen credit hours to teach, and during two terms I taught courses I myself had not studied previously. I also learned a new respect for professors, which I had not always had at Vanderbilt. I worked very hard with little free time, but it was a worthwhile and happy year.

Many of my students were older than I. Ninety-five percent of the staff were Chinese and 100 percent of the students. We used the best English texts, and I taught in English. But I wished to learn more Chinese, especially in the Mandarin dialect rather than my native Suzhou dialect. So I arranged to have lunch each day with the students and younger faculty members. This also gave me a chance to eat Chinese food, which I loved. I had breakfast and supper with a missionary professor and his wife, the Days, with whom I lived.

I was too busy for many outside activities, but I did help the university stop its water reservoir from leaking, and now and then I got into a soccer game with the students and younger staff. Dr. McMullen, comptroller of the university, took me under his wing, and I enjoyed his advice and man-to-man fellowship.

Hangzhou University, located on remote hilly land overlooking a beautiful river, was having trouble with bands of wild dogs roaming its rural campus. Already a number of the students had been bitten, and there was much fear of the dogs and of the potential of contracting rabies. Dr. McMullen knew of my prowess as a hunter and man of action, so he asked if I would try to solve the problem. I used two methods to get rid of the dogs. First, a safely administered poison did a rather good job, but it still left a residue of animals. Second, I used my high-powered rifle, for I was quite a good shot. That, too, worked.

One day as I made my routine rounds with my rifle I spotted two dogs that I had not seen before but which appeared to be the type of wild dogs I had been encountering. Although they were some distance from me, I took careful aim and killed them both. The next day I was called into Dr. McMullen's office and informed that we should discontinue the program. I had killed the two prize dogs belonging to the Chinese minister of foreign affairs. Although I had done it unwittingly, to me fell the difficult task of making a personal apology. Fortunately, I was forgiven for my mistake.

All fall my dad and I had been making some big plans. There was nothing either of us liked better than to hunt together. I had hunted pheasants, ducks, rabbits, and deer with Dad in the Suzhou area one hundred miles away since I was old enough to walk along with him at age six. We had often talked about going after big game, namely wild hog and tiger, but there were none of these in our area. We would have to go to Fujian Province, about five hundred miles south of Hangzhou, for this kind of hunting. We knew well a Mr. Caldwell, who was a missionary in Fuging near Fuzhou. Over the years he had become quite famous as a tiger hunter and had written a book, *Blue Tiger*. In his area tigers were not only plentiful but dreaded by the native Chinese, as most were man eaters.

To get to Fuzhou was not easy. One had to go first to Shanghai and take a coastal steamer, which took about three days and was a very rough trip. Dad and I also shared a love for adventure and reasoned we could go overland to Fuzhou first and then go tiger hunting. As far as anyone knew, the overland trip had never been made by a white man or a Chinese. Roads only went about 60 percent of the way. We guessed that there must be at least some kind of a path the rest of the way over which a motorcycle could pass. The map also showed rivers which were in part navigable. The famous Min River with its gorges was traveled by steam launches.

The more we talked about the adventure the more it appealed to us and the more we were determined to attempt it. We figured that our best bet was to buy a good used Harley Davidson with a sidecar, and when the paths got too bad for a sidecar we would abandon it and ride back to back. The Chinese new year holiday period coincided with our school vacation in late January, which would give us about three weeks for the trip.

First we purchased a motorcycle. But, as we found out, used motorcycles are almost never satisfactory, and we got it too late to find and correct its faults. We had three serious breakdowns on the way. First we needed to replace our drive chain, which was badly worn. We were still at a location where a replacement could be brought in by train. The second problem, more serious, was the magneto, and we had almost four days to wait on parts. The third time we were beyond the point where we could order needed parts and decided to abandon the motorcycle until such time as I could return later and pick it up. All that was left for us was the worst of all buses, which would travel for less than fifty miles every several days.

In a rather short time we came to the end of the road altogether. Fortunately, we were over the continental divide between Zhejiang Province, in which Hangzhou was located, and Fujien Province, where Fuzhou and Fuzhing were located. We discovered a small mountain river there and were told that a little flat-bottomed boat would be going down the rapids in a few days, mainly to carry the mail. We lost no time negotiating the three-day passage on this boat. It would terminate at a little town on the Ming River. From there we would take the steam launch to Fuzhou.

The next three days we moved down the small swift river through beautiful dense forests. Our boatman knew every mile of the river and just how to shoot the rapids in his lightweight boat. Three times a day we ate the same fare: rice, dried fish, and cabbage. By the second day we thought that it would be good to supplement the diet with duck, which we found on the river every once in a while. In the absence of a shotgun we had to use my 3006 Remington deer rifle.

Every ten to twenty miles was a small village where was stationed a military force to keep the peace and protect the village from bandits. We were white foreigners traveling in one of the wildest parts of China, so it was only logical that the military looked upon us with considerable suspicion. On two occasions it was nip and tuck until we showed them our passports, got to know them, and told them the reason for our mission and the misfortunes we had along the way. They then warned us of the many bandits in the area.

During one day-long wait we decided to hunt to pass the time. Although we saw no game as we tramped through some rather strange and wild country, we did run into a group of bandits. Those on the outskirts of the village tending their fields saw us with our fine-looking guns. They attempted to lure us into their village where they would have the manpower and firepower to relieve us of our guns and perhaps do more. We did not learn of their complete way of operation until we had returned to our starting point and were told by the friendly villagers there that we were lucky not to have been overpowered. Fortunately, we had sensed the danger when we first encountered the few men on the edge of the bandit village.

Our little boat reached the big Min River, and we just caught the crowded steam launch headed for Fuzhou. The river was rather fast flowing and in places not too deep. There the only way the launch could pass safely was for all the passengers to get off and walk around the shallow portion of the river, then reembark. Another hazard was the chance of being shot at by bandits on the banks, especially when the boat moved through some of the deeper gorges. There was little protection for the passengers, since all we had was deck space with nothing to sit on but the deck.

We had badly miscalculated the time it would take us to reach Fuzhou. Instead of three days it had taken thirteen. Our friends on both ends of the trip had thought the worst, namely, that we had been captured by bandits. The big mission hospital in Fuzhou had two difficult operations lined up for my dad to perform. Also, we had to see what kind of tiger hunting we could accomplish in the few days left before the coastal steamer left for Shanghai. But finally we and Mr. Caldwell were ready to go for the big one.

Only two weeks before we came to Fuzhing there had been a lot of excitement in the area. One of the villagers was walking along a lonely path when he encountered a 350-pound tiger asleep in a secluded place. It was the feared man eater, which in the last two years had killed over forty of his friends and relatives. The hunter hastened back to the village and solicited three other hunters with their old-fashioned guns. They found the tiger still asleep. They all took aim and counted to three before shooting. But the tiger woke up and in the confusion of the next few minutes killed three of the four men. The fourth escaped by climbing a tree from which he put the two final bullets in the tiger. There was much grief in the village but also relief that this tiger was now history.

The villagers had seen a lot of another tiger who, it was said, had already killed ten people. He was estimated to be somewhat smaller but very dangerous. This cat we would go after.

First we staked out two goats about a mile apart. Caldwell and I built a blind near one goat, and my father and Mr. Hayes, also of our party, built one near the other goat. The area was typically excellent tiger country with narrow trails, twenty-foot-tall sword grass everywhere, and almost no open areas.

After Caldwell and I had staked out the goat and moved across a small gully about seventy-five feet away where we built the blind we settled down to wait. Caldwell had a new 8 mm movie camera and was very eager to get movies of his prize gun, a 250-3000 Savage, killing a tiger. The Savage Arms Company had a special relationship with Caldwell ever since he had killed a Kodiak bear in Alaska several years before, and they had given him all the ammunition that he could use. Caldwell had already shot over twelve tigers himself, so he planned to take movies while I shot with his gun. I was used to a 250-3000 Savage for deer hunting in Suzhou and liked it, but I felt it was a bit lightweight for a tiger and had brought my own 30-06 Remington.

First an hour went by, then another, and it started to rain lightly. From our vantage point we could see up the narrow trail to a bend about one hundred feet away. We could also see the goat and then, beyond it, only about fifty feet of the trail to where it disappeared in the tall sword grass. There was a lot of excitement and patient waiting but so far no tiger. The rain caused Caldwell to put his new movie camera in the case to protect it. The goat was not cooperating by bleating as loudly and as often as Caldwell thought he should, so he would imitate the bleat himself, and the goat would answer feebly. Time dragged on, and I began to wonder whether there were really tigers here, when all of a sudden Caldwell punched me and whispered, "Get ready; he is coming."

The plan had been for us to let the tiger kill the goat, to get as much movie footage as possible, then to shoot it and get more footage. However, in the excitement Caldwell couldn't get the fastener on the camera case open. When he finally did get the camera out, the tiger heard and saw us and decided to forget about killing the goat. Instead, it jumped over the goat and was about to escape down the path when I fired my first shot right to where I thought his heart should be. It seemed to be a complete miss. I had a chance at just one more shot before he would disappear around the bend on the path.

This time I aimed a little more forward. The tiger let out a terrible roar and appeared to fall into the gully alongside the path. Now we knew we had a wounded tiger on our hands so forgot about further movie taking.

Caldwell took his Savage and I took my Remington and we moved cautiously down the path to see where the tiger may have gone. We stood alongside each other on the path not far from the point where the tiger had fallen down into the shallow gully, when all of a sudden there was a spine-tingling roar and out charged the tiger right for us. Instinctively, we raised our guns, aimed, and fired, and the tiger fell only eight feet from us.

It had been a close one. My shot had hit it in the neck, and Caldwell injured its backbone just below the front shoulders. The tiger was still very much alive but paralyzed below his shoulders. My second shot had destroyed his left shoulder and, we learned later, the first shot had gone through both lungs missing his heart by a mere half inch. In fact, if the softnose bullet had not been defective, it would have spread, as it was designed to do, and shattered his heart.

Now Caldwell and I decided to investigate what the tiger had actually done and where it had hidden before attacking us. We left the tiger on the trail where it had fallen, still very much alive but helpless. In the meantime, Dad and Mr. Hayes had heard all the shooting and had come up the trail to see what was going on. They noticed us some fifty feet away from the tiger and thought we did not see it. They could also see that the tiger was still alive, so Dad drew aim on its moving head and pulled the trigger, but his gun failed to fire. It was good in a way, because it would have ruined the face and head of the tiger, but we were all a bit shook up to have had two defective shells in the same day. Internal bleeding brought about the tiger's death in the next few minutes.

There was much celebrating when we learned that this was indeed the cat everyone feared for having already killed ten people in the village nearby. Furthermore, it was the one which a year before had bitten into a meat-baited homemade bomb and had its lower jaw broken on both sides. The jaw was now completely healed, but the bones were mismatched by almost half an inch. During the period of healing its mate must have fed it. Now, almost sixty years later, we still have the mounted head and skin only a bit the worse for wear.

We had only another half day to hunt tiger before we had to

catch the steamer back to Shanghai. Although I had gotten my tiger, I was sorry that Dad had not even had a shot at one. Needless to say, on the way home we were already making plans for a return trip. Despite all our delays and difficulties the trip was a rousing success. It truly was one of the best times Dad and I had together and the most exciting of my memories.

During a particularly hectic teaching period of that year I got to thinking, "Would it not be nice after this extra busy week to take a quick trip home?" My decision resulted in my spending the strangest night of my life.

It was only a hundred miles, about two and half hours by motorbike from Hangzhou University to my parents' home in Suzhou. I had not seen them since our tiger hunt in Fujian Province, and the taxidermist by this time might even have the skin and head mounted.

I had been on that road only once before. It was part of Chiang Kai-shek's new road system built in part to protect China from the growing menace of a full-scale Japanese invasion. I filled up the two and a half gallon gas tank on my motorbike and checked the oil. I then strapped on a canvas overnight bag complete with a few clothes, tools, pump, and a flashlight. It was four in the afternoon on a beautiful spring day when I finally left the campus. By China standards this was an excellent road, gravel to be sure and only about fifteen feet wide, but it served an excellent purpose. Traffic was light and consisted mostly of heavily loaded wheelbarrows, rickshaws, donkeys, and an occasional truck or old car. Some farmers were setting out rice plants, and others were adding liquid "night soil" to fertilize, demonstrating that China has been recycling for four thousand years.

I had been on the road about an hour when my bike acted strangely and then came to a halt. I discovered that the top of the carburetor had become loose, and all of the gas had leaked out. The road was much too new for gas stations. The only obvious solution to my dilemma was to push my little bike in neutral, which I did.

An hour and a half and five miles later I arrived at a fork in the road, all hot and tired. The branch turned off to a little village, and the main road went on to Suzhou. There at the fork was a little bus station with living quarters for the bus attendant. I introduced myself and my predicament to the attendant, Mr. Lee, and asked his advice about going into the village for gas and perhaps a night's lodging.

Mr. Lee was very cordial and sorry to inform me that the village had neither gas nor lodging. "Darkness is coming on," he said. "You must be my guest tonight in my humble abode. I shall telephone the bus station in Suzhou and have them put on two gallons of gas. The bus will be here at eight in the morning, and you can then be on your way." I was overwhelmed by his hospitality and interest in me. After some polite hesitation in my broken Chinese I accepted his offer.

Mr. Lee had a very modest one-room abode which served for cooking, eating, sleeping, and the bus business. My Suzhou dialect, in the vocabulary of a ten-year-old, was constantly becoming mixed up with the quite different Mandarin dialect that I had been trying to pick up while teaching at Hangzhou University, which was Mr. Lee's dialect. Despite these differences we got along beautifully.

After supper Mr. Lee explained that he had a commitment in the village and would be back about ten. He insisted that I use his nice traditional string mattress bed, which was completely surrounded by a combination heavy curtain and mosquito net, and that he would sleep on the hard bamboo couch. After Mr. Lee had left I hung my clothes on two hooks at one end of the couch and tried out his bed. Despite the strange bed and surroundings I fell sound asleep almost immediately.

At about eleven o'clock my host, Mr. Lee, returned and prepared to go to bed on the bamboo couch. Although his movements had awakened me, I was reluctant to allow myself to become wide awake, as I was very tired. Therefore, I pretended to be asleep by imitating the deep slow breathing of a sleeping person.

Mr. Lee had been drinking heavily, for I could smell the heavy scent of the wine, and his movements were quite unsteady. Before he lay down on his creaky couch I could clearly hear him rummage through my belongings hanging up on the wall. My sleepiness quickly gave way to an alertness and a sense of danger. Why was he looking through my clothes? The only reason I could think of was my wallet.

Fortunately, I had taken the precaution of removing the wallet from my trousers and placing it under my pillow. Now I awaited his next move. It seemed he had given up the search as he crawled onto his creaky couch. But my ears clearly told me that he was not going to sleep, just quietly waiting. This intensified my pretense of being asleep. After about twenty minutes Mr. Lee's bed again creaked as he got up. He moved in a kind of shuffle across the room as he came toward the head of my bed. In these few seconds a sense of real danger came over me. No one except Lee knew that I was there. What was his intent? Perhaps to feel under my pillow for the wallet, but could he take it without waking me? Perhaps his plan was the safer way—to use a knife first and then take the money.

I knew I had to do something quickly. Suddenly a voice in my ear seemed to say, "Pretend I am waking; see what he will do." It worked! Mr. Lee heard me, retreated to his couch, and lay down. I could see nothing through the heavy curtains, but my ears told me all I needed to know. He wanted my wallet, but he wanted to take it when I was asleep.

To confirm my theory I resumed my rather good imitation of a sleeping man. After about a half hour Mr. Lee again got up from his creaky couch and edged his way across the room toward my bed. Again came a compelling thought. "It worked before. Try it again." And I did just that. My pretense of waking must have seemed very real to Mr. Lee, for he retreated rather hastily to the creaky couch and tried his best to get in quietly.

He must know by now that I was a light sleeper and that his plan would not work. But again, could I take a chance and really fall asleep? I needed sleep, but under these conditions it wasn't safe for me. I must continue to play the game.

This time I needed to let more time pass and try to imitate an extra-deep sleep. It was hard to know about time; maybe two or three hours went by. By listening to Mr. Lee's breathing I was convinced that he was not really going to sleep and therefore must still be waiting for a final try for his plan. All the thoughts of being stabbed and buried in his back yard ran through my head once again. I tried to think through the details of extra-deep sleep and how that would sound different, and I decided this was the time to try it. It seemed to work, for after about five minutes of this, Mr. Lee stirred. I continued my convincing sounds. His arising was slower and more cautious, but there was no question that he had gotten to his feet and was preparing to come toward me once again.

As he neared the head of my bed there seemed to be unusual movement of his feet. I knew for sure he was just outside the heavy curtain and that time was short. My pretense at waking was almost precipitous, and again it stopped Mr. Lee dead in his tracks. He quickly retreated to his couch and got onto it slowly, but those telltale creaks came as before, and we each found ourselves back to the point of beginning. He undoubtedly thought that his American friend had an uncanny sixth sense or even a foreign angel looking over him. By this time I was convinced of the angel and thanked God for watching over me.

Some of the night was left, yet now I had an inner confidence and felt I could handle it with safety. All I need do was stay awake, not the easiest thing, for I was very tired and had had almost no sleep thus far. I forced myself to think about things such as engineering problems, and time, perhaps an hour, passed slowly. All at once a piercing cry reached my ears. It was the first crow of the rooster just outside the window. It was a most welcome noise, repeated every five minutes. My battle was over, for there was no way I could fall asleep again

Daylight was now creeping through the heavy curtains. Soon Mr. Lee's voice came forth in a very pleasant way: "Tsaw" (Good morning) and "Ch tsaw fan" (Let's eat breakfast). I responded in my poor Chinese with great politeness and relief. Our breakfast was the simple Chinese fare of soft rice with a few pickled vegetables and peanuts. Our conversation was friendly small talk.

Soon it was eight o'clock, and the bus came and delivered my two gallons of gas. I paid the driver for it, thanked him deeply, and put it in the English bike. There was the usual polite thanks and another offer to pay my host something for his kindness and hospitality. It was then a good-bye in my best Chinese, and I hopped on the bike and sped down the road toward Suzhou. An hour and a half later I was home.

When I look back on this strangest night of my life I think of the two main things my dad would tell me on our trips together: to love your fellow man and to be guided by God. If this was being guided by God, it was not only very exciting but very practical as well.

The rest of the school year went quickly. I was kept busy, in part by the rewarding visits I made to my parents. During their vacation times from the Shanghai American School I could see and enjoy my two younger brothers, Walter and Fred, and they visited me at Hangzhou one weekend. Finally it came time to return to the United States for graduate school. I had been accepted at Cornell University to study sanitary engineering and looked forward to later serving in China in that field.

I had saved almost enough money to carry me through the first year of graduate school and figured if I could get a job working my way across the Pacific I would come out just right. Fortunately, an American sailor jumped ship in Shanghai, and through the American consulate I was able to take his place as an ordinary seaman for forty-five dollars per month. The trip was an experience of a different sort. Here I was a graduate engineer but knew nothing about sailing an ocean liner and did not want to appear stupid. The test came the first night when the officer in charge gave me a rather long and complex order, then turned and left, expecting me to obey it. Not understanding what he had said but remembering his words I hightailed it to another ordinary seaman. I asked him what the order meant and how I should carry it out, explaining that this was my first experience on a ship. The plan worked, and after trying it the same way a number times I soon learned what was what and got along well. During the course of three weeks we must have painted half of the gear on deck. I got a swell sunburn, to say nothing of some good meals and about forty dollars for my labor, but most important I got free passage and saved that money toward school. In fact, when I got to San Francisco I had saved enough so that instead of hitchhiking across the country to Nashville I went by bus for almost nothing.

It had been a full and wonderful year. What more could I have packed into it? One very significant thing happened. During the spring of 1935 a small group of dedicated businessmen from

Shanghai visited Hangzhou University for a weekend. They called themselves the Oxford Group. I attended their meetings and was deeply impressed. They measured their living by Christ's Sermon on the Mount, or the four absolute standards of honesty, purity, love, and unselfishness. They not only believed in change but that God guides people toward the greatest plan for their lives. I decided to try this way, to give my life to God, to live a new life. But the seeds planted within me that weekend were like those seeds which fell on rocky soil and wilted in a few weeks. In part, this was because I had no fellowship to help me live to my commitment. Nonetheless, this experience paved the way for a permanent change, for at graduate school God would give me a second chance through others to change my life forever.

The second indelible imprint on my mind and heart happened to me that year in China. Dad had always been very close to me, but this was the year that I got to know him for the first time on a man-to-man basis. Dad had a way of sharing his deepest thoughts and convictions so as to lift people to their highest. He was a surgeon of considerable renown. It was his habit to pray for God's help and skill before every operation. He was not a minister, but he lived out his Christian faith in such a way that he need not preach; his life was his sermon. My times with Dad that year had given me spiritual and motivating guideposts for the rest of my life.

I was now ready to start a new phase of my life.

CHAPTER FIVE

Graduate Student at Illinois and Harvard

When I arrived in Nashville it was my intent to stay only a few weeks and then proceed to Cornell to take up graduate study in sanitary engineering. I visited with some of my former professors at Vanderbilt to tell them about my year of teaching in China and my graduate school plans. Professor Hutchinson, having just returned from a six-week survey tour of the leading universities, said I should immediately change my plans and go to the University of Illinois. He convinced me that its engineering faculty and program were way ahead of Cornell's. With his help I made the switch and was admitted just in time to register at Illinois.

It was a pleasure to meet and discuss my course plans with Professor Babbitt, who with Professor Doland was co-author of the widely used book *Water Supply*, which I had used in my basic course work at Vanderbilt and from which I had taught at Hangzhou University. I laid out a course of study taking most of Babbitt's graduate courses, including his sanitary laboratory courses. Also, I registered in the top professors' graduate courses in hydraulics and hydrology and in an advanced course in structural analysis under the world-renowned Hardy Cross. I still had a strong interest in structures and needed more knowledge in that area to be a good sanitary engineer. I would also need to write a master's thesis under Babbitt on the dewatering of sewage sludge.

I had saved enough money teaching at Hangzhou to see my way through two semesters if I was thrifty, which was not hard for me. I arranged to live in a cooperative dormitory-house called the Cosmopolitan Club, where about half the residents were foreign graduate students. The house cut back on its charges to students by using the regular rooms for living and study and requiring everyone to sleep in a large unheated attic. Here I had my first contact with a communist, though I viewed him as an armchair communist.

In the spring the Illinois varsity soccer team approached us to see if we could pull together a team of foreign students with soccer experience and play an exhibition match. There was no time to learn to play together as a team, but we held the match and beat the varsity 3-0. This showed us all that to play soccer well one had to start learning it quite young, which was the case with the foreign students and me.

My youth was still evident, as I was prone to take bets about daring to do some crazy things. I won five dollars one night when the thermometer had fallen to a record low of -23 degrees F by running all the way around the block stripped to my waist.

During this year the head of the Student Young Men's Christian Association, "Chief" Wilson, got me interested in its foreign student program. I headed a special program that sponsored a series of foreign-related talks with prominent speakers, which drew large crowds. During Christmas vacation another Student Volunteer Movement quadrennial meeting was to be held in Indianapolis, and I was a delegate from Illinois. It was better than the Buffalo conference four years earlier. One thing that made it outstanding was that Florence had come as a delegate from Johns Hopkins, where she had gone on into nursing after graduating from Queens College. Before the meetings were over and it was time to part we had gained a mutual feeling for each other that had not been there before and which followed into our letter writing for the next years. But we were not ready to become engaged, for each of us had a lot more graduate work to complete. But it was comforting to me that I now had a girl I could feel serious about with some real assurance for our future.

I had acquired an inexpensive full-size Harley Davidson

motorcycle and used it to get around. I biked over to Baltimore to see Florence for a couple of days. The bike broke down before I could start back. Shop repairs were expensive, so I crated and trucked it back to the Illinois campus where I could fix it myself inexpensively. Before the summer was over I discovered that I was using the bike more than was warranted for a young self-supporting graduate student. I also had one close call, and in two bike mishaps one friend had broken his leg and the other was killed. So I made the right decision and sold mine. While I was still in the learning stage friends and I would now and then use the bike for double dating, riding in tandem. On one occasion we went to a small circus, and I was challenged to allow an 850-pound lady to sit on my lap but without any serious or lasting bad effect.

My academic work at Illinois was in every way a great experience. Graduate school was much harder than undergraduate, but my interest in each subject was fired up so that I studied exceptionally hard and made excellent grades. During my course under Hardy Cross in structural analysis there developed a real and uncommon rapport between him and me. He would take great delight in prodding some of the older bright students in the class after they had not answered his question to his full satisfaction by saying, "Well, now, let's see what the fellow from Vanderbilt has to say about it." I couldn't study hard enough for him and gained a great deal from his class. Right at that time he came up with a new theory for solving flow distribution problems in complex pipe networks, which was really a carryover from his already famous theory in designing rigid frame buildings.

Professor Cross knew of my strong interest in sanitary engineering under Professor Babbitt and also my taking hydraulics under the dean. So he approached me to see if I would be interested in taking this new theory he had worked out and running a check on it before he had it published I felt greatly honored and did so. It is now used worldwide.

Professor Babbitt also approached me to see if I would be interested in running the sanitary engineering department's renowned pilot-scale research experiment station for the summer for a nice salary. I certainly needed the money for my second year of graduate study and knew that I would also learn a great deal. So I accepted the position. I dealt mainly with rather large-scale anaerobic digestion experiments for both sewage sludge and ground-up household garbage. That was when serious thought was first being given to widespread use of garbage grinders in the home. We also had a whole series of experiments using the so-called activated sludge treatment for raw or settled sewage. This method was beginning to become popular and widely used by municipalities. In undertaking these experiments I had to give overall supervision (under the professors' guidance) and also had to run the laboratory tests and keep records. I did have one tough but rather crude laborer whose job it was to do most of the day-to-day manual labor. We would each bring our lunches and eat them together, but I could never get used to his coming right out of the nasty sewage and sludge tanks, rinsing his hands in the polluted unchlorinated plant effluent, and then eating his sandwich. He often looked sickly, I thought, but as far as I knew he never came down with any of the waterborne diseases.

In the spring, two important things happened which affected me for the rest of my life. First, I had been giving a lot of thought as to whether I should continue beyond a master's level in my graduate work, and if I did, if it should be at Illinois or at Harvard, which I had been hearing more and more about. The Illinois sanitary department, good as it was, had only three or four graduate students and only one studying for his Ph.D. Harvard, on the other hand, had in the last few years moved way out front of all the universities in the field of sanitary engineering. It had over fifty master's level students and three doctor's level. Furthermore, I had been offered scholarships by both schools, so which would it be? The two leading professors at these two institutions were the best in the country. I concluded that I had been well exposed to Professor Babbitt for a year, and there would be a lot of merit now in going to Harvard and learning what I could from Professor Gordon Fair and his distinguished colleagues. So I made plans to try for a doctor's degree at Harvard.

The second event affecting the rest of my life was the crushing blow of my dad's premature death in mid-March. It was by far the most grievous time in my life, and if it hadn't been for the closeness and caring of Chief Wilson it would have been much worse. The mission board, too, was sensitive to my situation by sending me two, rather than one, cables. The first said that my father was critically ill; the second expressed their deep sympathy in his death.

Some weeks later I learned the details of his passing. He was always strong and of vigorous health, even though he pushed himself very hard in his work. About two weeks before he died, he was sick in bed with what everyone thought was a very severe cold. Three critically ill patients came into the hospital, each requiring major surgery. No one else at the hospital could handle the complexities of these cases, so Dad got out of bed to perform the surgery himself. He was only able to complete two before he was forced back to bed. He was then diagnosed to have pulmonary pneumonia. This being well before the day of the wonder drugs, he died within two weeks at the age of fifty-six.

I have always had a hard time trying to rationalize why God would allow one who had worked so hard and successfully to be of service to his fellow man to die so young. However, who are we to complain about the infinite wisdom of God? After ten years I at least partly understood some of this divine timing. Within a year of Dad's death the Japanese started their four-year war and invasion of much of China. Suzhou was one of the first areas to go. Dad detested the inhumane ways in which the Japanese treated the Chinese people. It would have been impossible for him to have worked at the Suzhou Hospital after the city was taken over by the Japanese. And following Pearl Harbor, if he had still been in Suzhou, he very likely would have been placed in a concentration camp until the end of World War II. At any rate, following the war he may have had two or three years when he could have again served the Chinese people before the Communists took over the country. So perhaps divine wisdom did, in fact, spare him much pain.

I had looked forward to discussing with my father the question of my going to Harvard. I felt I would have been encouraged by his saying, "Yes, you can handle it. Don't worry. You have it in you." Although I had to make the final decision without consultation with Dad I was left with his heritage and the very best thoughts a father can leave his son. Now I again could hear him say, "The two greatest things in life are to be guided by God and to love your fellow man." These principles became an integral part of my decision to go on for a doctor's degree at Harvard. Behind that decision was a love of the people of the third world, especially of China. The commitment became my driving force and gave me the daily energy to work hard enough to succeed in this goal, and the goal was to serve China just as my father had, not in medicine but in sanitary engineering or preventive medicine.

And so it was in the fall of 1936 that this country boy, now approaching the age of twenty-five, found his way to Cambridge, Massachusetts. I had earned enough money in my three months running the sanitary-experiment station at Illinois to carry me through the first year, and I had a tuition scholarship. Now, all I needed was a small part-time job and a good economical place to stay. After meeting some of the professors I was led to a boarding house run by a dear older lady, Mrs. Beckwith, on Wendell St. She was a kind, motherly type, and her third-story room and two meals a day were what my budget needed. She told me she was short of the number of students she had been able to sign up for meals that year. If I brought in a few more boarders she would subtract a 10 percent commission for each from my own bill. That was equivalent to a good job in itself, and I brought in enough to pay half of my bill.

The next day Professor Whipple offered me just the job I needed: assistant sanitary inspector for the university. I was limited to about forty hours a month, but I had to visit each of the university's four swimming pools and eight kitchens collecting samples. These I tested in our laboratories for the quality of the water and of the dairy products. At seventy-five cents per hour this job was not only the best-paying student job on campus but it had a most remarkable fringe benefit. Whenever I completed my laboratory testing I wound up with three quarters of a gallon of a mixture of milk, cream, whipping cream, and ice cream, with an average butterfat content of about 20 percent. Mixed with chocolate malt powder it was so tasty and rich that one could safely drink no more than two glasses. It became a delight to invite guests to share the rich drink in my room, but we learned all too frequently the penalties of being gluttons. By sad experience we found that one who succumbed to the third glass of the rich mixture would be unable to sleep that night.

Another benefit from my stay at Mrs. Beckwith's was that 90 percent of her boarders were law students. Being the only one not in law, I was constantly asked to be the judge when they tried the law cases they were studying that week. One thing I learned was that, for the most part, law is 90 percent common sense. But even more important, from among these law students I made several lifelong friends.

Although I missed the spacious campus and stately old elm trees of Illinois, those surroundings were more than made up for by the international reputation and the three hundred years of tradition of Harvard, just getting ready to celebrate its tricentennial. Widner Library was the best university library in the United States and second only to the Library of Congress in size. The home of the business school was about the most impressive building I had seen, and the law school, right across a grass quadrangle from the old engineering building, was stately. Harvard had only about four thousand undergraduate students yet had another four thousand graduate students. Our engineering school had no undergraduate student body at all, and so it was with many of the other schools, including the traditional law and medical schools. Even though the campus had only about half the land compared with other universities of equal size, it was pleasingly laid out and shrouded in tradition. It was no trouble walking from one part of the campus to another. Besides, walking was good exercise, and there was no need for cars or student buses. In my sanitary inspector's job I had to get around to about every part of the campus and learned to love it.

My objectives for the next two years were clearly defined: pass selected courses by grade B or better; pick my major area of interest and begin laboratory research under my major professor, to culminate in the writing of a two-to-three-hundred-page scholarly thesis with tables, graphs, and a summary of my work; survey the extensive literature on my subject; take two and one half days of written examinations called "pre-lims" (required after about a year into the program); pass a test in the reading of scientific literature in two related and approved foreign languages, which in my case were French and German (the requirement I feared most).

After getting started on this program, I thought I would take an immediate try at the pre-lims and spent a few weeks using all my time studying for them, even though the field was much too broad to study for. Fortunately, I passed and celebrated having that major hurdle behind me.

When it came time for the foreign language requirements, I decided to take French first and employed a tutor, studied hard in my spare time, and took the exam. I came up short of Harvard's standard as to how scientific French should be translated into English. However, the professors had to admit that there were no really worthwhile, pertinent technical articles in sanitary engineering in French; hence, the practical question: Why should I waste more time studying French when there was nothing to read in that language? The professors came up with a very practical answer: Let Snell by at a low grade in French but let him concentrate on German and do well in that. There was quite a lot of worthwhile German technical literature. Greatly relieved, I set aside eight weeks to be free of all other study and work so I could give my full attention to the task of learning to read scientific German. My major professor, Gordon Fair, was part German and wrote and spoke freely in the language. He and Professor Imhof had written a book which appeared in both English and German, and he was willing to use that book for me to take my reading test of translating German into English. I passed the exam satisfactorily and used the knowledge for reading a number of good German technical articles. But after I left Harvard I freely told people that it had taken me eight weeks of concentrated effort to learn to read German and eight days to forget it.

I knew from the beginning that I wished to concentrate my research and thesis on the biggest health problem in China: the spreading of human wastes onto edible crops—without pretreatment—which resulted in a massive spread of pathogens through many phases of the people's lives. This long but interesting program of laboratory experiments got under way right after my pre-lims and extended over a period of a year and a half.

On some days I had to do my special mixing of the separate samples of human urine and fecal matter that had been collected. Actually, I could mix the refrigerated samples only at night, for it would literally "stink up" the whole building. I had to take a lot of kidding for this work.

I was able to find out why this undiluted mix of human wastes defied being broken down by the anaerobic-digestion bacteria that live in it naturally, a well-understood process that normally stabilizes most organic waste. I discovered that the urine waste broke down quite quickly into ammonium carbonate, which was alkaline enough to place the methane digestion phase in a "stuck" position where nothing could happen. Further research revealed that adding other organic waste substances would produce large volumes of carbon dioxide which neutralized the alkaline carbonates to a much less alkaline compound: bicarbonate. Then the process could continue in a desirable fashion.

Since rice straw was plentiful and not used to much advantage in China, I thought it would be the most practical waste that could be used to accomplish the neutralizing task; hence, I included it in our laboratory experiments with real success. Thus we had the theoretical and the practical basis for the future field use of the process in China and other oriental countries. In fact, during World War II three technical articles relating to my thesis were published, and when I was in Japan soon thereafter as a special United Nations consultant on composting I learned that they had seen these articles and already had built waste treatment facilities using, for the benefit of ten million people, the bulk of the knowledge I had discovered at Harvard.

Every hard-earned degree program must to some extent be softened with a certain amount of physical exercise and recreation or one can, in fact, go crazy. I got much of my exercise by walking on my official job and also ran several times a week, for that gave me the most exercise in the least time. Many of my friends and I were thrilled by long outdoor hikes, such as we would plan in the White Mountains of New Hampshire. We overdid some of these trips to such an extent that it took weeks to overcome the effects. On one occasion a young fellow in our party got lost from the rest, so we searched all day and night before we located him. Another time a friend bet me that I could not climb from the starting-off point at Pinkham Notch, elevation 2,030 feet, to the peak of Mount Washington, elevation 6,280 feet, in two hours. It was my hardest-earned ten dollars, but I did the 4,350-foot vertical ascent, which was about six miles via the trail, in an hour and three quarters. My climbing companion was in nowhere as good shape as I and had to quit at about the halfway point.

By the end of the first school year I was low on funds. Professor Philip Drinker, head of industrial health at the Harvard School of Public Health, asked if I would like to work under his supervision for the three summer months doing research on nitrous oxide emission from motion picture projection booths, which used carbon arc lights. It was excellent experience and a good break from the routine of my regular school program.

During much of my first year I was so involved with the academic battle that I neglected the spiritual part of my life, which had always been important to me. I did attend the Wesley Foundation and even church now and then, but I felt I needed more. About that time Moral Re-Armament (MRA) became quite active in the area. One day I picked up an attractive magazine called *Rising Tide*. I studied it in detail then looked up one of the people in the area and attended a number of their meetings. The thing I noted that was different from the regular brand of Christianity I was used to was that these people did not just talk about it but lived it. These new friends were part of the same worldwide movement that had held meetings at Hangzhou University about two years before, where I had overlooked Christian fellowship. Eventually I felt led to talk at length with David White, a student in the graduate school of business. He told me about his own life, frustrations, and deep change when he surrendered his life to God. It was then that I knew God had his finger on me. He was giving me a second chance to make up for the time I had failed at Hangzhou. With the high quality of fellowship that was available to me here in the greater Boston area I should certainly be able to hold to a commitment. I became a born-again Christian that day.

That decision affected the rest of my life. God became real to me, and I spent time each day for spiritual study and two-way prayer. I formed the habit of writing down my thoughts each morning, which has helped guide my life on the right course. Also, making God's guidance real and alive meant my going over my life in detail and measuring it against the four standards in the Sermon on the Mount: absolute honesty, purity, unselfishness, and love. Although I had always prided myself on being honest, I got a certain conviction when I thought in terms of absolute honesty as my new standard. I had to go to my major professor to tell him that during the previous months I had taken certain paper and pencil supplies from the university store shelves and used them for my personal needs. Although he was an agnostic, he could see a change in me, and it brought a further closeness between us.

This change in my life gave me an inner peace with myself and enabled me to organize my life and bring about the efficiency and commitment I needed to finish all phases of my doctoral program and get my degree at Harvard.

My second year at Harvard I was elected president of the Wesley Foundation, which meant taking quite a bit of responsibility for its weekly meetings. The students in the organization also saw a change in me. This not only affected the quality of the program, but other individuals began to change as well.

The second year I also found the right time for a weekend visit to Florence in Baltimore, where she was still studying nursing at Johns Hopkins. Although I still had a strong feeling toward her, I was also willing to put things on hold until the right time.

CHAPTER SIX

Andes Adventures

The good news could not have come at a better time. I had survived four weeks of my self-imposed schedule for finishing my thesis and taking my exam on it as soon as possible. The progress toward this end had been slowed by the need to keep body and soul together. I decided to borrow money to hold me until I could finish, then pay back that sum from a good full-time job, instead of subsisting on fifty-to-seventy-five-cents-per-hour campus jobs. It was a sound decision, but the regimen had begun to wear me down. I worked nineteen hours a day, did the essentials of life in an hour, and slept four hours. I had read that the most efficient way was to divide the four hours of sleep into two two-hour portions—ten to twelve PM and six to eight AM.

So when my major professor called me into his office to ask whether I might be interested in taking a job with a longtime friend of his in Venezuela and told me all the details, I was elated. I do believe it was that news which enabled me to hold to my tight schedule for the remaining four weeks.

Venezuela at that time furnished the United States more oil imports than did any other country, and we were trying to help it improve its infrastructure in return. I would be assigned to an American consulting team designing water supplies for many of the cities in the Andes region of the country, an area with ideal climate—not the heat of the tropics. The design team needed more reliable field data if they were to do a good job, and they thought that a qualified young American would fill that bill. The job would pay two and a half times an equivalent stateside job plus all expenses when I was outside of Caracas, which would be most of the time.

I could not stay in Cambridge to attend graduation exercises but had to catch the *Santa Paula* of the Grace Line out of New York to get down there in time. The five-day luxury voyage to LaGuaira, port for Caracas, was a delight and also served as a period of recuperation to a normal lifestyle of eating, sleeping, and working.

My first two weeks in Venezuela I was being briefed about what the American team was doing and on my own work. Roy Welter, chief engineer and designer, took me in tow and taught me a great deal and, as it turned out, became a lifelong friend. The design team was about to move into high gear on its largest job to date—the complete design of all aspects of a new water system for the city of Merida. I was to spend eight to ten weeks gathering the needed information. I was given a complete, brand new set of surveying equipment, along with a new car and a Spanish-speaking driver. But there were no other technical people to fill out my needs when I had to survey.

The big problem was that my Spanish vocabulary had only grown to about fifty words, and my driver's knowledge of English was zero. I had a small English-Spanish dictionary but was otherwise expected to find a way to get the job done. Needless to say, it didn't take long to learn how to order eggs and bacon for breakfast. And I soon learned things to do besides just make motions with my hands, especially when it came to training a four-man totally green crew how to hold a surveyor's rod or steel chain in such a way that the end results were accurate. So I took full advantage of my driver. By every sign-language means possible I told the crew what needed to be done, then asked my driver to tell them in simple Spanish what to do or what I had just tried to say. I listened and then, as best as I could, repeated it to see if they did the same thing the next time around. In this way it wasn't too long before my conversation grew to such an extent that I could get along with the crew with less and less of the driver's help.

I was eager to get the information to the American design team as soon as possible, but I hadn't been in Merida more than a day before I learned its water supply was so polluted that in the city of twelve thousand people there were an average of ten cases of typhoid fever a week. It would be at least a couple of years before the new water supply system could be designed and built and put into operation.

Something had to be done. I couldn't just go about my assigned business and ignore the present typhoid fever epidemic. Merida had a fine smaller university and hospital, so I looked up the chief medical officer to discuss with him what I saw as a very grave problem needing correction. Fortunately, the doctor spoke passable English. After a few introductory remarks about what I had heard regarding the typhoid epidemic and my assigned mission of helping in the long-term solution for the water supply, I posed this question to him: "What do you think we should do about the present emergency?"

He responded that the problem was grave and felt the solution would be to blow the concrete cover off the water reservoir at the high point of the city so the sun could shine on the water and, by passing through it, purify it of the typhoid germs. Having just come from the best sanitary engineering school in the world, I struggled to keep a poker face and replied, "The reservoir holds only about twelve hours of follow-through, and the sun could only shine on the water half the time. There are many days with no sun shining at all."

He then very politely asked me what I might suggest as a solution. This was my opportunity to outline my plan to install a good gas chlorinator, even if it took a month to be sent from Caracas. We could ask the Obras Publicas National to approve the plan and send one as soon as possible. I would be able to install it and get it running. After agreeing on this we next discussed what could be done immediately. I suggested that if he gave the go-ahead I would make a reliable homemade chlorinator using a fifty-five gallon oil drum, fabricate a constant head orifice, and fill it with chlorine bleach powder dissolved in water. That would give immediate protection.

The overall plan was cabled to Caracas and a favorable reply received. I got the homemade chlorinator working, and in less than two days the water supply was being safely chlorinated. The incidence of typhoid fell to zero, much to everyone's surprise.

In about a month the new English-made Patterson chlorinator arrived. I took off a day from my survey work to install it, and it worked very well. I relaxed, thinking the problem was now permanently solved. About eight to ten one-hundred-fifty-pound chlorine cylinders had been sent up with the new chlorinator, which were expected to last about four months. During this time there were no more typhoid cases, and everyone felt safe. Those who had boiled their water before stopped, for the chlorine alone was doing a good job. By the time the chlorine ran out, I had gone back to Caracas and had been assigned to other remote places and other tasks. However, no one took the responsibility of noting they were about to run out of chlorine cylinders and to order more from Caracas. Even worse, no one took the responsibility of notifying the citizens of the city of Merida, who were then relying on the chlorinating system to make the water safe. But it was no longer safe because of this neglect. In the United States such action or lack of action was looked upon as criminal neglect. Needless to say, a surge of new typhoid cases resulted, but the situation was corrected eventually.

The routine surveying work and other technical decisions and information for the design of a new water intake, water treatment plant, and water distribution system went rather well, and I finished the work on time. But before I left Merida I made two attempts as an inexperienced amateur to climb Pico Bolivar (the Peak of Bolivar). On the first try a friend and I thought we would try climbing the peak on a two-day venture. The peak is 16,426 feet altitude (Merida is about 6,000 feet). But to climb the peak we first had to drop about 800 feet into a valley before starting the real climb.

We left midmorning and spent the night with our sleeping bags at the last little native house on the well-used foot trail, about a mile before it crossed over the pass at the highest point at roughly 12,000 feet. The next morning we continued the ascent, first on the trail, then around the edge of a large valley between us and the peak to a point where the terrain appeared to slope at a climbable grade right up to the snow-covered peak. The farther we climbed the more beautiful the scenery became, for we could see peak after peak in the Andean chain. We could even look over into Colombia and see several of the snow-covered peaks there.

At this point we became concerned about how we would climb onto the snow and icecap of the mountain to make it all the way to the top and, if the cloud cover came in as it often did about midday, whether we could safely find our way back down the slopes and rocks to the trail. We were close to 16,000 feet elevation and noticed that breathing was much harder and our rate of climb a lot slower. Instead of the route we had picked leading on to the snow peak, it led to a sheer cliff with a drop down of about 800 feet before it ascended to the peak again. We had needed a good map but didn't have one.

Simultaneously the clouds came in, and it didn't take us long to make the wise decision to retrace our steps to the main trail just before the fog became too dense for us to find our way. Once we reached the trail we lost no time making the long hike back to Merida.

I looked upon this first attempt as an exploratory trip. The next should be planned with experienced climbers of the peak, and I found a mountain climbing club at Merida University. None of the members had been up the Peak of Bolivar, but three decided to join me on the next climb. They learned that the best way up to the peak was to go farther around and approach it from the south, thus avoiding the 1000 foot drop-off.

We would leave the city before midnight, take the well-used trail in the dark, and arrive at the point where we would strike out across the rough mountain slopes about daylight, then go nonstop to the peak and retrace our steps to the trail before dark. There we could decide whether to come all the way back or rest first, but at least we would have accomplished our goal.

The four of us started off with great enthusiasm. We hiked so fast we reached the point where we were to leave the trail and had to wait an hour before daylight to start over the rough terrain. We were well above timberline, where the ground was covered with scrubby evergreens and edelweiss. The rocky mountain slope was steep, but the scenery was terrific.

As we gained altitude and the sun got higher we became warm and had to rest frequently to catch our breaths. We picked a spot we could find on the way back where we left about a third of the weight of our backpacks.

But here a minor tragedy occurred. While packing that morning one of my companions had shoved my new razor-sharp machete into my backpack with little thought as to whether it could slip out. In unloading our gear, I felt something coming loose and instinctively reached behind me to catch it. I pressed the sharp edge of the blade so that it cut my left palm to the bone by my left thumb. The deep cut bled profusely, but we finally made the wound stable by tightly tying a large handkerchief to hold the thumb firmly against my palm.

Although the cut could get much worse before we got back to Merida, and the condition of my hand would handicap my further rock climbing, I decided that I could keep up and continued on with the group.

We began to wonder how good were the instructions we had been given. Nothing looked like it should, and we had to lose altitude in several places to circle to the point where we would ascend the peak from the south. After four more hours we had eaten lunch and twice left more clothes and weight from our backpacks. We realized we had gone out of our way by a considerable distance, and if we had not left our belongings in these three places we could have returned to the pass on the main trail by an easier, shorter route.

Now the clouds showed strong signs of covering the peak before the day was over. But there was still a chance the weather would improve, so we pushed on. In the next two hours we got to the point where we would soon climb up onto the glacier covering the peak, only about a two-hundred to three-hundred-foot vertical climb. But the clouds were gradually lowering from the peak and soon to engulf us. After a bit of soul searching of what we wanted to do and what we knew was the safe thing to do, we decided to descend quickly to the well-marked trail. I suggested that the other three take the better shorter way back and that I go by myself at as fast a pace as I could and pick up the belongings we had left behind.

It was about three in the afternoon, and by six thirty it would be dark. It had taken us almost eight hours to come up from where we had left the trail. Even though my return trip was considerably longer than the route the others were taking, I had advantages. I had memorized landmarks so that I could find my way even with the partial cloud cover, and I had the incentive to get back to care for my injury.

Going downhill with a light load was easier, and I took long fast strides in a kind of gallop. I found the piles of clothes, but by the time I approached the last one the cloud cover became much worse and I had to wait about a quarter of an hour before I could go on. I finally reached the trail about six o'clock. My hand was becoming more uncomfortable. I got to the small stone shelter on the trail where I was to meet the others and unloaded the clothes and waited.

The others should have been there, and I worried that they may have taken a wrong turn or been hampered by the clouds. In a few minutes it was dark, and I wondered if their two small flashlights were adequate. I dozed for an hour, mistakenly thought I heard people once, and my hand throbbed so much I longed to get to the Merida hospital. About seven thirty I knew I should not wait until morning to go back to Merida, so I left a note on the pile of belongings and started down the trail, which had taken us seven hours to climb earlier that morning.

I had only one small flashlight and needed to conserve it for the more difficult parts of the trail. I made my best time employing the same gallop I had used earlier. Amazingly, I made it all the way back to my hotel by ten o'clock. Twenty-three hours had passed since we had left the night before.

My friend the German proprietor of the hotel took me directly to the hospital. Fortunately, a young intern was on duty. He cleaned the wound on my hand and said he should also take about ten stitches to close it. Because of the late hour and no other staff there, he was unable to give me a local anesthetic; would I like it to be sewed up anyway? I said yes, and my friend offered his next-best form of anesthesia: He put his two thumbs into my ears and pushed so hard the pain diverted my mind from the surgical needle the intern pushed through the thick skin of my palm about twenty times. Despite the throbbing ache I managed to sleep, for my mind was at ease and I knew I had done the right thing in coming back by myself.

Late the next afternoon my three friends made their way back to the hotel. They had gotten lost and when darkness fell were not sure where the trail might be so huddled in a small cave until daylight. When they reached the little rock shelter they were sure I had gone on to Merida but failed to look inside and find my note and their belongings. The following weekend two of us climbed back up the trail to recover their things.

I was disappointed that we had not succeeded either time to reach the Peak of Bolivar. However, we had played the game right and safely and had enjoyed every bit of our time. And I was grateful my first assignment in Venezuela had been in Merida, thus making the climbs possible.

CHAPTER SEVEN

The Ultimate Adventure

A lthough Merida had been an excellent place to start my training in Venezuela, I was ready for the break afforded by two weeks in Caracas where I was first debriefed on Merida and then briefed as to the nature of my next two assignments in Valera and Trujillo. Both cities were bigger and more sophisticated than Merida. Each had its own problems, field decisions to be made, and lines to be surveyed.

By this time my Spanish had greatly improved. Even with my limited vocabulary and poor grammar, I could make my points much better and understand what was being said to me. Likewise, I had been able to communicate more effectively with the American design team and give them exactly what they needed for their best designs.

Valera was surrounded by much cattle land, and our surveying took us through too much. The area was full of ticks. Hundreds of thousands would be picked up in passing through the shrubbery. Every night on returning to the hotel I was red with bites all around my waist and elsewhere. I had heard that these ticks carried Rocky Mountain spotted fever and thought it was important to take precautions. I had a jumpsuit custom made for me, which zipped up each arm and leg and was tight around my neck. When I went through the underbrush and a couple of hundred ticks landed midbody, they started crawling in every direction. As soon as I was aware of this I pulled a small whisk broom out of my back pocket and brushed them off. In this way I was able to reduce the actual bites to about 5 percent of what they had been. Yet in about three weeks I got quite sick and was told by the local doctor I had Rocky Mountain spotted fever. He prescribed shots of a French medicine in glass vials and a lot of raw vegetables. The shots didn't seem to have either a good or bad effect on my fever, but the contamination on the vegetables brought on a lot of diarrhea. After a couple of days in bed I went back to work but felt weak or somewhat ill for several weeks.

The natives of the Andes region most feared the snakes, including pythons, which were quite common. The pythons looked frightening, but it was really some of the small, hard-to-see snakes that were dangerous and even deadly. I used high leather boots so felt rather safe, and generally the two helpers with their machetes up front cutting a pathway for us to use in the survey were in more danger. There were also on a number of occasions encounters with tarantula spiders; if they got a chance to bite they were rather dangerous but seldom deadly. We were not in an area for malaria, for the climate in the Andes was ten to fifteen degrees cooler than that in the tropical forests of Venezuela.

As a single person thrust into a foreign country for two years I had many adjustments to make. Evenings and weekends needed to be constructively filled, not just the forty-hour work week. In the interior of Venezuela almost no one spoke English, and my limited command of Spanish lent little to a social life. The radio, all in Spanish, did help me learn to speak better. I had brought along a good short wave radio and was able to get several of the British Broadcasting Corporation and United States news and music programs.

My major professor at Harvard had urged me to waste no time condensing the best data in my doctoral thesis into three technical articles for publication. This involved a lot of work, and my little portable typewriter, used in writing the thesis in the first place, was indispensable; but I couldn't spend all my free time on this task, worthwhile as it was.

The disciplined time I spent studying Spanish vocabulary, grammar, and speech had gratifying results, but two phenomena were soon noted. First, I found myself constantly substituting my native Chinese words in place of what was intended to be Spanish and wondered why people couldn't understand me. The second phenomenon came a little later as I became more proficient in Spanish. When I would meet a Chinese friend and try to practice my Suzhou dialect, which I formerly spoke with ease, I for the life of me couldn't say a thing. All I could think of was Spanish, and I was very embarrassed. With the passing of the years my Chinese, the language I learned as a child, came back, and the Spanish, learned the hard way and much later, faded. Even today I get the words mixed up and still make mispronounced substitutions but no longer to the point of complete frustration.

Reading and letter writing also took up much of my spare time, and for recreation and relaxation I sought out games of chess. I remember especially Ken Brown who represented several United States firms in Venezuela and traveled in the interior. He was an excellent chess player, and we would engage each other whenever possible. Ken used to be a "hooked" player spending every possible moment in a chess club. Then one day he looked around and came to an important discovery. There were over fifty members in the chess club, all good players but not one a successful businessman, for each was so captivated with the game he neglected other important parts of his life. Then and there Ken made the decision to give up chess, which he did until he found time on his hands in the interior of Venezuela. I, too, have learned from Ken's experience not to let anything like chess obsess me.

The driving force within me, the direction and source of motivation, came out of my morning periods of meditation and my practice of having quiet times, or two-way prayer. Writing down my thoughts each day had become habitual over the last two years at Harvard, and this allowed me to look at the thoughts more in detail and helped me to separate the wheat from the chaff of my human thinking and self-will. I did very much miss the close fellowship I had enjoyed and found most beneficial in Cambridge. There we often got guidance for each other. When two or more had the same guidance on the same subject, the content of that thinking could be relied upon as opposed to one's own inner thinking, which was much more likely to become blurred with one's desire and self-will. So in my isolation in the heart of the Venezuelan Andes I missed the necessary strength of spiritual fellowship. I especially needed the right thinking for my very best girlfriend, Florence Moffett.

After six months of having been rather isolated in Venezuela, somewhat to my surprise I kept getting guidance that it was the right time to ask Florence to be my life partner. These thoughts persisted to the point where I knew in my heart it was much more than desire or self-will. The thought then came to check this important decision with a very close friend, Francis Bradley, in Boston. Francis had known me very well over the last two years, and I could trust him and his guided checking of this important question: Should I or should I not ask Florence to marry me?

I was truly elated when I received Francis's affirmative response and lost little time composing my letter to Florence with the big question: "Will you be my loving wife?" I added, "If the answer is yes, I will call you long distance and I will ask you again and personally hear your wonderful yes."

So it came to be. We planned for Florence to join me in Venezuela in six months and for us to spend my last year there together. To me this was the ultimate gift—God's selection of a man and woman as each other's lifelong partners. This, of course, was the most important decision I had ever made. My feeling is that the same kind of decision, along with the same certainty and happiness, is truly available to all prospective husbands and wives, and it is the best conviction I can pass to the next generation.

During the next six months my step was light and my heart full of joy as I continued my field work for the government of Venezuela and at the same time made countless detailed plans for Florence's departure from Richmond, Virginia, where she was a public health nurse, and her arrival in Caracas. I arranged with my bosses for me to be in the field only a quarter as much time after Florence arrived. We planned for a car, a house, and furniture, some of which she would bring down with her.

Getting married in Venezuela had certain complications. The law stated that a foreigner arriving in the country would have to wait six weeks to be legally married. The solution to this problem was for each of us to appoint a legal proxy and have them go through the wedding steps on our behalf prior to Florence's arrival in December. So friends of mine, Mr. and Mrs. Usacho, did this for us, and when Florence arrived on December 7, 1939, we were already legally married. The law further required us to have a state wedding before a magistrate, which was all in Spanish. Naturally, we wanted a church wedding. A close friend of mine, Rev. Bancroft Reifsnyder, who headed a Presbyterian mission in Venezuela, tied the sacred knot. He and his family and other members of their mission went all out to make us feel welcome. They even made available to us for our honeymoon their mountain hideaway at Los Teques, a small village about fifty miles away.

"Cloud nine" was much too low a cloud to describe our honeymoon. We had seven years of time to go over, from the time we first had been drawn to each other but had been held back by some hidden force or infinite wisdom from full participation of life together. We had the joy of living one day at a time, which was upon us, and the fun of looking into the future as one instead of as two.

We had a rented car and enjoyed seeing the area together as well as spending a glorious day on the white sand and in the surf of a nearby beach. We shared with each other the depths of our lives— both the good things and the bad—and felt better and closer for it. We prayed and thanked God for the gifts he had given us, especially the gift of each other. We dedicated our lives to the Almighty and started having periods of meditation together, a practice that over the years has given us direction, unity, and purpose for living. It was a wonderful beginning of what at this writing has lasted fifty-seven years.

Upon our return to Caracas we spent two weeks in a pension, a small, family-style hotel, and then a nice little house turned up in La Florida, a suburb of Caracas, where we made our first home. The Obras Publicas National was true to its promise to use my services in the Caracas office most of the time and only sent me to the field when something important came up which they thought I should handle. I enjoyed this change of work from the field to the office. It broadened my practical experience and also made me more valuable to the government when I was assigned to the field. Most of the time I was under the number two Venezuelan engineer, Dr. Leon, and I enjoyed our close working relationship. Our major emphasis was in the design of water distribution systems rather than the treatment plants that were being handled by the American design team.

During the next year Florence and I were especially active with the American community in Caracas, which had grown to over five hundred. We joined the country club, which was not too expensive, visited with friends in homes, and took an occasional day at one of the nearby beautiful beaches. Every once in a while we attended a concert or a movie in Spanish or English with Spanish subtitles. What brought us the most satisfaction, however, was the organizing of an American Protestant church, which soon grew to well over one hundred members.

One day a fine looking young Austrian fellow, a refugee named Bill Cornides, came to the church to worship with us. After church as I was visiting with him I had a very strong feeling about him. It came to me very clearly that I needed to spend some time with him and should ask him to join me on a hike up the nine-thousand-foot range between Caracas and the sea. He accepted, and we had a rewarding day together, during which time I talked about my life, my defeats, my victories, and how God had helped me change and become a much more effective person. Before the day was over I was shown why I had been led to have this time with my new friend. He told me that he had planned to take his own life the very next day, but now he was confident that God was real and had a plan for him. Bill became a regular active member of our church, and eventually he became a priest. I feel that God taught me as much that day as he did Bill—the importance of being open to the inner voice and what obeying it can mean for others and for oneself.

Florence and I were able to see some of the places in the interior where I had spent a lot of time by myself. She could take the unpleasant things along with the pleasant, and these experiences we had together helped us to grow and become one.

We got so that we rated all the hotels we stayed in by the kind of napkins they put on the table. First was the cloth-napkin hotel, of which we had only one. Second was the whole-paper-napkin hotel, then the half-paper-napkin hotel. Finally, in a little town of five hundred named La Grita at an elevation of about six thousand feet we had a quarter-napkin hotel, where we stayed for about ten days. I had located the town's best new source of drinking water from a large and beautifully clean spring up in the mountains about three miles away and had to survey the line and grade of the supply line to be built.

Generally the quarter- and half-napkin hotels had other distinguishing marks of excellence, or lack of excellence, such as cows sleeping in the patio or unmentionable qualities in the showers and rest rooms. The main thing is that we survived and learned about life in the third world. We became ever more desirous of serving as missionaries in China as had our parents.

I was especially grateful that one of our field trips took us to the city of Merida, where we stayed in the Hotel Aleman and each morning were greeted by the inspiring view from the patio of the snowcapped Peak of Bolivar. We not only enjoyed our stay in Merida but couldn't help starting to plan a third attempt at climbing the summit.

Based on my experience of the last two tries we were able to plan well. I arranged for two mules—one for our excess gear and the other for Florence. These we took as far as the last house on the well-worn mountain trail at an elevation of about twelve thousand feet, and from there we moved on foot. Leaving the trail we dropped down and crossed a lower valley, then continued up into a high and almost level area just below the talus that reached the start of the snow and icecap. Here we made camp and used a large supply of edelweiss, which with our blankets made up a warm and comfortable bed. At that altitude—fourteen thousand feet— temperatures fell to well below freezing, and ice was everywhere in the morning. The night gave us a glorious view of the stars, the likes of which we have not seen since.

After breakfast we left most of our things at the camp, made our way slowly up the rough and steep talus, and came to the base of the ice cap. Up close it looked much more ominous than it had at a distance. The edge looked about like I would expect the edge of a one-hundred-foot glacier to look, and the problem was how to get from there up onto the slope of the cap itself so that we could make our way to the summit. We lacked ropes and ice grapples for our boots, and the only thing I had thought to bring along to cut steps in the ice was my trusty machete. I did have a proper leather case for it this time.

After some search we found a kind of crevasse or break in the wall of ice, where we could safely climb up from the talus to the surface of the cap of ice and snow. Once we were on the cap we were both relieved. It appeared that it would be only a matter of another hour before we climbed the last two hundred fifty vertical feet to the summit. Our progress, however, was greatly slowed by the fact that each step had to be made by chopping it with my rather light machete. There was a lot more ice than we had anticipated.

We had advanced on the cap perhaps a third of the way toward our goal when my dark glasses fell off and broke so that they could not be used. We were already being bothered by the extreme brightness of the sun, which was greatly intensified by the altitude and the white snow and ice. Breathing became difficult and now, besides the sunburn, which was getting to us, we had the worry of my not being able to see and possibly going blind. We struggled on for another fifty feet and then once again reviewed our options. If we went on we might make our goal, but we might do serious damage to ourselves, especially our eyes. The worst scenario would end the beginning of a long life together. The vote was unanimous: We would turn around, short of our goal, but opting for a long and sure life together.

The trip down was uneventful except for our having to nurse very painful sunburns and somewhat deflated egos, but we knew that we had made the right decision. Certainly there are other things in life more important than climbing to the top of the Peak of Bolivar. Over the years we have found many. This was a part of our growing up and putting first things first, especially putting God's will for us first.

During the remainder of 1940, Florence's first year with me, the war in Europe grew more and more serious and gave us both concern. For some time we had talked about serving as missionaries in China. Dr. McMullen, the comptroller at Hangzhou University, where I had taught in 1934-35, wanted us to join the Presbyterian mission and be part of the university staff, and now we made formal application to the mission board. A few months later we were accepted and urged by the board to shorten our stay in Venezuela by two months to be ready to join the staff for the beginning of the second semester. By early October it appeared that our future was all set, and we made plans to sell our belongings in Venezuela and return to New York.

Our plan was first to visit our friends in the Boston area for several days and then take in North Carolina and Tennessee to see all of our relatives before we set sail for China. It was the end of a wonderful first year together. Could the rest of our life possibly be as gratifying? We already had the beginning of a new life within Florence and were grateful for it. We had given it the nickname Chico, "little boy" in Spanish. Chico was a constant reminder of our first year together in Latin America.

CHAPTER EIGHT

From Theory to Practice

We had been looking forward to the five-day return voyage to the States for weeks—another honeymoon, including a glorious day in Bermuda. Instead, a different plan evolved. Florence's prenatal doctor told us all was not well with her pregnancy, that she should have complete bedrest on the ship and have another doctor's opinion as soon as we reached Boston. Although disappointed, we accepted the situation with courage and optimism and prayed that soon all would be well and normal again. I felt bad that only I could enjoy the luxuries of the ship and see the sights in Bermuda, and all Florence got were verbal reports from me. By the time we were scheduled to dock in New York, Florence seemed so much better that it appeared she was about well again.

As the big ship drew up to the dock we looked down from the deck and saw my good friend John Honnold, an honor student from the Harvard Law School, and his new wife waving at us. John now had a job with a prestigious New York law firm. We had become very close friends through the Wesley Foundation at Harvard. We were close not only intellectually and spiritually, but in other ways, including our sense of humor.

John knew the reputation of Venezuela as a world producer of diamonds, and he called up to me on the deck, "What did you do with the diamonds?"

Embarrassed by his not-too-well-considered humor I tried to shut him off and said, "Don't worry!" It turned out that we were the last to be cleared in customs, for someone had reported the brief exchange. That bit of humor cost us an hour and a half delay.

After our two-day visit, the Honnolds put us on the train to Boston, and just two hours later we were with my Uncle Arthur Brikett and Aunt Flora, who with my three cousins had made me feel at home during my stay at Harvard. This was to be our base for several days while we saw a few friends in the greater Boston area. Florence's brother Alex was at that time doing a residency at Beth Israel Hospital, so our visit with him was a priority. He put us in touch with the right obstetrician to check on Florence's condition, which once again had become more acute. Her new doctor's prognosis was that the pregnancy was not going at all well and that the only right step at this point was to terminate it. Although greatly disappointed, we both accepted the wisdom of this excellent obstetrician. The next day Florence entered the hospital and had the procedure. We were indeed fortunate to have the quiet love and care of my uncle and aunt in their lovely Natick home, where Florence regained her strength the following week.

During this week of Florence's recovery I looked up friends in Boston, Cambridge, and at Harvard. During my two-year absence much had happened, and it was good to get caught up. The war situation was getting more serious each week, and it was a question as to how long before America would be in actual combat. Already the "Arsenal for Democracy" was in high gear; we were helping our friends and getting ready for the day we also would be fighting.

Against this backdrop I was approached by a friend of mine asking if I would like to take a job at Metcalf and Eddy, probably the most prestigious environmental firm in the world. We would work on a top-priority research job the War Department had given them, and they were looking for the right qualified man to work with them.

TNT plants were being built all over the country in preparation for the war. The manufacture of TNT produced a strong toxic waste which was difficult to treat. The experts seemed to think the waste might be treated using anaerobic digestion if it could be made to digest properly. The news of my having spent over two years of research on the general subject of anaerobic digestion at Harvard had gotten around. Although it was only a three-month assignment I knew its importance and decided to accept.

This job, coming out of the blue, changed our whole planning for the future. We decided to stay in Boston for at least three months and perhaps six, delaying our trip to Nashville. As to when it would be right to go to China with the mission board was somewhat in question because of the war situation, which reinforced our decision to stay in Boston.

We found a nice third-floor apartment in Cambridge overlooking the Harvard graduate school tennis courts and settled in with the new job, location, and friends. Metcalf and Eddy had the eleventh floor of the Statler Building overlooking Boston Commons, and it was a simple quick run on the subway from home to work. I enjoyed working directly under one of the partners of the firm and with its chief chemist. By the end of the three months we had the answers to the problem and had submitted a confidential report to the War Department. Naturally, I had an interest in staying on longer with Metcalf and Eddy. Although their work in the Boston office had dropped off to just a trickle, they decided to keep me on, partly as a reward for the good job I had just completed.

During the next three months I learned the way a big consulting firm handles the design of sewage treatment plants for small to moderate-size towns. This kind of work was all new to me and, therefore, very interesting. But it was not closely tied to the war effort and made me feel I was not in the mainstream of things. M&E, as it was called, had a big office in Bermuda, which was connected to the war effort. All the old-time and essential employees were being encouraged to transfer to Bermuda.

There were three rather large and very well-known consulting firms in Boston, known as the "big three." The partners of these three firms knew each other well, and with the war work going on they worked even more closely together. Instead of being inefficient and holding onto the middle and lower-level employees, they shared them so that the resources of all three firms were used to a maximum. I fell into this category and felt that not only was I getting a real break but that the most crucial war work was getting done much faster and better than it would have otherwise.

Since many of the M&E workers were being transferred to Bermuda, I interviewed at Fay, Spofford and Thorndyke and was offered a comparable job with them. They had a large rush war job designing a new dry-dock for the Boston Shipyards. They needed help especially in hydraulics, for a dry-dock is full of pipes and pumps. By this time I had learned that the big three firms had a peacetime practice to keep beginners on the drawing board, even though they usually were not trained draftsmen but trained engineers. The thought was that to learn engineering correctly you had to learn to be a draftsman first. I did not feel this was right or efficient, and I didn't care about drafting either. By doing drafting instead of engineering I was not getting top experience soon enough.

The other thing I learned was that most of the people in the big three thought well of practical-type engineers but poorly of academic-type engineers, especially those with advanced degrees. Hence, I learned not to let anyone know that I had a master's degree from Illinois and a doctorate from Harvard, and I got along fine. I took care of the "draftsman-first" problem by not drafting too well, but I carefully helped some of the designers in checking their engineering calculations.

During my first summer at Fay, Spofford and Thorndyke, the firm brought in a famous Massachusetts Institute of Technology (MIT) professor to give them a hand on the hydraulic design for three war bases, storm drainage pipes, and other like facilities. At the end of the summer the man went back to teaching. Needing to have all work in an engineering office checked by a second independent engineer, they picked me, for by that time they had confidence in my ability to handle problems in hydraulics. The assignment turned out to be very embarrassing. I had not been on the task very long before I found that the renowned professor had made a series of serious errors, and now I was the young inexperienced guy questioning his authority. Fortunately, I found an engineer with some standing in the firm who could understand what the differences were all about and that, despite my junior status, I was 100 percent right and the professor had been thinking about other things when he got into those design problems. The differences were large, and the mistakes, if left uncorrected, would have been costly. The experience did greatly enhance my standing in the firm, and I was asked to either design or check all the designs in hydraulics from then on.

At FS&T I had one of the best supervisors I have ever had, Bill Hyland. He knew not only his engineering but how to handle people as well. He could inspire them, get 120 percent of a day's work out of those working under him, and tell them how to do something better while not making them feel bad. He deeply cared for all those he supervised. In later years I wished I had had more time under him and learned to more fully master his techniques so that I would be able to do the same for my younger employees.

The next big push in design related to the war, which the United States had entered by that time, was with the largest of the big three firms, the one that had a reputation of combining design with the construction phase. The project had to move so fast that there was no time to finish the design phase, take bids, and then get on with the construction. Instead, the project was done on a cost-plus basis all at the same time. Although things usually cost a bit more this way, they could be completed in about half the time. So it was that I became an employee of the famed Stone and Webster Engineering firm and helped with not only one but three large TNT plants in various parts of the country. I learned much about how the big three did things and did them well and why they were sought by clients from all over the world to engineer big projects. I truly felt blessed to have worked for these three firms a total of two years on a variety of important war-related projects.

The disaster at Pearl Harbor on December 7, 1941, came just about four months before I started work with Stone and Webster. Our first child, Dorothea, was born March 19, 1942, just as I was making the move. By fall 1942 I was trying to discover how my time and talents could best fit into and make their biggest contribution to the war effort. All sanitary engineers, as we were called, were assigned to an area of maximum use to that effort. Although I was subject to the draft and had a low draft number, the decision made for sanitary engineers was supposed to be of higher authority than the decisions of the draft boards, although the draft boards did not always follow this policy. At this critical time I was approached by a friend, Frank Flood, formerly of Metcalf and Eddy who was now in charge of the water, waste water, and solid waste sections, plus pest control, of the First Service Command, which included all army and air force posts and outposts in the six New England states and Long Island. He wanted a right-hand man and trainee for his job. Compared with the work I had been doing, this seemed more important to the war effort. Though still a civilian, I would be in the Army Corps of Engineers and working with the military on a day-to-day basis. Furthermore, I would be using all of my knowledge in the effort and at the same time filling out my experience record with special emphasis in the operations area that was important to good design. The further satisfaction of this new work was that it was, for all practical purposes, draft proof for the duration.

The First Service Command, one of eight commands in the United States, included fifty major posts, three with populations of over fifty thousand, and over three hundred outposts along special coastal points of military importance. Important programs undertaken on all bases (where they applied) were as follows: 1) superchlorination of the drinking water to prevent enemy contamination; 2) corrosion control of the water distribution systems to keep the rate of flow up to standard and greatly extend the life of the wartime-used black-iron hot water pipes; 3) cathodic protection of corrosion in all the elevated water storage tanks; 4) repair of underground leaks in the water distributions; 5) replacement of seaside outposts' deep salty wells with shallow fresh ones; 6) replacement of dangerous cyanide gas to control vermin in the barracks with the newly discovered, highly effective DDT. We also gave more detailed technical supervision to the operators of the eight larger sewage treatment plants, and analyzed and solved special problems that came up.

One such problem was unique. At the air base at Presque Isle, Maine, our northernmost point, the water supply taken from the Presque Isle River became so grossly contaminated with potato starch wastes from a large factory that it was much stronger smelling and more offensive than stale raw sewage. To discover the cause and correct the problem, it was necessary to travel upriver with the ambient temperature at -25 degrees F and on none other than a dogsled, taking samples of the water through the twenty-four inches of ice as we went. There was no way to sweep the decaying potato starch out of the bottom of the river before the spring freshet came, so a temporary way of making this impossible water potable had to be found. Superchlorination was ineffective, but a new compound, chlorine dioxide, had just become available and turned out to be most effective.

Another experience, this with the commanding general at Fort Devens, created a lot of stir but was happily resolved. We had successfully replaced the former burning dumps at the three other large posts with the new concept of sanitary landfills. However, the general at Fort Devens wanted nothing to do with this newfangled idea. One day I had a call from him, and he said, "You can put that sanitary landfill in any time you like." I asked him why the change of heart. He told me they had a bad fire at the dump, and when the fire department came to put it out, there were so many rats running everywhere that the firemen were afraid to get off their truck. So before we could install the new sanitary landfill system where no burning was allowed but where the fresh refuse brought in each day was first compacted and then covered with a layer of compacted earth, it was first necessary to poison the existing rats so they could not migrate to other parts of the base. To everyone's surprise this poisoning program resulted in the killing of an estimated twenty thousand rats, which formed a pile over six feet high. From then on we got nothing but praise from the commanding general.

The corps had a fine trailer laboratory, manned by competent service personnel, which was very useful in helping to solve many problems. Everything we did and saw was confidential, and it was exciting to be at the forefront of the staging area for the war in

Europe. It was a thrill to visit the Strategic Air Force base at Westover Field Air Base and see the new giant bombers and transport planes that had such a big part in winning the air war. It was also a sobering experience to visit the forty-thousand-person base known as Camp Myles Standish, from which troops to Europe were sent. They would board special trains—about twenty thousand at a time—for ships in New York or elsewhere to go to Europe.

Often I thought, "But for the grace of God I should be on one of those putting my life squarely on the line." Although emotionally I wanted to go all the way to the front like so many others, I knew that being one of a rather scarce breed of sanitary engineers I had few options. The board in control of our limited number of sanitary engineers said (and I agreed) that I was doing the best thing for our country by serving in the Corps of Engineers, though I was still a civilian. Should I join the army as an officer, which I could do; I would be assigned to the so-called sanitary corps, and my tasks would be inspection of mess halls and vermin control in barracks, which would be far less useful than the job I was already in.

Almost three years went by, and it was not until V-E Day that my priorities changed, and I had to rethink everything. In the meantime, Florence and I had two more beautiful daughters, Karen and Martha, now three girls in all, and my chance of being drafted dropped, for all practical purposes, to zero. With the war in Europe over, the job I was in had turned from a staging area to one of bringing the boys back from Europe. Now the emphasis was on the war in the Far East to bring Japan to her knees. The place in which I could be most useful was China, where I knew the people and something of the language. The United States Public Health Service (USPHS) was part of the armed forces, and it held out what seemed to me a strategically important position. It would mean being an officer doing work comparable to my existing job. In China I would be part of the war effort and eventually of the bigger reconstruction program as soon as the Japanese were defeated. To me this was far more important than being an inspector of army mess halls and would again use all of my talents as a sanitary engineer.

Because this meant leaving Florence and our three young

daughters for perhaps a year or longer, we gave the matter a lot of thought and prayer and checked it with some of our new friends in Moral Re-Armament in the Boston area. When it became very clear that this was the right thing to do, I accepted the commission as a major in the USPHS in June 1945.

The war with Japan came to a rather sudden and abrupt halt with the dropping of the two atomic bombs, and V-J Day came on September 14, 1945. My pretraining with the USPHS continued in the States, and instead of being flown from Burma over the "Hump" into China, I waited for the first ship to leave for China to pick up some of the First Marine Division. It was November before I set sail from San Francisco.

I have related the professional side of my life covering the five years when I moved from my academic training to my work. But there was also our family life, which was in many ways as important, if not more important. During these five years we went from a one-bedroom apartment in Cambridge to a two-bedroom apartment when our first daughter was born. Within a few months we found a nice little rental house in Melrose, a bedroom suburb to Boston, and there we had our third daughter, Martha, our strawberry blond. Martha was only about eleven months old when I took off for my year in China.

In Melrose, five of us families were active in MRA. Never in our life before or since have we had such close friends each of whom would do anything for the others. We all looked to the Lord for our strength and were open books with each other, which, of course, made it much easier to live an effective spiritual life. The five couples were Bob and Jean Russell (Bob was an executive in the telephone company); Ralph and Helen Gage (Ralph was also with the phone company); Arthur and Cecyle Hackendorf (Arthur was an employee of the U. S. Department of Agriculture); Badger and Betty True (Badger was manager of a large can-manufacturing company).

We all had kids about the same age and saw a lot of each other. We even shared a large vegetable garden that we worked together. This produce was a big help in putting food on the table during wartime, specially when we took advantage of the at-cost commercial cans for preserving our surplus food for the winter. These friendships are strong today, more than fifty years later.

In 1940, about the time Florence and I returned to Boston from Venezuela, the activity of MRA became very intense. While at Harvard I had known a number of people in the work and was drawn closer to the work along with Florence. MRA launched a number of morale building plays and reviews, which drew much positive national attention, including strong endorsements from national leaders and generals. An excellent review of the work during that and the postwar period is the book by Garth Lean, *On the Tail of a Comet*. MRA involved world leaders from many countries as well as ordinary people who with the power of God were able to do extraordinary things otherwise impossible.

The spiritual strength I gained during various phases of my life stemmed largely from my relationship with the people associated with MRA. There is a distinction between the importance of this kind of close spiritual fellowship, where each one holds the others up to the high standards set for us in the Sermon on the Mount and to the importance of inner personal discipline, and where each individual is strengthened by reading the Bible and other spiritual literature, daily meditation, and two-way prayer or guidance of the Holy Spirit. Both phases are essential, or things are likely to drift off into a way of life not relevant to the needs of the real world today.

My adventures as a major in the USPHS in an unsettled China were to show how the good Lord can use an ordinary, very imperfect guy like me in exciting experiences.

CHAPTER NINE

China Again

I lost no time enlisting in the army's United Sates Public Health Service (USPHS) to serve in China in whatever capacity I was needed. The original plan was for me to fly from Burma over the "Hump" to Chongquing (Chungking) in West China. With the dropping of the atomic bomb, V-J Day came overnight, and the United States' whole China Theater plans changed with it. So it was determined that I should go to Shanghai on the first troop ship sent over to bring the fighting men home, and on November 8, 1945, I set sail on a "liberty" ship with only eight passengers, mostly correspondents.

My hometown, Suzhou, was only fifty-five miles from Shanghai, where I was first stationed. Early in my stay I had a free weekend and used the opportunity to take the jeep, carbine, and .45 pistol and drive up to Suzhou by myself. It had been over ten years since I was last there, and eight years of this time the Japanese and Chinese had been at war. It was an exciting trip, in part because, in the confusion of the surrender and the lack of repatriating ships, the Japanese were still in command in Suzhou. I must admit I felt a little strange—in fact, a little insecure—seeing twenty thousand Japanese everywhere and my being the only American. In true Japanese style they would stand and salute me as I passed alone in my jeep. I wanted to make a quick inspection of our home, which until a few weeks before had been the residence of a high-ranking Japanese officer. It had been well kept, but what interested me most was to see whether anyone had been up under the rafters where my folks had hidden our hunting guns and other valuables. Unfortunately, someone had found them and removed everything. Later in my stay I got back to Suzhou and looked up some friends.

On arriving in Shanghai I was assigned to serve in the United Nations Relief and Rehabilitation Organization (UNRRA) and the Chinese counterpart called CINRRA. The former was set up to be the advisors and the latter the doers in the field. However, in sanitary engineering there were virtually no qualified Chinese; hence, I was asked to perform a dual role for both organizations. I was one of eight USPHS personnel assigned to China. There was one other sanitary engineer, and the rest were medical doctors and dentists. We were all informally supervised by a medical man who was known previously to have been a right-hand man of Tito, the well-known Communist leader in Yugoslavia. It also became quite apparent after I had been there for only a few days that I was the only one of the group who did not have strong Communistic leanings. It seemed they had been especially recruited or brainwashed after their arrival to help the cause of the Chinese Communists in every way possible.

This tightly knit group not only worked as a team but had many perks worked out for themselves, including the following: the best rooms and housing in the area, fine cars and drivers, free food from the army mess at the same time they drew illegal per diem pay from the USPHS, the sharing of a good-looking white call girl, and trips to Hunan—the western Communist headquarters where some of them had been given nice gifts and plaques by Mao himself. Pressure was put on me from each of these men to comply with their goals and objectives, and they were openly hostile when I would not bend from my convictions and high moral standards. They really blew their collective tops when I went to the army officer and paid him for my meals, for we were already getting per diem for our meals in our paychecks. Even though I informed them of this ahead of time it created some fear among them, for they had found a man they could not mould to their pattern, and each of the seven in the USPHS now knew they had a serious problem with the military over per diem.

I was then called before the Yugoslavian Communist leader of all the health-oriented personnel and asked many questions as to why I would not go along with their ways of doing things. He ordered me back to Washington, but I said that I had come to be of service to China and intended to stay and that it was questionable whether he had any real authority over me. He then became very hostile, saying that I would either go back to Washington or go to North China and work up there (where I would be out of their way). I felt I was given the correct answer for him and said, "I have never been to North China, and I think I would like it up there."

The UN bureaucracy in North China was not stacked toward the Communist cause as it was at the Shanghai headquarters. Nonetheless, they were not without their influence. I was stationed at Tianjin (Tientsin), the UN headquarters for the five northern provinces of China. The UNRRA office had twenty-five people, while the CINRRA office had about three hundred eighty people. My assigned duty was to give technical supervision to the program in both offices to reconstruct the major water, waste water, and solid waste facilities in the five northern provinces.

Our two largest projects in the region were a program to clean out all the sewers in the city of Tianjin (over a million population) and a program to remove eight years of accumulated garbage in the city of Beijing (Peking). During the war between China and Japan no garbage trucks had been allocated to collect and remove garbage in the city; instead it was just dumped on designated streets over a distance of about twenty miles. The average cross section of these piles was four feet deep on the edges and twenty feet deep in the middle—a lot of garbage—but most of it had dried out or become composted with time except for that part that was being added each day. We set up portable narrow-gauge rails, loaded the garbage into small carts, and pushed these carts out of the city to fill low-lying areas in the country. For each project the UN gave us three thousand workers. Each of these workers was supposed to receive three pounds of flour, imported from the United States. They would take this and, using the difference in market price, trade their three pounds for ten pounds of native poor quality flour.

My seven men in the sanitary division were responsible only for the technical side of these two large projects as well as a number of varied smaller jobs. But one can imagine that with handling as much money as the project did there would be a great temptation for corruption even higher up. So it turned out to be. I knew that if I did not take some serious responsibility for this matter no one would, and the projects would not only run out of funds but were already getting a very bad name.

My personal investigations led me to one of my own men, a Chinese minister's son who gave technical supervision to a large part of the garbage removal job. I suspected he knew a lot about what was going on behind the scenes. So I spent an afternoon with this young fellow and explained quite a bit about my own inner convictions and thoughts about God. Finally he broke down and told me that he had been bought off and knew much of the inside workings of the graft group. He decided to turn states witness. I took him to the Chinese director of CINRRA, whom I knew to be an honest man, along with the deputy director. The five department heads under the director were known by the public to be crooked. In fact, the situation had become so bad by then the people in the area had nicknamed CINRRA "Relief for Self."

Around this time another very important thing happened. It seems that God answered our prayers to help solve the problem through a young Chinese man by the name of Paul Lee. During my time in Tianjin I was fortunate to be rooming with Dr. Jim Yee, a young American-born Chinese doctor who was also a Christian who practiced his faith. We, along with a small consecrated group of Chinese, would meet together from time to time to pray, meditate, and seek guidance as to what each of us should do, especially about this corruption situation. There came to our attention a young Chinese, a former bandit, who had about fifty men under him. Besides fighting the Japanese they had adopted some of the practices of Robin Hood by now, that is, robbing from the rich and giving to the poor. This fellow, named Lee Ying, was reported to have personally shot over fifty people and was also the grandson of a famous general, not now living. His mother was a devout Christian. One day Lee entered a small Chinese church and sat down in the back by himself during the service, which was in progress. As a result of what Lee heard from the minister and of a sense of the plan God had for him, Lee deeply felt all that goes with the experience of becoming a born-again Christian. On top of this experience was another, much more startling: Lee lost his eyesight, just as Paul did on his way to Damascus. All of this happening, along with Lee's nefarious past, gave the congregation and minister a lot to worry about, and they really didn't know what to do with him.

When Jim Yee and I heard about Lee, we had a strong feeling that Lee was changed for some special purpose concerning our situation. So we got in touch with him and invited him up to our room to hear the details of his story. Jim's knowledge of Chinese, although imperfect, was far better than mine. By this time Lee's sight had come back, but the congregation was very much afraid of him. Jim and I not only listened to Lee but prayed with him and sat down and sought guidance for his future. Strangely enough, we all had about the same thoughts, namely, that I should not only tell our CINRRA director about Lee but arrange for the director to interview him for a job. Jim and I strongly felt that Lee would have an important part in cleaning up the corruption.

A couple of days later the director and I met with Lee, and he was asked to personally tell his story to the director. The director was impressed and said to Lee, "We would like to hire you; however, you are not to report to anyone but me." This was the turning point in solving the corruption problem. I would see Lee in disguise on various parts of the job, and he would signal to me or Jim, and I would see him from time to time in our room. But it was all strictly confidential among Jim, me, the director, and his deputy (who was a devout Christian and part of our fellowship).

We got to know Lee very well. Because of the manner of his conversion we gave him a Christian name, Paul, which stuck with him for the rest of his life.

After a few weeks the director was satisfied that he had all the proof needed to convict each of his five department heads, but he had another problem. Politically, each of these crooked department heads was the director's superior, and special plans were needed to remove them. So he called in his deputy director and told him the situation. Then he said he was going on a week's vacation, leaving the deputy in charge, and by the time he got back he wanted all five department heads dismissed and charges brought against them. This action made a lot of stir, but it was the beginning of the housecleaning that went through the whole organization.

Paul stayed on after I left Beijing, but that was only the beginning of a long friendship between us. Five years later I was instrumental in getting Paul under a special congressional bill to come to the United States. We took him under our wing, taught him English, and got him jobs. For over twenty years he worked for the FBI on many delicate matters pertaining to the ideology among foreign students in this country. He is now retired, partially paralyzed from a stroke, but is a fighter and determined to continue to help bring friendship and understanding between the United States and the new China, which is emerging into free enterprise and toward democracy.

Ever since I was six and invited to accompany my dad on hunting trips, hunting had become for me the ultimate thing to do and to look forward to. Its magnetism grew stronger as I matured. I loved to hunt any kind of wild deer, rabbits, or game birds, including pheasant, quail, snipe, and duck, but duck hunting gave me the biggest thrill. There was nothing like ducks coming in fast and low with a whirring noise all their own. Invariably the sound would send chills up and down my spine. The key to success was to be ready, to be a good shot, and to know how much to lead them so that the shot would hit the fast-moving targets and not pass behind them. It was even more of a thrill when there was time to take aim on and bring down two ducks from a single flock. The other thrill was to then command the dog to go out into the paddy field and retrieve them.

Since I had been back in China I had not had the time nor the place to hunt as I used to. Then one day I heard about a lake twenty miles east of Tianjin where the duck hunting was reported to be excellent. I found out as much as I could about it. I learned that there was both good news and bad news. The good news was that it was a shallow lake about three feet deep and about three miles across. During the early morning hours and the late afternoon hours the duck were so thick that they darkened the sky when they were frightened and took off.

I also learned that the lake was used to advantage by one or more commercial hunters. They had camouflaged bamboo rafts on which they had mounted two homemade cannons using homemade shot consisting of stones, nails, and about anything the hunter could find and fire from two-inch pipes with black powder. Combining the cannons' tilts, a fuse between the two cannons cut just the right length, and correct aim and timing, the hunters usually took an average of one hundred ducks. They then waited a day or two before they ventured out and changed their camouflage.

The day finally came when one of my best friends, Marty, and I went out together. Marty was a former navy man who had joined CINRRA to help the Chinese he had learned to love during this particularly difficult time of postwar reconstruction. He had led several convoys of medical supplies into the interior and had many hair-raising experiences. One time Marty came back from one of the missions and told me how the Communists had ambushed the convoy and shot a passenger in the lead truck, whom they supposed to be the convoy leader. Marty had not half an hour earlier taken over from his driver to give him a bit of a rest, and the Communists, therefore, shot his driver rather than Marty himself. The strangest part was that his convoy was taking medical supplies to the part of the country that was already under Communist control, for CINRRA by treaty was to bring humanitarian aid to both the Nationalists and the Communists. The Communists burned all the medical supplies in the five trucks not knowing they were on the way to being delivered to their own people.

Marty's and my first trip to this duck-laden lake met all the expectations that had been building up in my mind for weeks. The hunting was more than the usual thrill for me. On the way home we had fun planning the next trip, with whom to share our twenty-five ducks, and where I could borrow a better shotgun next time. Along with all these good thoughts Marty told me some of the bad

news about the lake. On the northwest edge of the lake the First
Marine Division, who controlled that part of China during this
period, had their main ammunition depot with enough men to
protect it. On the southeast edge of the lake a band of Communist
irregulars had gathered, at first just to see what was going on. Later,
when their strength reached about five hundred, they would stage
night raids and make it much more difficult for the marines. Often
the marines declared the lake off limits to all its personnel. In a
number of instances the informal fighting took on the resemblance
of all-out war. Although officially the Americans had neutral status,
everyone knew that America was backing Chiang Kai-shek—also
the unofficial policy of the United Nations. The danger was
nonetheless there, and we not only had to be aware of it but had to
keep track of and obey the off-limits orders of the marine command.

Even with the marines occasionally closing the lake to
recreation, Marty and I, and now and then others, planned duck
hunting trips there. It was always something to look forward to.
One night Marty gave me a call and with great enthusiasm told me
of a hunt which a group of his friends were planning for the
following Saturday. Fourteen were to go in three jeeps. Several
marine friends had been included. Would I put it on my calendar
and be sure to be part of the group? I very much wanted to go and
had that day free. But on Sunday when I saw Marty I told him I
would not be going on the hunt. It was not easy to explain to him
why, especially since I had no other date that conflicted, and he
knew how crazy I was about hunting at that lake. I said I just felt
strongly that it was not right for me to go at that time.

The real reason for my decision not to go was that during a
daily period of Bible reading, meditation, and prayer that
direction had come very clearly to me, even though it was
somewhat of a shock. Why wouldn't the Lord want me to join
my friends and have fun as I had many times before? With all the
complexities in my life my quiet times had become essential, and
I learned that when I obeyed the thoughts that came to me I
could count on the right things happening to me and my work.
Disappointing as it was, twice again the thought came clearly:
Don't go with them on Saturday. My decision was firm.

A necessary business trip to Tonggu with stops by the lake to hunt both on the way there in the morning and again on the way back in the evening seemed a better plan. So on Wednesday my interpreter and I took my jeep and left rather early for Tonggu. We found time both going and returning to stop and get in some really good hunting. Moderate sized flocks circled around and came nicely into range as I stood in three feet of water a hundred yards offshore. The evening sky was especially beautiful. My two hunts that day were most satisfying.

On Friday Marty called to ask if I would not change my mind and go with them, which I declined. The next thing I knew it was Saturday afternoon. Marty dropped in on me to give me all the news. "Gee, it's a good thing you didn't come. If you had you wouldn't be here now," he said. "There were thirteen of us all together, eight civilians working with the UN and five marines, including two sergeants and three privates. I took my UN jeep and the marines brought two of theirs. We hadn't been at the lake ten minutes and were putting on our hunting clothes and waterproof boots when we were suddenly surrounded by about a hundred armed Communist irregulars. There was no use trying to get our guns and use them. We had no alternative but to do exactly what they told us. They admired our hunting gear and our shotguns and made us put all of them in one of the marine jeeps. They didn't know how to drive the jeeps and made the marine drivers drive the two jeeps away for them with some of their armed men and all of our gear. They permitted us to keep my UN jeep, and I was allowed to take the eleven remaining men back to Tientsin. They also said that after the two marine drivers had taken the jeeps to where the Communists wanted them the marines would be brought back to this point and I could take them back to Tianjin. They made it clear that I was to come back alone and without notifying anyone, or real harm would come to the two marines."

Two hours later Marty was back again to pick up the two marines. They were not there, but a couple of dozen of the Communists were waiting. They said that the marines would be held captive indefinitely, and how did Marty dare to go back on his word and report the happenings and send reinforcements? He told them no such thing had happened.

Back at Tianjin Marty learned that three navy men in uniform had shown up for some duck hunting not ten minutes after the eleven in his jeep had left the lake. They had been unable to borrow shotguns so brought their automatic tommy guns to shoot duck. As the three sailors innocently drove up, the Communists thought they were there to rescue the two marines and opened fire. The sailors instinctively jumped from their jeep, hit the ground, and started to return fire. Before long, the sailors had killed several of the Communists, but they quickly realized that instead of there being only a handful there were a hundred. Again the sailors acted instinctively and with their guns blazing jumped back in their jeep and took off without getting wounded.

Marty paused and grew very serious, "John, it's a mighty good thing you decided not to come with us. Your being a major in uniform, they would have taken you captive in the first place, and now who knows the fate of the two marines? You must have had an awfully strong sixth sense about this."

I then fully explained the clear warning not to go I had received in my daily morning quiet time. It took more than eight weeks of the highest level of diplomacy to bring about a release of the two marines. My faith in two-way prayer was greatly strengthened to the point where I never again doubted its reality and the wisdom of a power beyond ourselves.

Every several weeks I had to go to Beijing to supervise the big refuse removal project. There were problems and further rumors of mishandling of the money. Even though my duties were officially related only to the technical side of the project I could not help but be alert to all aspects. Planning for the project took place mostly in the day, but now and then inspirational thoughts would come to me in my morning quiet times. So it was on this particular day. My plan had been to take my jeep as I had done countless times. It facilitated my getting around Beijing. On the other hand, I enjoyed the quiet ride on the train when I went that way, and it did allow me time to read and relax.

The distance between the two big cities was about eighty miles, and a good two-lane concrete road connected them. At two well-known places a deep ditch cut right across the highway through the concrete. They were used from time to time by the authorities as roadblocks. Also on occasion the same roadblocks had been used by the Communist irregulars, and a number of people had been stopped and searched and sometimes even shot or killed. I had been through these roadblocks many times by myself but was always relieved after I had safely passed without incident.

The morning of that day I had to decide whether to go by train or jeep, it came to me in my quiet time I should go by train. I knew it was a real message to me and wrote it down.

That evening my good friend Marty gave me a call and said that he had to go to Beijing the same day I was going and wouldn't it be fun if we drove there and back together. He would take his UN jeep and I could relax and we could have a good visit together. I told Marty that I very much appreciated his invitation and under normal circumstances would be delighted to go with him.

Marty asked, "Well, why can't you go this time? Is there some special reason?"

I told Marty about the clear direction I had written down in the morning and that I thought I had better go by train.

On Thursday I had a wonderful train trip there and back and accomplished my mission with dispatch. After supper I was resting in my room when in walked Marty in a very disturbed state of mind. He burst out, "Gee, it's a good thing you didn't go with me! You would undoubtedly have been shot! There must be something to this direction you wrote down to go by train."

On his way back from Beijing he had come to the roadblock and noticed that all was not well. As he was about to drive around the edge of the three-foot trench in the pavement, he was ordered by two men with rifles and headbands to stop. He knew instinctively they were Communists. He was about to stop, but his previous experiences raced through his mind, and in only seconds he decided not to stop, for he was sure they had bad things in mind for him. To throw them off and to get by the area where the two men with guns stood, he suddenly stepped on the gas as hard as he could and aimed for one of them. The man jumped out of the way but lost his balance and fell to the ground. They were both so surprised that at first they didn't know what to do. They could see that Marty was a civilian UN person and that his jeep was a UN vehicle. When they came to their senses, they shot four or five times, mostly over his head. But two shots hit the back of the jeep.

Marty was all right, but he said, "That would not have been the case if you had accepted my invitation to ride with me. It would have been obvious to those irregulars that you were an American officer, and you know how they hate the Americans for taking up the Nationalists' side against them. There is absolutely no question in my mind but that one of their bullets would have found its mark and that you would have been a dead man!"

Nothing could be done about Marty's encounter that day, for officially the Communist irregulars did not exist, even though their strength and numbers increased each month. Becoming clear to Marty and me was that we would do well to seek a wisdom greater than our own. I felt that I was winning a real spiritual teammate in Marty.

Because I had moved from Shanghai at the order of the chief medical officer there—the Yugoslavian Communist—did not mean that I was free of that group's influence. I had been reported to Washington by them as one who was undesirable and should be removed. The United Sates military knew of my solid background but thought they should have one of their intelligence agents in the army's G2 look me over. After some considerable undercover investigation they concluded that I was okay and that there was a lot wrong with the others in the USPHS group. Then the G2 man and I exchanged pertinent information. He had found many things the pro-Communists were up to, including smuggling gasoline and other war materials in UNRRA vehicles, and otherwise helping the Chinese Communists' cause. Our contact, plus mine with the FBI, continued for two years, well after I had returned home. Several of these USPHS personnel were reprimanded severely, and one was sent to prison for five years for no less than treason.

On two occasions I had to go deep into the Communist-held territories within our jurisdiction. The UN was neutral, and we were supposed to give humanitarian help to both sides regardless of their ideological persuasion. On both of these trips I did have some excitement but never really felt that I was in danger. On one trip my interpreter and I went by jeep. As we came to the Communist lines we were apprehended, and two armed guards were assigned to our jeep the whole time we were in their territory. I had told my interpreter not to tell anyone that I understood quite a bit of Chinese, for I wanted to learn what I could from their speaking with each other when I was within earshot.

On another trip farther into the interior we went by train. There had been a lot of trouble with the Communists cutting the railroad track and shooting up the trains; hence, a machine gun was mounted on the cow catcher, and I had the pleasure of riding on the cow catcher for several hours during the trip going. The railway had been cut, but the day after, we were able to go through. However, the breaks were so large that the train would not be back in service for two to three weeks. I felt that my services were needed back in Tianjin so requested that the man the UN had assigned to the city purchase air tickets for me and my interpreter. Unfortunately, the man in charge of the office was a Communist sympathizer although a fellow American, and he thought that the longer he kept me inactive in his city the better and refused to buy a ticket. Since I was an army major in USPHS uniform I decided to contact the military base and had no trouble getting free plane rides out for both of us. Again, the subversive group learned they had been foiled.

During my stay in China I took several opportunities to visit with Dr. Leighton Stuart, who was a longtime missionary, former president of Yen Ching University, and then the United States ambassador to China before the Communists took over. (He also happened to be Florence's uncle.) I also had occasion to meet and talk confidentially with several high ranking army and marine officers (full colonels) in North China. Most people were not aware of what was going on in China at that critical period of history. I, of course, was not privileged to most of the critical information, but a couple of things, I believe, the American people should understand.

Evidently our State Department was quite well infiltrated or these things could not have happened. At the end of the war with Japan, Chiang's crack division, armed with our best weapons, was sent to Mukden as a symbol of holding the line in Manchuria for the Nationalists. But in the State Department the decision was also made that this division was not to be given any munitions. The result of this underhanded action was that the city fell to the Communists without much trouble, which was the beginning of the end of the Nationalists' control in Manchuria. A second thing, told to me by two army colonels, was the Communists' strategy for taking Manchuria city by city with the cooperation of our State Department. In each of about twenty areas there was assigned a team of three as a peacekeeping force: one Communists colonel, one Nationalist colonel, and one American colonel. Whenever either side started an attack, the three were to meet together and order military activities to halt. The trouble was that this only worked when the Nationalists attacked. When the Communists attacked, the Communist colonel got sick and delayed the action of the three until their military objectives had been accomplished; then the fighting was stopped. For practical military reasons, the army colonels told me, this was the main cause of the victory of the Communists in taking over Manchuria.

Who is to say what history will show in the long run about the Chinese Communists' takeover of China? Certainly it is good that we saw fit to make friends with the Chinese at the right time, and it is my humble opinion that in the long run China will turn to democracy and more fully to the free enterprise system and become an even better friend of the United States.

Just before Christmas 1946 I returned home. I had learned a lot about China and its needs during my tour of duty as a major in the USPHS assigned to the UN reconstruction of North China. The trip back home was not like that going over on the liberty ship; it was by Pan American "flying boat" via Manila, taking three days and stopping only for gas. Top speed was one hundred seventy miles per hour, and at night passengers were put up in berths like on a train. Today we make the same trip in twelve hours.

It was great to get home for Christmas and enjoy it after a year of separation from Florence and our three small girls.

CHAPTER TEN

The Dream That Failed

During the last half of my tour of active duty in China the seeds of a great dream began to grow in my mind. I had once thought that my life work might be teaching sanitary engineering at Hangzhou University under the auspices of the mission board. But would it be enough help to China and be in time?

In 1946 China was the sleeping giant of the world powers. As she was aroused and grew in strength economically and politically she must grow out of her four-thousand-year-old way of life. Her poor infrastructure and poor public health were just two areas in which to begin. The latter would have to be based on water supplies and waste treatment. For example, my hometown, Souzhou, a city of over a half million, had not even the beginning of a water supply or sewer system. My father had devoted his life to bringing medicine to the country and upgrading it. But for every patient who could be treated in a hospital, one thousand needed to be helped by a giant public health program. Our postwar year of working on sanitary engineering in China had been little more than a demonstration of a task that needed to be planned and carried out on a very large scale over an extended period of time.

So began my big plan, which eventually developed into the China Sanitary Engineering Service, Inc. (CSES). At first only one other person shared my thinking, D.S. Abell, the chief sanitary engineer for the United Nations Relief and Rehabilitation Administration (UNRRA), who was located in Shanghai. Abell was sixteen years older than I and had a lot of public health experience. He also was a committed Christian. During his tour of duty in China he had fallen in love with the country and its people and wanted to stay there to work in sanitary engineering. We met only occasionally but corresponded frequently.

Before I left China, Abell and I met with an officer with the First Marine Division who became one of the inner circle in the big plan. No project, however big or good, could succeed in China without having talented and dedicated Chinese as a controlling part of it. From among the many capable Chinese we had gotten to know and work with that year we picked four to bring into the program from the start: W. C. Ching as construction engineer, Lanier Young as secretary, and T.Y. Koo and S.F. Wang as members of the board. Also it was not long before Roy Welter, chief design engineer in my former Venezuela project, was enlisted to become at the right time the chief engineer. We now had an organization which I would serve as chief of training, testing, and research for the broad spectrum of sanitary engineering, while Abell would be president until the right Chinese person could be trained for the job.

We discussed the proposed company with several influential government officials, with a number of practicing water engineers in the large cities, and with Dr. Leighton Stuart, the United States ambassador to China. Each gave us very enthusiastic responses.

I got permission to return to the United States two months early to spend full time organizing that side of the operation. Abell agreed to remain in his post with UNRRA for some time and continue with the China side of the plan.

Upon my return home, Florence and I took stock of our finances and decided that our total savings were sufficient to support our family and pay my expenses for a full twelve months while I developed CSES. With the help of a part-time secretary, Florence, and others, we incorporated as a not-for-profit corporation in Delaware. We put together thirty pages of descriptive data and an attractive illustrated prospectus. We drew up a four-year financial plan, for it was hard to see ahead any further than that, especially with the growing turmoil in China. Ambassador Stuart kept me informed of the impending troubles between the Nationalists and Communists. Increasingly the question was, would the situation get better so the program could go ahead safely, or would it get worse, perhaps so bad that the program would have to be put on hold or even scrapped?

Having worked with many major suppliers of both equipment and chemicals while with the Army First Service Command for three years, and having a number of senior-engineer friends, I was able to make up a list of about fifty manufacturers of sanitary engineering equipment and supplies to enlist in our China program. I contacted all of them by mail or personally, and the response was gratifying. We refused to take even any seed money from these American corporations until the project would actively start in China.

Our broad multipurpose program to bring about the construction and operation of water supplies and sewerage systems throughout China would, however, ultimately lean heavily on many of the American manufacturers that represented the latest state of the art in every phase of the field. We would either import their equipment and supplies and take a standard fair commission to support our research, training, and engineering phases or, in the long run, arrange for joint-venture manufacturing in China.

The not-for-profit CSES was conceived to be the catalyst for making things happen in the water and waste water field between the present time of no activity and some point in time, say twenty years hence, when the marketplace had taken over in a natural free-enterprise way. The CSES needed to do all this but also had to undertake a lot of needed research to learn what was the best way to apply today's knowledge to China's unique problems and accomplish the task with a very limited budget. We also needed to do a lot of training and promotion work with both the Chinese and international institutions.

Because of my eighteen months with the United States Public Health Service, which was a branch of the armed forces, I was entitled to the educational provisions of the G.I. Bill. To me a real need, important in preparing for the China work, was to learn to fly. I wanted to get the newest but not-too-expensive amphibious plane, as there were almost no runways in China but many broad canals. I took one hundred ten hours of solo time on the G.I. Bill and saved the last forty hours until we could get the amphibious plane. It was a great experience, and I enjoyed every minute of it. I looked forward to the time when we could afford our first plane.

Although the political-military situation in China was looking less and less promising for our program, there was still some hope that it would stabilize. The plan was ready to be implemented, but we did not want to get all set up and going well in China and then have the civil war shut us down. I finally wrote each of the fifty American manufacturers we were planning to work with, telling them of the dangers of the present situation and asking them to put our relationship on hold. All but one agreed. About a year later this temporary waiting period went into a shutting down of the planned program.

While still in this waiting phase I knew we had used up our family savings and that I must find work. A new firm, Burns and Kenerson, needed a project engineer, and I was fortunate enough to get the position. Kenerson had just returned from two years in China with the Army Corps of Engineers, where he supervised the construction of dozens of military airfields that were strategic in keeping the Japanese from overrunning West China. He was considered an expert on small airfields and had designed and supervised the construction of several of them around New England.

I used to talk with Ken about the possibility of my renting the little Cessna in which I had learned to fly and taking it up to one of their jobs, doing what had to be done, and flying back all in the same day, thus saving one or two days over his driving time. Finally, he told me to go up to Berlin, New Hampshire, gather the data he needed, and come back the same day. That would put my idea to the test. I was delighted with the assignment, and although my cross-country experience was quite limited, I set out very confidently.

To go from Boston to Berlin I had to cross over the White Mountains, many of which are about six thousand feet elevation. I saw no problem with this, but I had not counted on the possibility of strong downdrafts. As I approached and tried to climb over the chain of mountains, the plane did not seem to make much progress toward the needed altitude. In fact, for a while I actually lost altitude, even though I was climbing to the plane's full ability. Finally, the reason became clear—deadly downdrafts—and the solution became clear as well: make a wide circle back from the mountain range, gain more altitude above the draft and out of its reach, and then proceed over the peaks, but not without a loss of about a half hour and considerable pride and self-assurance. The task was completed with dispatch, but Kenerson would no longer be badgered by an overconfident freshman flier to pioneer an efficient way to make his field trips for him.

During my year with Burns and Kenerson the firm acquired the task of designing the new bridge to be built over the Charles River separating Boston from Cambridge where on its banks lay Harvard University and Massachusetts Institute of Technology.

I was elated when Ken asked me to be the project engineer on this bridge, which would have to match or excel the beauty of the several other graceful brick arched bridges that were the pride of the area. The ingenuity of the designer would be taxed, for it would be difficult if not impossible to build true structural arches over this part of the river because of poor and soft foundations. I agreed to accept the assignment providing I was free to pick the man who would be largely responsible for the details of the design. "Tiny" Thompson was a talented engineer I had gotten to admire while working at Fay, Spofford and Thorndyke and who was now freelancing. If anyone could accomplish the difficult day-to-day detailed design he could. My request to include him was granted, and Tiny and I, along with one draftsman, completed the bridge design in less than the allotted time. The job was structurally complex, as we had to make a rigid-frame continuous steel truss and then cover it with a facade of three beautiful brick arches. I could never have done it by myself at that stage in my professional life, but with the technical depth of Tiny's experience and my leadership, the team was able to do what seemed to many like a miracle. Everyone was more than pleased, and after construction was completed there was no question that the Eliot Bridge was now the most attractive over the river.

As the year drew to a close, Burns and Kenerson's work fell off a bit. I was feeling confident that I could do as well or better on my own. If I could get the jobs and do them well, I would not be dependent on others for my employment or security. By that time Florence and I had recovered financially, but our having just spent all our life's savings the previous year on CSES left us only enough money to support us for three months. But I was ready and decided to hang out my own shingle.

Along with the excitement of starting on my own was the bad news about China. All of us who had worked to organize CSES knew that all of China would almost certainly be taken over by the Communists. Under such a regime we would not be able to launch CSES. We now know that China under Communism would not have accepted our big plan. But China is currently undergoing another economic revolution and is on the verge of a still bigger revolution of democracy and human rights. Perhaps someday soon the essence of our plan will still be played out. I have faith that China will end up a victorious democratic world leader and a fast friend of America. All our efforts will not have been in vain.

So life went on. We would find other ways to be of service in the developing world where environmental engineering was so much needed. Just a month before my one-man office was opened in a spare room of a friend's home, John, Jr., was born on November 13, 1948. Our three girls were ages six, five, and three, and our little rented house was filled completely. We now had quite a family to love and enjoy, and Florence had more than a normal mother's load. We were all tremendously happy, for we were sure it was God's plan that we have each child and that great things lay ahead for each of them. We were fully confident of the future of my new consulting engineering office.

In all things we trusted in God.

CHAPTER ELEVEN

Hanging Up My Shingle

On Monday, November 28, 1948, having cut all my security ties of working for others, I became a new, one-man consulting engineering firm in a two-hundred-fifty-square-foot office in a friend's home a block from our house. During the past year of employment at Burns and Kenerson I had saved three months' salary toward this new venture and had prepared myself emotionally for the break and a new start.

At age thirty-five I was mature and confident. Besides my seven years of academic study and training I had ten years of varied and excellent experience. My weak points were that I had no business or speaking training and that my nature was to be introverted and a bit shy. Also, I had four children and a wife to support. But the decision to go on my own was made from a firm conviction after much praying, checking with my close spiritual friends, and soul searching. I knew it was right to open this new chapter of Florence's and my destiny and opportunity to be of service to our maker.

Normally the work of a consulting sanitary engineer comes mostly from government. To get government work in the New England area meant having to kick back one tenth to one third of one's fee to the politicians. But because I was totally unwilling to compromise in this way my only alternatives were to take industrial or commercial work or to subcontract work from fellow engineers and architects.

117

Fortunately, two of my good architect friends had a large veterans' housing project. They needed the help of an engineer in the site planning and design, as well as for their structural, surveying, and soils work. A lot of this kind of work was going on at the time, and not every engineering firm was qualified or interested in "subbing" the work. This job well done led to other architects with similar jobs, so by the end of a year I had over ten such jobs completed or under way.

One larger more political architect gave me all his work and also treated me as his protege'. He would take me out to lunch to discuss his work and then often wax eloquently on his philosophy. "There are three important things in architecture. The first is to get the job. The next is to get the job. And the next is to *get the job!*" I knew just what he was talking about. The difference between us was that the politicians were helping him get his jobs, and the good Lord was looking after me.

One architect for whom I had utmost respect was a deeply spiritual man. I did a variety of work for him, including some important structural steel design for commercial and school jobs. One day he came into the office and said the city of Revere had elected a reform government that was looking for a good architecture-engineering firm to design and supervise construction of its new municipal stadium. We made a good presentation together and were given the job, our first municipal job. With the reform slate, it was totally clean and free from kickbacks.

More than a year later our engineer-architect team was about 80 percent finished with the design when we heard that in a new election the reform group had been replaced by an old-style corrupt group. The next thing we knew the new people called us to report on the progress of our work and then told us they wanted us to pay them personally $15,000. We had suspected as much and were prepared for the worst. We asked them, "Do you mind telling us where this money will go?"

They said, "No; five is for the mayor, five for the council, and five for us."

We replied that we could not accept this way of doing professional work and suggested that we bring our work to a halt, that they turn it over to another firm they might select, and we would bill them only for work done to date. Our response came as a big surprise to them. They went into an hour of private discussion, then came forth and asked us to forget everything they had said and finish the work, and they would make no further requests for money.

The corrupt group lived up to their word to us. But as we got into the bidding and construction phase another new plan began to unfold. They made arrangements with the only contractor to bid to take about half his fee, or about $300,000, from him rather than the $15,000 from us.

Malden and Sumerville were two medium-sized cities near Melrose where I lived and had my office. Their departments of public works had heard of my experience in sanitary landfills with the First Service Command during the war. They needed a good way to dispose of their municipal refuse and looked me up because I was the only professional in the state who could be of service to them. There was no mention of kickbacks. I was given a year's contract to design and provide day-to-day supervision of construction. The two cities had about twenty acres of tidal flats between the Malden River and Main Street, the four-lane, north-south highway that also served one of their best residential areas. We computed not only how much the refuse would be compacted over time but also the compaction of fifteen feet of bog under it with the extra weight of trash on it. Each settled at a different rate over time. Leachate was kept out of the river by an appropriate solid-fill dike along its edge. They got a first-class job without any citizen complaints. The well-compacted refuse after a year's further settling was just right to be filled with two feet of hard soil, and the whole area became the site of one of their first shopping malls.

I had a strong interest in a good chemical and bacteriological lab and bought the lab that Coca Cola had made up but never really used. This was the only portable lab in the region. The word got around, and I had more calls for its service than it could handle. So after a year I built a stationary lab as well. I had two excellent trained chemists who were able to man these two facilities. The portable lab was assigned to solve a number of complex industrial waste-treatment and disposal problems, some given to us by our friendly competitors who had no lab themselves. We also took away from the Metcalf and Eddy Company a good-sized sanitary survey and study of the Concord River, which was overloaded with municipal sewage. In another case, the portable lab was tied up at an industrial plant on a rather tough problem for almost six months.

Before the end of the first year it was clear that the one-room office was going to be totally inadequate. By then we had our fifth child, David, so the little house which had been our home for seven years was also inadequate. We found a beautiful eighteen-room house in the best part of Melrose (with half an acre of land) that no one wanted, and bought it for a song. The third-floor "game area" with twelve hundred square feet made an ideal office; another five hundred square feet in the basement housed our stationary chemical laboratory. The on-site carriage house held our mobile lab when it was a home. By the end of the second year the operation had grown to a staff of eight people and had begun to gain a good reputation.

Dr. Rolf Ellison, who headed the Sanitary Engineering Option at Massachusetts Institute of Technology, invited me to teach one course a semester. This was not only stimulating, but it gave me a lot of new contacts and brought many new consulting jobs. These were mostly small but very interesting and often quite complex and sometimes led to further and often larger jobs.

Fay, Spofford and Thorndyke, one of the big three consulting firms in the greater Boston area for whom I had worked several years previously, had a big contract with the Defense Department to design three major military bases in Newfoundland. This was during the Korean War, when many feared that the Soviets would pull a surprise attack on us through that area. Everything was rush-rush and hush-hush. They asked if I would handle the water and wastewater aspects of these three bases for them under their contract, which I did.

During my third and last year as a consultant in the Boston area I was selected to be the expert witness in a large and controversial court case, *The People vs. The Boston Consolidated Gas Co.* A week before the case came to trial, it was obvious that we would lose unless I was able to prove physical negligence by the gas company. About two years before, gas from a bad leak in the main had seeped underground into a residential basement. Several people were injured and one killed. An older photograph showed a tree that had since been removed. After getting permission from the city department of public works, I had the street dug up to uncover the gas main next to where the tree had been. My excavation showed that, before the tree was removed and the evidence all but destroyed by the gas company, a large root had grown in such a way as to dislodge and crack the gas pipe, thus causing the leak and resulting tragedy. Photographs of the remaining root and repairs showed beyond doubt what had taken place. The gas company had been negligent in not making periodic inspections along the line with its gas-leak detector and was keeping all this under wraps.

The gas company's lawyer was one of the better known in the city. He tried to prove to the court that I was too young and inexperienced to be an expert witness and thus should be disqualified. He pulled a number of unfair tricks without success. Then, in an attempt to trap me, the gas company engineer fed him a very complex technical question. Although I knew the answer, I felt it was time I put the lawyer in his place. Knowing that he did not understand the question passed to him by his engineer, I asked him to clarify it. Suddenly he realized I had him in a tight spot. He lost his temper and a great deal of prestige with it. Needless to say, our side won the case.

Florence and I remained active in our community, church, and especially Moral Re-Armament. We continued to be close to the families in Melrose who met frequently in spiritual fellowship to hold each other to our highest and to find God's will for our lives and for our greater community.

At this time I felt compelled to prod the engineers of the country to think about moral and philosophical things in addition to the humdrum of technical decision making and wrote a one-page article for the July 1950 issue of *The Bent*, the official publication of the engineering honorary Tau Beta Pi, titled, "A Rational Approach to the H-Bomb," which created vigorous discussion. It pointed out that while God is in control of universal actions and reactions such as occur in the sun, he will allow people to retain their freedom of will over the things they control such as the knowledge and lust for power that led to the development of the hydrogen bomb. People can, however, choose to turn the control over to God by tapping his source of wisdom and power and truth and making them essential to human decisions.

The article was read by the acting dean of engineering at Michigan State University, which was looking for a new head of its department of civil and environmental engineering. This led to an invitation for me to accept the position. I initially turned it down, received an invitation to visit with the dean and staff, and got a call from President Hannah that convinced me to go and see. I came away deeply impressed with not only the institution and its leadership but the opportunities they offered. The deciding factor was my deep sense of God's direction that it was the next place for me to be of service. Thus in December 1950 we sold our house and engineering firm, packed up the family, and drove to Michigan after having lived in Massachusetts for thirteen years.

In the fall of 1950 I had been urged to run for alderman for the city of Melrose. I did so and had just gotten into the feel of the election when it became evident that soon I would depart for Michigan. I placed a letter in the city newspaper that challenged the candidates to do their best and stated that I was withdrawing for new work in Michigan. Despite my withdrawal (and to my amazement) I was almost elected.

CHAPTER TWELVE

Professor and Department Head

Our move from Boston to East Lansing, Michigan, home of Michigan State University, opened up a whole new life, not only for me professionally but for the family. It was not just a geographical move of over eight hundred miles to the west but a move from the three-hundred-year-old New England tradition and culture, some good and some fallen into an abyss of corruption. Our newly adopted Midwest, by comparison, was vibrant, open to new ideas and, as we soon learned, virtually free from corruption. It was the home of the birth of Henry Ford's automobile and mass production yet still contained vast forests, lakes, beautiful scenery, and wildlife. Here we brought our five young children into a new and healthier atmosphere in which to enjoy their childhood, receive the right education, and be better prepared for their adult lives.

I moved from an eighty-hour work week starting a young private practice to a fifty- or sixty-hour week in my new academic endeavors, which was also very good for the whole family. I had more time for the pleasures and duties of a father of five young kids who needed me a lot.

Our move also brought me away from the practice of engineering in a private consulting firm to a new commitment to work with others in a Big Ten university to teach students to become good practicing engineers. My part-time teaching at

Massachusetts Institute of Technology had helped prepare me for the transition.

Furthermore, I had the opportunity to upgrade the research and development work that I loved so much. An important part of my former consulting work had been to give clients a quick and practical fix to their particular problems. But now I advanced to the more worthwhile research and development conducted in a university, where our first goal was to push the walls of knowledge ahead. My salesmanship abilities were still needed for acquiring research funds, but now I was part of a big university with the full support of the dean and the president behind me. There were so many pluses in this move that, as time went on, I became more and more convinced that it was the divine plan for the next step in my life, and I was eager to pursue it.

I had spent all of December at Michigan State University getting my feet on the ground, and when Christmas vacation came I flew home and looked after the final closing of the office and our business affairs. In my absence Florence sold our eighteen-room house for almost two thousand dollars more than I had been asking for it. Our furniture and trunks were shipped out to our new home and would arrive in about eight days. We used the time to see relatives in North Carolina and Alabama. Then, early on the morning of December 31 we set out on a nonstop drive of nine hundred twenty miles from Selma, Alabama, to East Lansing, Michigan, in our Chevy with all five kids neatly packed in. At night the three girls slept on the back seat extended and made level with luggage in front of it, and the two boys, ages one and two, slept on a plywood chalkboard reaching from the back window to the top of the front seat like an upper bunk. We made the trip in just under twenty-nine hours, including gas and rest stops and driving the last three hundred miles in dense fog—all without expressways. We arrived about noon on January 1, with a foot of snow on the ground.

We had always wanted to live on a lake, and now finally we did. Lake Lansing was a shallow four hundred fifty acres, by far the largest lake in the area. The swimming, fishing, and sailboating were excellent, and we enjoyed the colorful sunsets and their reflections on the lake. As spring and summer came our new homestead became the ideal place to bring up the family, with a sanded beach, sea wall, docks, fishing boat, and even a nice little sailboat, which it didn't take long for all the family to learn to use and enjoy.

Michigan State University also brought great satisfaction to my professional life. At the end of World War II it was sleepy little Michigan Agricultural College with fewer than five thousand students. Under the leadership of President John Hannah and the team he built around him, it grew to over forty thousand students in only twenty years. The campus was very large and one of the most beautiful in the country. With the returning veterans there was a tremendous need for both new dormitories and married student housing. Dr. Hannah built these with mortgage money rather than tax money. The institution grew not only in the number of students but in distinguished faculty and prestige. During my second year there it officially became a university, and the old name of "Cow College" became history, even though MSU still maintains a major agricultural college. Along with its academic growth the university developed its athletics program. While I was there it became part of the Big Ten, won twenty-three football games with no losses or ties, and went to the Rose Bowl twice.

University life has its own interesting and worthwhile programs and things to keep one busy. As a department head I had to do a lot of speaking, which I learned to enjoy, for it was an opportunity to pass worthwhile thoughts to the students and to my peers. My experiences back in New England with graft in the government still haunted me, so I decided to write an article exposing the practice and get it published in a well-read municipal publication such as *American City* or *Public Works*. The article was rejected, however, not because it would not be of interest but because it would make waves and perhaps make some readers very unhappy. I finally sent it to the *Journal of Engineering Education*, for there it would educate professors and in turn students and perhaps ultimately help to turn the situation around. They published not only the first article but, after all the reader response, wanted a second article as well.

Our building, Olds Hall, was one of the older less attractive on the campus. It was very operational but visually did little to inspire those who held classes and labs there day in and day out. One day an idea came to me, which eventually became reality. The bare expansive walls of the hallways on two floors we filled solid with beautiful four-by-eight-foot murals that pictured everything in the field of engineering—civil engineering in particular—which would be of interest to and inspire the students and staff. The murals were photographs of successful engineering projects blown up and mounted on a special wallboard.

As a department head it was part of my duty to talk with many of the so-called problem students. I considered this an excellent opportunity to help. Sometimes their problems were purely financial, sometimes low grades resulting from not enough study, sometimes personal, sometimes a combination. The good news was that 95 percent of the time there was a right solution to the student's problem and it was a matter of helping the person to find it, put it into operation, and stick with it.

I also learned valuable and satisfying things about teaching and tried to pass them on to our staff members. One thrill for a good teacher is to get to know, capture the interest of, and inspire a C student to make straight A's, a change inside him which usually has a carryover to the rest of his life. Another thing I learned was that most students can carry a full-time school load along with a half-time outside job and do a first-class job of both. Or, they can go to school half time and work full time. Now and then I would have students who supported a family while working full time and going to school full time as well. But only a few could do this and make good grades too, for it took too much out of them. One of the most interesting occurrences was when we had in the department a father and his son studying civil engineering at the same time who also graduated together.

Getting various divisions of the civil engineering department upgraded so that they could be approved for first a master's level of work and in some cases for a doctor's level was of special interest to me. Undergraduate work was important and needed to be upgraded also, but having a staff which attracted graduate students did a lot for the whole program and made for improvements at all levels. Likewise, I had an interest in attracting good foreign students. They not only were tops in their own countries but were an inspiration to the American students and to our staff as well. Now forty years later a number of these former students come to the United States for business and look me up or keep in touch by mail, or their sons have come to study at MSU.

Dr. Sachiho Naito graduated with an M.S. in sanitary engineering in June 1955. We kept in close touch and worked together on international projects. In January 1995 he was chairman of the board of a 40,000 private Japanese educational institution and visited us in East Lansing for two days.

Whenever an institution makes the phenomenal growth MSU made in the late forties and early fifties, it is impossible to raise the standards as rapidly throughout the whole university. This was seen in the school of engineering. My selection and employment was part of the growth and upgrading process, and both Dean Miller and President Hannah expected me to live up to their expectations for the university. They had given me the highest engineering-school salary (except for the dean's), a nice office, and as secretary, and there were some very talented men already on the civil engineering faculty. Our civil and environmental department was on about the same level of improvement as the mechanical, electrical, and chemical engineering departments. The newly formed applied mechanics department was headed by a good new professor with a strong plan for academic advancement. Research and development projects were almost nonexistent in all the departments. But the administration's view was that research and development were the key to stimulating the processes of academic growth and prestige and the building of an engineering school which would be sought after by students, especially graduate students. Other parts of their program were to weed out the staff and bring in new people with good reputations and potential for building the quality of the institution.

Although my experience in administration had been very limited, I felt that I had the underlying talents and feel for the job. I certainly had the backing and, to a degree, some coaching from Dean Miller as well as strong general and moral support from

President Hannah. The first term I did no teaching but spent my time getting to know the faculty both within and outside the department. In a number of staff meetings we discussed how we could reorganize our curriculum to bring it more into line with the needs of the profession. Subsections planned for the department were structures, soils, hydraulics, transportation, surveying, and construction, and within a year we were able to upgrade and add an environmental section. For each area there was selected a faculty member to set the pace and advise the students with special interest in that area. We also introduced a research program in each area, explored such natural interests which existed, and tried to instill interest where it was dormant or weak. By the end of the first year we had added three new men: Dr. Wu in soil mechanics, Dr. McCaulley in environmental, and Ken Kenerson—formerly with the United States Corps of Engineers and more recently from the consulting firm in Boston, Burns and Kenerson, where I had worked some five years previously. Kenerson formed and brought his expertise to our new construction section, which attracted many students wishing to get into construction work. Another area in which MSU began to make a reputation was ground water hydraulics. Only one other school in the country, Colorado, taught courses in that area. Fortunately, we had living in Lansing the man who taught all the United State geological personnel their technological know-how. He was very good, and I arranged for him to teach a beginning and an advanced course in the field.

In the early fifties almost every civil engineering department in the country had a common problem: where to find room in an already crowded curriculum to teach surveying—an area of knowledge that was essential to a civil engineer yet was also starting to be considered subprofessional to civil engineering. The theory and advanced theory for surveying in highways and a lot of field instruction and practice were needed before someone could make dependable use of these tools. After much faculty discussion and talks with the forestry department it was decided that the civil engineers would offer their main surveying courses at the already existing but underused forestry camp in Michigan's Upper Peninsula. This concept had been practiced for years at Vanderbilt

1. Dr. and Mrs. John A. Snell, 1907 About to go to China.
2. Rev. and Mrs. Lacy Moffett
3. Dr. John A. Snell at Suzhou Home 1930
4. Snell Family in Suzhou 1920
5. Grace Snell 1936 Nashville
6. Moffett Family from Kiang Yin 1924 Florence 2nd from right

1. John R. Snell age 2
2. Snell's home in Suzhou
3. Lura and Dorothy Snell take a ride
4. Outpatient Building, Suzhou Hospital 1925
5. Main Building 250 bed Suzhou Hospital
   1925
6. Superintendent, and Chief Surgeon
7. Florence Moffett 1932 Queen's College

1. John [5th from right] played both varsity soccer and American football
2. John's model sailboat he made in shops, 24 inches long
3. Girl's dormitory, Community Church, and Administration Building SAS
4. John at top of pyramid traveling from China through Europe 1930
5. Administration building SAS

1. Dr. John A. Snell graduating from Vanderbilt Medical School 1907
2. John Raymond Snell graduating in Engineering from Vanderbilt 1934
3. Vanderbilt Administration building
4. At age 72, John comes in 10th of 50 in a mile "Fun Run" Vandy's 50th
5. Gordon M. Fair, John's major professor at Harvard
6. 50th anniversary at Vanderbilt visit to engineering school

1. Civil Engineering Faculty at Hangzhou University 1934-1935
2. Tiger shot by John at Fuzhing China in 1935. It had killed 10 in village
3. Tiger Hill Pagoda, Suzhou. Visited by Snells in 1979
4. Suzhou University Administration Building 1979
5. Ink Pagoda Near Suzhou Hospital

1. Peak of Bolivar, 16,350ft. Merida, Venezuela from Trail
2. Peak of Bolivar, from up on the snow line, 200 feet from top
3. Engineering reconnaissance for one of a number of water supplies in the Andies
4. Florence arriving on the Santa Rosa Dec. 6th 1939
5. Maracay, Venesuela, Dec. 1939
6. Maracay, Venezuela, Dec. 1939
7. Instructor, part time at MIT
8. Project engineering on new "Eliot" bridge crossing the Charles river

1. 18 room Melrose home and office 1948-1950
2. Three girls, right to left: Chica, Karen, and Martha
3. Five kids on the porch of The Big House
4. First Melrose home
5. Major Snell USPHS assigned to the UN reconstruction of water wastewater, & solid wastes in the five northern provinces
6. Lee-Ying, "Born Again" Paul Lee., Underground Fighter, cleans up corruption in CINRRA
7. Paul Lee, visiting us in East Lansing from his work with the FBI

1. Michigan State Beaumont Bell Tower 1952
2. "Sparti" on MSU campus
3. Inspecting a surveying class
4. Snell's office in Olds Hall
5. Fort Mackinac
6. Grand Hotel, Mackinac Isalnd Moral Re-Armament. MRA, Conference 1955
7. MRA Delegates included two "Changed" Ex-communist coal miners
8. New MRA auditorium and headquarters on Mackinac Island.
9. Snell as Director of Eight Nation 30 day Conference in Tiawan in 1955
10. Snell Meets Generalissimo Chiang-Kai-Shek

1. Family in front of Lake Lansing house
2. Family in front of Garage Lake Lansing house
3. Five kids and Blelocks at Lake Lansing
4. Family by Car at Lake Lansing
5. Sledding down an incline and hill
6. Residence in East Lansing 1975 to present

1. Family reunion at Blue Lake—Dad, Karen, John, Florence, Chica, Martha & David
2. Family Reunion at Blue Lake—with most of the grand children present
3. One of the beaches at Blue Lake
4. Skiing in the back woods at Blue Lake
5. Snorkeling for 5 pound bass
6. Relaxing, after working on Lot clearing and sales

1. Drafting room in 120 year old church converted into an office
2. Some of the officers A] John R. Snell, Pres. B] John O'Malia, VP, C]
   Mi Cheng, Assoc. D] Kurt Gutter, Assoc. E] Hugh Corrough, Assoc.
3. New office at 911 May St. with 30,000 square feet of space
4. Expansion at Detroit Metro Air National Guard Apron
5. East Pakistan Agricultural University—From paddy fields to 8,000
   students

1. 300 ton per day high tech compost facility at Huston, TX
2. 400 ton per day composting of cattle manure & bedding. All fed back to cattle
   So Charleston, OH
3. Under The World Health Organization, WHO, Snell was a special consultant
   to Japan on composting
4. Expressways, interstates, overpasses, & bridges
5. Snells study in fall 1995 for Buenos Airres, Argentina as to how to treat and
   utilize sludge from 6,000,000 people
6. An innovative way, without Taxes, to produce much new waterfront
   development in Michigan.
7. Dredging Long Lake, Mich. SEG led the consultants in Lake restoration.

1. Aerial of 270 acres of stocked shrimp ponds in Belieze—next to sea
2. 500 pounds of shrimp being harvested with each net full.
3. Sennis River—four miles from houses to the sea
4. Corn being raised under the bootstrap project for small farms
5. Typical coast and bay in Belize
6. Map of Belize

1. Snells and Dr. & Mrs. Tien led China tour to China 1979 at the Great Wall
2. Snells at the Tiger Hill Pagoda in Suzhou in 1979
3. 800 year old bridge over the Grand Canal at Suzhou in 1979
4. Guiling, limestone hills along the Lee River, with water buffalo
5. Native dancers at Bali, Indonesia—SEG undertook world bank project for complete facilities for 12 private hotels

1. Snell Grandparents and 12 Grandchildren 1995
2. John and Florence Snell
3. John and Florence with John, David, Karen, Martha, and Chica
4. Eight horsepower one cylinder diesel tractor and trailer 1981
5. Florence with nurse who worked with her brother Dr. Alex Moffett 1981
6. Snells at Temple of Heaven, Beijing, China 1979

when I was there and had served other useful purposes such as building an esprit de corps among the civils.

One of the more difficult tasks of my position was to accomplish the weeding necessary to upgrade a program. Two or three on our staff had come into the program during rapid growth without consideration of their potential for future excellence. Most did not as yet have tenure, but one with tenure had no better qualifications. I saw two sides to each of these situations: the interest of the university and the interest and rights of the staff members themselves. Each man desired to stay on staff, for to leave could be a backward movement professionally. Yet to stay on and not be able to keep up to the faster academic pace of the new department would eventually catch up with them, making for unhappiness and ultimate departure. My approach was a series of frank and caring sessions with each person. After they came to see the future options more clearly, we worked closely together to see that they made the right moves for their own professional betterment as well. Even the assistant professor with tenure saw that a move was in his best interests and made a planned departure, still keeping his good reputation. We remained close friends for years.

Faculty research was almost nonexistent in all the departments of the school of engineering. Dean Miller and President Hannah both saw in me a strong interest in research, and I had the confidence that, with the right encouragement and support, I could help make research an integral part of our program, which would raise levels of professionalism and attract better students, especially at the graduate level. The school had minigrants for preliminary testing of the staff's bright ideas, using graduate students as a first step toward a research project. Yet initially it was not easy to stir up enough interest in faculty members to take the extra time and effort and risk of failure to pursue the mysteries of research.

In the early fifties the cold war was warming up, and the funding agencies placed more emphasis on defense-related projects. Our nation had not as yet learned how bad off we were in the environmental field. We solved our problems in longhand, using slide rules and mechanical calculators. Computers were just being invented but were not yet practical nor affordable. A computer that could do half as much as a $1500 personal computer does today, in those days took up the space of a large room and cost about $150,000, or one hundred times as much.

The prospect of developing research was one of the strong drawing cards that had made me accept the position at MSU. Over my recent years of experience I had encountered many interesting problems which were important to our profession and were still unsolved. Especially in the environmental field the potential was great, yet no one seemed to be grappling with these problems.

The question was where to start. How could we define these problems in a way to catch the interest of financial sources, prepare scholarly requests for funds, and try to sell the idea where there was a reasonable chance of interest? When our staff had no one with the qualifications or special interests it was necessary to find a qualified person elsewhere who was willing to leave his job and take a temporary research job with a school with no research reputation. The job seemed difficult at first, but my interests were strong, my administrative backing solid, and I did have my share of good fortune. My background at MIT and Harvard helped, especially with some of the national funding agencies. While at MIT I had considerable contact with industry, some of which involved research using one of the two small laboratories owned by my consulting firm.

Then there was the composting of organic wastes, which had endlessly fascinated me during the last year of my consulting practice in New England. I now remembered Dr. Earp-Thomas from Australia, who in 1949 had contacted me when I was living in Boston to see if I would like to help him in an engineering way in the field of composting organic wastes. Earp-Thomas was originally a dentist, but since coming to the United States and living in New Jersey he had devoted all his time to the exploration of the possibilities of composting and wastewater treatment. In our first meeting he had endeavored to interest me as I listened for twelve hours to his tall stories about the almost magical attributes of composting. Several weeks later we had a repeat twelve-hour discussion. I was convinced that the uncertainties about his claims amounted to about 90 percent chaff but that there was about 10 percent wheat. The problem was to tell the difference between the two. I had been too busy at the time to become involved on his terms and uncover such differences back then. Yet I had always said to myself that if I ever got the chance I would put the process to the scientific test.

Now at MSU the time to take the chance seemed to be right. Because of the nature of composting I decided to start right off with a combined pilot program and a rather extensive laboratory bench-scale program. I located a well-qualified chemist-biologist, Dr. Carl Schulse, and another with considerable practical experience, plus several graduate students, including one who toward the end worked on his Ph.D. degree under me. Earp-Thomas gave his knowledge and cooperation, and I decided to use his basic digester design with some common-sense modifications so that we would know scientifically what was going on. I also convinced the city of East Lansing, within which the MSU campus lies, to put up the money for the pilot plant if we would take its five tons of separated food wastes each day and run them through the plant. Dr. Hannah had a cement-block building built next to the East Lansing sewage plant to house the project. A grinder was given to the project by Mitts and Merrill. Conveyors, motors, and drives were contributed by other companies. The department of microbiology and the school of agriculture each had a strong interest in what we wanted to do and pledged their support on peripheral aspects of the program.

Dr. Earp-Thomas bragged that his secret bacteria were essential to the success of the project, but that turned out to be a big part of the chaff which had no truth to it. With everything running smoothly we were able to get good composting in only four days at temperatures of up to 160 degrees, which was high enough to pasteurize any pathogenic organisms and to kill weed seeds as well. Once during the experimental program the microbiology department's special incinerator broke down for a week, and they had no place to dispose of their infected chicken carcasses, so we were asked to run them through our pilot plant. The feathers were so rich in nitrogen that the temperatures rose ten degrees above normal but with no bad effects.

The University of California at Berkeley had also taken up an interest in composting but started its program with the thought that it would only take a short time to demonstrate that it was fraudulent. Instead, they soon found that it really worked. Their work was confined to piles of refuse and other organic material in long windrows. They had little to do with bench-scale work and nothing to do with high-rate digester composting. We wished to gather some independent experience with the so-called windrow composting, hence had a parallel project going in the back forty acres of the university's experimental fields. We found that there it took as long as six to eight weeks as opposed to four to six days in our mechanical digester.

Although the pilot part of the project created the most outside interest, the hard advancements in science were made in our extensive laboratory bench-scale work, where we determined in detail how composting was affected by temperature, moisture, fineness of grind, pH, seeding, aeration, essential nutrients, and many other factors. By these experiments we built up the bank of knowledge needed to more fully understand what was going on, what was essential, and what was not. One advantage of the laboratory work was that there were so many facets to the work that a master's degree candidate could bite off an appropriately sized portion and make a good thesis from it.

Although several universities and the United States Public Health Service undertook a lot of further research and development on the subject, it was the extensive initial work done at MSU which put composting on the map as a viable solid-waste treatment option and has made it practical and workable today. Because of our initiative, the World Health Organization invited me to join with the national compost committee in Japan to undertake a rather extensive research and development program there and to help the city of Kobe design and build a plant for the treatment and utilization of their organic wastes. I also wrote a series of articles and eventually became a co-author of two nationally used books. However, this project was to cause considerable later controversy.

Dean Miller's health was not good, and he was eager to find the right replacement for himself, someone who would also help to further upgrade the school of engineering. He secured Dean Potter, who had just retired from Purdue University, to seek and recommend suitable candidates for the position. Dean Potter did a good job in picking a man of academic standing and action but evidently did not check his skills in human relations. At about the end of my third year the new dean started his job at MSU, and about a year later I decided to move on. Five years later the Michigan Engineering Society had put enough pressure in the right places to bring about his resignation.

As is natural, I initially gave the new dean a lot of support, even though he appeared to have a few rough edges. We did need change in the school of engineering, and everyone has his own way of making things happen. But as the new dean's dealings with each of the departments increased, controversy increased also, especially in the department of electrical engineering, which was his field. There it boiled over. I happened to know the department head quite well and heard more about the problems than most people.

The new dean also probed into the heart of every other department, and our civil and environmental department was no exception. He knew of President Hannah's desire to bring in more research, and he was quite aware of my success bringing in so much that we then had more new research and development than the rest of the departments combined. The two of us had talks every once in a while about all kinds of things within our department. At first I thought he had some ideas worthy of doing, but some of his suggestions were very distasteful to both me and members of my department.

One day he really surprised me, telling me I would have to give back a research grant for our composting project from a nationally renowned foundation, which we had not yet spent but which was creating a lot of scientific interest all around the country. Furthermore, he made it clear that this particular project would have to come to a quick conclusion and that it was not the kind of research and development the university should do. He gave me no choice but to go to the foundation and make up a story as to why we must return the money. I discussed this with some of our staff members, and it disturbed them as well.

Dean Miller was not available to talk over the matter, so I went to the other person who had twisted my arm to come to MSU, President Hannah. I thought he would have some words of advice and a plan for the situation, but the dean's request, including a demand that I lie to the foundation, bothered him even more than it had me. The next thing I knew, in my presence he called up the dean and made it quite clear to him that I be allowed to keep the research and development money.

I knew before I went to Dr. Hannah that the impasse would likely lead to my leaving the university, even though I had tenure the day I started. But it was time to draw a line in the sand, and I did. The question was whether the dean would mend his ways in dealing with the internal affairs of each department. He chose instead to take revenge and escalate the controversy, and within a few days his assistant replaced me as department head. This created quite a stir not only in our department but in others as well. (Because of my tenure he could not relieve me from being a professor at MSU.)

I foresaw things getting a lot worse in the school of engineering before they got better. I had much better things to do in life than to put up with this kind of negative thought and action. It was just the opposite of what I had come to MSU for and for which I had enjoyed the last four years.

These happenings in life need more than simple human wisdom. In the weeks leading up to it I had prayed much about the whole matter. Now the thought came as clearly as possible that I should resign and get back into consulting work but this time in Michigan where things were clean. I explained this to President Hannah. He was very disappointed in the way the dean had handled matters in our department and in the others. Dr. Hannah said, "If you are leaving, the least I can do is to give you a terminal leave with six months' salary. This should be helpful in getting you started in the consulting field."

From then on I avoided any discussions with the staff over the subject of the dean. I also avoided all discussions of it, which became quite hot, in the Michigan Society of Professional Engineers, which became very incensed over the way the dean was upsetting the reputation of the university. About four to five years later he decided to resign, and he was replaced by a very able man who ran things well for the next thirty years.

I will always look back on this time of being a professor and department head with good feelings, except for the last few months. I am convinced that had something negative like this not happened to me I would have stayed there probably until retirement and the new sagas of my life would never have unfolded. MSU had been a new and very productive and happy part of my life. But my new and exciting life to come could only take place when the confines of my former ceiling and walls at the university were removed and I was given the whole world in which to venture and work.

CHAPTER THIRTEEN

The Start of a Lifetime Career

New Years Day 1956 was the beginning of a new life for me. I had completed four happy and productive years as a professor and department head in one of the largest and fastest growing universities in the country. These years provided not only complete security for myself and the whole family but a very satisfying period of professional growth.

During my last few weeks at Michigan State University I had carefully considered which of the two branches of the fork in the road ahead I should take—private research and development or consulting engineering. I knew it was right to venture into uncharted regions, but what about a whole new professional life in research and development? There were many things I had learned to love about this field in the previous years, especially the intrigue of the unknown and the challenge of discovering new and needed knowledge. Was this the way I was meant to help humankind in the future? As much as I was attracted to research, it became clear to me the last weeks in December that my career should instead be down the other branch of the road, in engineering consulting, and that research would fill a satisfying part of that venture. Not only had this logic led me to this conclusion, but I had put the question squarely before the Lord and now had my answer.

As I reviewed my situation on this New Years Day I realized that

137

things were much more favorable for starting a new firm than they had been seven years before when, in the corrupt atmosphere of New England, I had begun that successful venture. I had not only some savings but, thanks to Dr. Hannah, six months of terminal-leave salary which would keep things together while I brought in consulting jobs and converted them into a reasonable steady stream of income. I was beginning to be known in Michigan, where there was not then a problem with corruption.

The year before, I had dug out the crawl space under our lakeside home and built a big table-high train room for our two boys (and myself) for Christmas. I had gone on and dug out a large room for an office, complete with a spacious inside flower bed using overhead fluorescent lights. Here and in the upstairs study I would start the new firm John R. Snell and Associates. (Even though I had no associates, I soon would.)

A four-thousand-year-old Chinese proverb was a guiding light: "The longest journey starts with the first step." I needed that first job I could sink my teeth into to be able to pay some of the bills in another month or two, then the second job and the third and so on, and there must be no end of them. I had my eyes and ears open and saw a potential job coming up in the little village of Ashley, population five hundred, some forty miles to the north. It needed an elevated storage tank for its water system but could not really afford a new one. After I met with the village council they decided to put their fate in my hands and appointed me to make a preliminary study for $1,000. Fortunately, I was able to find for them a good used tank, which was being replaced in a larger community. Ashley got it free for taking it down and reinstalling it, thus saving 80 percent of the cost of a new one.

By the time the Ashley job was done I had visited many places and lined up and even finished several other small municipal jobs. I took advantage of all my contacts to say that I was now in full-time consulting work and ask if they had any work coming up in the near future or knew who might. This, along with leaving an experience record, seemed to strike a number of responsive chords, for it was only a matter of a few weeks before I had a lot more work than I could complete by myself. Now I had to think about whom

I should hire immediately to do good work and be an asset for the future. Two at the top of my list were John Williams and Dick Emerson, both of whom had worked for me in Boston. John was an exceptionally bright and highly trained young engineer and good at design, especially structures and soils. Dick also was bright, talented at design and drafting up the design so that it was clear and meaningful to the client and the contractor. John arrived in Lansing on March 11 and Dick a few weeks later. By summer we had added three Michigan men. The six of us were running out of space in our home, even though we had taken over some of the living area by then.

What started the unusual rate of growth was not the one-by-one municipal jobs I acquired but my calling on the Michigan Department of Highways. I had talked to my highway friends and explained my new circumstance, then asked what they would think of trying me out with one of their bridges to design. They let out a lot of bridges but all to large and well-established firms, most of whom had their head offices out of state. The department's response came as a surprise and a challenge: "Do you think that you could handle three bridges?" I didn't know all the details of how I would do it but had the confidence that I could. That started a long and satisfactory relationship between the young Snell firm and the Michigan Department of Highways, which resulted in many miles of interstate road and bridge design, plus occasional county road and bridge work.

It is one thing to get the first job, but it is another to produce a satisfied client and have the work continue. This simple truth in consulting was deeply ingrained, and I wasn't about to forget it. I took the three bridge designs to the department for review, went back in a few days to check for myself, and asked, "How do our designs compare with those of your larger, old-time consultants?"

The response was a form of double negative designed not to let me get a big head: "They are no worse than any of the others we have. Would you like some more?" Before I could give the people the proper answer they expected, they asked, "Can you handle ten bridges? We have a group of them on the new I-94 west of Ann Arbor." I knew I could, so they signed up our little firm for the ten bridges, twice the work we had in hand.

About this time three things happened in rapid succession. First, I needed some credit at the bank. Second, I needed more good men. Third, I needed a new downtown office with a lot more space that would be flexible for enlargement, would not cost much per square foot, and would be acceptable for the employees and the occasional client who ventured into the office. The right place fell into our laps. A contractor friend of mine had just bought an old building which had been abandoned by the Michigan Farm Bureau. It had some twenty thousand square feet of space. He made us the fantastic deal of one third of the space for one dollar per square foot per year plus heat and lights. Furthermore, we could have first option on second and third sections of the building at the same price. The front was the executive portion of the complex, which included the president's office for me complete with a working fireplace. After some painting and fixing up we moved into the new quarters in late June of 1956, less than six months after we had opened our doors in our home office.

Having a good relationship with the president and others at the East Lansing State Bank I approached them for present and future credit that I could count on and live with and that would permit the rapid expansion I could foresee in the immediate future. One of the big problems in the consulting field was that it often took a long time for the clients to pay after we had completed and turned in the work. This could be from two months to over a year and, now and then, much longer if the client was held up in selling bonds or otherwise obtaining financing. We came to a fair and workable arrangement with the bank. They would loan us at an interest rate of prime plus 2 percent interest on 100 percent of the completed value of all highway or other state work and on 80 percent of any municipal work that we had finished and which had been formally accepted by our client. When these payments came in we naturally had to return those loans. To live within these rules was not always easy, and we constantly had to plan ahead, not only for each job but also before each payday for which jobs would be assigned in time so as to borrow enough to meet the payroll. Only once did one of our project managers fail to meet the completion deadline, an easy thing to do, which made it impossible to have the credit to borrow the money to meet the payroll.

The strain of putting it all together and keeping up with our incredible growth rate was such that two things happened. First, it seemed that I wore a groove in the sidewalk between the office and the bank; and second, I had all the strong symptoms and certainty that I was coming down with a bad case of ulcers. Fortunately, this was not the case. I decided I needed more mental and spiritual control over my life and started to alter my lifestyle accordingly. That was the end of ulcer symptoms for the rest of my long engineering career.

The third and most difficult aspect of the rapid growth was personnel and management. Fortunately, one cannot see too far ahead or the future challenges could be overwhelming. By planning for a slower and more rational growth fewer mistakes or miscalculations are made. It seemed right that when we moved to the new downtown office I was approached by Ken Kenerson, now Professor Kenerson, whom I had appointed to head the new division on construction at Michigan State University. He had had enough of the effects of the new dean, had decided to leave MSU, and was thinking of opening his own consulting office. After many hours of deliberation we decided to convert my rapidly growing firm into a partnership, call it Michigan Associates, and build together instead of becoming competitors. Furthermore, it looked like we were going to have all the bridge and highway work we could handle, and with Ken as a partner I could spend more of my own time getting and doing sanitary engineering work, which was of a great deal more interest to me.

In the meantime, I had contracted with the World Health Organization (WHO) to undertake a major assignment in the Far East starting in late August and running almost three months. I was to visit six Oriental countries—Taiwan, Korea, Macao, Hong Kong, Japan, and the Philippines—and then be the technical director of a thirty-day symposium on the treatment and utilization of organic wastes. (This was my second assignment for WHO. The first, while I was still at MSU, had been to help the Japanese design and build the composting plant in Kobe.) When the symposium convened in

Generalissimo Chiang's summer compound, two more countries' representatives were added: Sarawak and Guam. The visits to the six countries provided me with an update on the conditions there, to see their activities and interests, and to share some of my special knowledge on both anaerobic digestion and our new work of composting organic wastes. It was also a great chance to meet the right people for future work.

It was unfortunate that the arrangements with Kenerson had been made so rapidly and that I had to leave for the WHO work so soon thereafter. When I returned from the trip in November, I became aware immediately that things were not at all right. Most of Ken's experience had been with the United States Army Corps of Engineers, much of it under World War II conditions. His military approach was very different from mine. I leaned strongly toward the democratic approach to getting things done, with ideas and cooperation from everyone at every level. To put the matter bluntly, we had a revolt on our hands, and it was either arrange for Kenerson to go on his own or lose a lot of our people. That wasn't what we were in a position to do, for we had a large backlog of bridge and highway work to complete on a rather tight schedule or breech our contract. It was a hard decision and would have been difficult to work out except for Ken's and my close friendship and ability to communicate and treat each other fairly. We had all the second-management people we needed, and with more on the way we could perform without Ken. We settled by Ken taking 25 percent of the work on hand and my taking 75 percent, since I had been the one to start it all and to bring in the work. It turned out to be not only a fair solution but one where we could work our own natural ways and be happy. My firm continued to grow rapidly, and his by design chose to remain small.

With Michigan's aggressiveness in getting 90 percent federal funds to build its part of the tremendous interstate highway system, and with our pleasing the highway department by turning out good work for them on time, there seemed to be no end to the work we could handle. We added two more men, Frank Theroux and John McDermott. We were also growing, although not at breakneck speed, in water and wastewater jobs from municipalities and from a big Air Force base, and over the next year added Bill Harvey, John Fairall, and a former graduate student of mine, Bill Turney. By this time we also needed a lot of help in management and acquired Don Brown, who not only gave us the management we needed but had time to do consulting for clients in the field as well.

I had always looked upon municipal planners as professionals who should fit like a hand in a glove with engineers. I got to know them very well at MSU and had taught service courses in utilities for them. They were often the first to be employed by cities to plan several years ahead, and usually this planning included the type of projects done by the engineers. And so our firm took on a full-time relationship with a planner, Martin Frissel, who helped us both and continued until his untimely death.

In less than three years we had exercised our option on the whole twenty-thousand square feet of the building, for we were close to filling it. Our staff had grown to sixty-five. There things started to level off, not because we were not doing a good job with our clients but because of changes in the highway department under a new Democratic administration. The head of Michigan highways was an elective office in those days. When Mr. John Mackie, a Democrat, had first been elected the year before, we were sure that our work would be cut way back because we had been given so much work by the former Republican administration. The change of party control is always a worry for a consulting engineer. We had done nothing wrong, but we now were suspected of having in some way helped the former administration to be elected in the first place, which we had not. Most consultants, at least those in Michigan, played a fair game and did not contribute more than very nominally to either side. We played it down the middle and often counted on one member of the firm to get to know the opposition, especially if they put up a strong candidate and the outcome was in question.

And so it was when Mr. Mackie came to office. I took time to get to know him and understand some of the problems which lay ahead for him. The fact that I was not one of the old-time Republican firms but one emanating from Mr. Mackie's alma mater seemed to help. I was also able to give him the advice and support he needed to become a registered engineer, which was very meaningful to him. I am sure that the decision to do more of the work inside the department came from higher up, but it turned out to be bad news all the way around for the consultants. The department had decided to do most of the work in house instead of using consultants.

The standard fee for private consultants to design highways was 4 percent of the construction cost, and for bridges it was 4.5 percent. When the new program, in which all the design work was done within the highway department, got well under way, an unofficial look into the numbers showed that the department's internal cost of design jumped to the outlandish figure of 16 percent, or four times as much as the fee to consultants for the same work. It took a couple of years for all of this to become known and for the policy to again slowly reverse.

Most of the larger consulting firms doing work in Michigan were from out of state; hence the cutbacks affected only a small proportion of their business. But our loss represented a larger proportion of our business. The loss required a lot of adjustment but was not without its benefits as well. First, our growth had been unhealthy because of its phenomenal rate, and now this change would even things out. Second, our borrowing to finance the routine work as well as the growth was always on the dangerous edge. Now when work was completed there was some profit left over which accumulated and allowed us to operate on more of our own capital instead of that which was 100 percent borrowed. Third, we had always wanted the balance of less highway work and more sanitary work. Here at last that opportunity was with us, even though it was being forced on us. All in all, we had a lot to be thankful for when these positives were added together. We needed to solve the negative aspects, and all would be well.

This was our first experience with one of the worrisome aspects of consulting, namely, how to adjust to a declining market, especially when the decline was as radical as it was for us. The key was to realistically look at where we would likely be in the months and a year or so ahead, then move so as not to hurt either the firm or the employees. We hated to lose some of our best men to the highway department, especially when it was the reason for our cutbacks. But we had no choice. So several of our talented men made the move and rose to places of prominence with the state. But by that means the friendship with the department was strengthened, and when in the future other work was let to private consultants, we got our share. But it never again occupied an undue proportion of our business.

During the first three years of unbalanced growth we were still able to get a foothold into some interesting facets of the sanitary field, with more and more of the projects taking on greater size and respectability. Important cities were beginning to see the potential value of composting as a viable way to treat and utilize their organic wastes. My experience in the field of composting while at MSU and with WHO led to our firm doing studies at Baton Rouge, Toledo, Bogota, and Seoul.

Our strong interest in water resources led to our first study for the restoration of Lake Lansing, then for a boating channel through Strawberry Island in Lake St. Clair, and for the first sewage disposal system in Michigan by scientific dilution in the Great Lakes at Mackinac Island. Also we augured horizontal perforated pipes under the Chippewa River which became Mount Pleasant's new water supply and the largest well in Michigan.

We became prominent as expert witnesses in the court case of the *Six Lake States vs. Chicago* in that city's unsuccessful attempt to double the amount of Great Lakes diversion in the Chicago Drainage Canal in lieu of its treating the waste it dumped into the canal. It was not only a battle fought in the courts but in the United States Senate as well. We received a lot of favorable press from the case and were able to help defeat the attempt. During these early years we made a breakthrough with industry, which gave us an ongoing reputation in the following years. Prominent national companies, including A.O. Smith, Infilco, and Chicago Pump, each included us in interesting facets of their ongoing research and development. Omaha Stockyard, the largest in the country, engaged us to look into composting its manure. Post Cereals, the number two breakfast food corporation, engaged us to cut back its high organic wastes entering the Battle Creek sewage treatment plant.

We not only reduced the amount of the waste but eliminated it and also came up with more salable animal feed. Needless to say, the innovative approach we gave them opened us up to a lot of work with them in the years ahead.

Thus ended the first three of my twenty-seven years with the firm that someday would be called the Snell Environmental Group. The next fourteen years were to be marked by expansion geographically and innovation in the work. Adventure was at the center of it all.

CHAPTER FOURTEEN

The Adventure of Consulting

Adventure is made not just from the good things in life but from the tough things as well. On January 1, 1959, I took stock of where we were and where we were going and wrote my summary of the situation.

With no further work on bridges and highways we had cut the staff from sixty-five to thirty-five or fewer people. Because of the restructuring of the State of Michigan Highway Department there would be no work in that field in the foreseeable future. But our bridge and highway work was 90 percent completed and turned in and 70 percent paid for.

Most municipal and environmental work continued to go to the larger, well-entrenched sanitary firms both within and outside the state. It takes time for a new firm to cut in on the jobs which for years have gone to others, especially the enlargements rather than new work.

Most of our young, well-trained engineers and designers who had left our firm had already been hired by the state highway department, as good a place as they could go in the state of Michigan, and two especially became prominent in the department. Two others found good private jobs. We had worked closely with our employees to see that they were well placed.

To help increase our share of municipal and environmental

work, I and other staff members wrote journal articles on areas where we excelled and presented papers at national technical conferences. I also published my article, "Getting the Most Out of the Consulting Engineer." Two years earlier, my article on our Michigan State University research and development work in composting had been widely read. Furthermore, we redoubled our efforts to seek out new work with our followups on potential leads, including quite a few "cold" calls.

Because of my China background I had special interest in overseas work, but the art of being exposed to it and gathering in the work is quite different from domestic work. The good thing was that there was no significant competition in Michigan for overseas work, which put us a step ahead of the two larger firms with which we were competing for local work. We had already done a number of important and interesting jobs in other countries, the last in 1958 in Bogota, Colombia, designing a 700 tons per day (tpd) compost plant; smaller jobs had been done in Hong Kong and Japan. But we needed the right plan to seek and secure overseas work rather than just leave it to chance. Our special lawyer friend in the Philippines, whose brother was a former president, wanted to bring our special knowledge in composting to his country. My close friend from student days at Harvard, Y. M. Liu, then on his third two-year assignment for the United Nations in Pakistan, wanted to introduce me around. Pakistan seemed a possible substitute for China.

After four years of heavy earnings and keeping our expenses in check we had a capital surplus greater than was needed to support the shrinking office staff. Some of the capital had been invested in stocks and real estate, and our continuing expenses were pared down to the size of the work we had been able to bring in.

If necessary we would continue to cut back. Already we had built our firm to one that was well managed with good accounting, secretarial, sales, and public relations personnel, and enough good design engineers and draftsmen to turn out quality work on time. And we had reduced the office space according to the flexible arrangement with the owner.

This was where things stood at the beginning of 1959.

The year 1959 was our low point. The adventure was to stay

alive and not lose any more men. A number of little jobs fed us, and we bottomed out with about fifteen men. We made up our first printed brochure, which attractively presented our staff and its accomplishments. McDermott wrote a good article on low-cost bridges addressed to county roads people, and Bill Turney wrote one on an innovation of the activated sludge method of treating sewage. With these and other tools we fanned out and saw many city and town officials. This was our turning point.

In early 1960, two jobs came in from larger cities. The first came out of the blue through the city manager of Toledo, Ohio. He had read about our work in the municipal refuse field, especially in composting, and employed us to make an extensive study of that city's overall problems. We had to compare landfills and incineration with the newer composting approach and also improve their pickup and haul operations, for 75 percent of overall costs were in this area. We gave this opportunity all we had and came up with a one-hundred-fifty-page report full of drawings and tables and helpful recommendations. The city selected the more conservative landfill disposal method, for composting was too new and untried. Our study on collection and haul presented a lot of money-saving opportunities which it adopted. This put us on the map for new ways of using mathematical formulas to better understand what was taking place and how to save money.

Shortly after Toledo we had another break for the preliminary design of a compost plant in Guatemala City. Although little came of it, for they had no money, it was a clear indication to us that Latin America was interested in this new technology for which we had been in the forefront of development. Including our study for Baton Rouge, Louisiana, we now had developed this new alternate method of refuse treatment and utilization for three cities.

In July 1960, a rather unusual opportunity came along. The national government of Argentina put out a request for unique design proposals for compost plants for seventeen of their large and medium-size cities. It was a prize package such as is frequently offered architects for the preliminary design of special buildings. Each individual design would be studied by a national committee, and prizes would be offered, perhaps enough to pay for the actual work a firm had put into the job. One had to come in first or second to get a prize. The best part of the package was that the engineering firm winning first prize for any city would be selected to undertake the final design of the plant that city intended to build. We decided to enter. To have a better chance of winning and breaking even on the prize part, we selected nine of the seventeen plants and worked up as good a design as the state of the art would allow for each of the nine cities. The general approach for each was the same, but the sizes and costs were varied to suit the conditions, including the sizes of the grinders and recycling equipment which were part of each plant. We had to prepare all of this in Spanish and according to their special forms, but when we had finished we felt very satisfied and confident that something good would come of it.

The results of the competition were very pleasing to us. For the nine designs we submitted we were given four second prizes and five first prizes. We were told to wait until they found the money, at which time the plants would be built and we would be the engineers of record on five of them. In the meantime Argentina had a rather special problem of composting 200 tpd of market wastes in Buenos Aires and asked us to make a preliminary special design for that, which we did. It had to be different from composting refuse alone in view of the fact that market wastes were quite wet, which meant adding some dry material first so that the process would remain porous and aerobic. As things turned out, the early 1960s was a bad time for Argentina, and not until fifteen years later were they able to have us design a plant for them to build.

The Argentina work inspired us and gave us a lot of good data to put out a significant article in Spanish on the design of compost plants. This was useful to us and helped officials in Latin America to understand what composting was all about. I was also very busy as a co-author of a new book on refuse disposal published by the American Public Works Association, which was printed the following year but was already getting considerable publicity. For this I had monthly work meetings of the six co-authors; the other five were municipal officials who were experts on refuse disposal.

In 1960 smaller jobs continued to come into the firm and kept it alive financially. During this year several more papers and publications came out which were useful in exposing us as a young firm with a lot of new ideas worth trying. I was asked to speak on composting at the annual national meeting of the American Society of Civil Engineers (ASCE) in Knoxville and at a similar meeting in Canada. That year the extensive report on the eight-country environmental symposium, of which I had been technical director in Taiwan several years earlier, was printed.

About this time I took up the invitation of my Harvard friend Y. M. Liu to visit him in Pakistan and let him introduce me to some of the officials and local consulting engineering firms. I was very much impressed by the people and their hospitality in West Pakistan, where I first visited. My trip culminated in the signing of a joint-venture agreement with a young up-and-coming consulting firm that had exhibited potential and needed just the kind of technical help we could give them. They, in turn, could join us to sign up some government work and furnish us with engineering and drafting help done by their younger staff members. We called the joint venture Snell-Republic Associates Ltd. Before I left we made a few calls to city officials together.

Several years after World War II, and after much negotiation, India was given her independence. After still further negotiations, the areas which were mainly Muslim were made into one country, East and West Pakistan. However, West Pakistan had an Arab stock and was situated on the western edge of India, whereas East Pakistan on the eastern edge of India had her roots in Asia. Their languages, lands, economies, and almost everything about them were different except for their religion. I looked at Pakistan with optimism as a place where we could directly help the people themselves. This was my best substitute for China as a place to be of service, at least for the time being.

Eight months after my first visit Snell-Republic had work in hand and contracts to complete. The main job was to make a detailed study and preliminary design for the city of Hyderabad, population one-half million, for sewage collection and disposal, storm water collection and disposal, and refuse collection and utilization, employing composting so that the end product could be used with agriculture. Before we were through our first contract, it was extended to make composting studies for Lahore, population two million, and Lylapour, about half that size. It was one thing to sign up a job of this magnitude but another to find the competent man to supervise it in the field, make all the important decisions, and write up good feasibility reports.

For an American to live abroad in the hostile climate of West Pakistan's summer heat of up to 120 degrees would make the job even more difficult. The climate of East Pakistan was as hostile but different, with the temperature some degrees lower but the humidity close to 100 percent. And in those days there were no air conditioners. Furthermore, this obviously was not the last job we would have in the two Pakistans, so I needed to choose with care the man I would send there.

The year before, I had settled on Roy Welter as the best candidate to head our overseas work. I knew him well from my days in Venezuela, where he had been chief engineer. He was sixteen years older than I and well rounded in sanitary work. He had worked for a number of national and international firms. Roy agreed to come to us August 1, 1962, and we both knew what kind of overseas work we were getting into. He and his devoted young wife and ten-year-old daughter moved to Lansing. Roy got to know our firm well and was very helpful with a number of domestic projects in hand. In March 1963 he made his first trip for us to East and West Pakistan. His main task was to secure new work and follow up the contacts I had already made with the help of Y. M. Liu. This trip was a success, and he returned by July fourth.

We had gained enthusiasm for working in that country and were eager to move things along. By early October the Hyderabad project was calling for attention, so Roy agreed to work up the feasibility report and left for Lahore, West Pakistan, on October 12. Unfortunately for us, our Pakistan joint-venture partner was very new in the field and did not have a clear idea as to how to get our job started efficiently, so much valuable time and money were lost. Had Roy been in the United Sates he would have known exactly what to do and would have led the way. But in Pakistan things were entirely different, and Roy waited in vain for our native partner to lead. The first thing needed in writing a feasibility study is to gather a mountain of reliable data. Roy met with frustration time and again. By mid-December the material gathering was only partially complete, and he was falling way behind in his initial schedule to accomplish the whole task.

I had been hoping for a turn for the better each week, but the lack of progress bothered us both, especially with the deadline for project completion being only about four months away. Christmas Day came, and to my surprise I had a call from Roy. He was at home in Lansing. Our new friend and future partner, Mr. Rafical Huq in East Pakistan, had seen through Roy's problem with our West Pakistan man. He figured that Roy needed to get away from it for a couple of weeks so insisted that Roy vacation at home.

Roy came into the office to update me on the job, and his two-week vacation didn't seem like too bad an idea. Certainly it was one he needed. When the end of January came and went and Roy was still with us, however, I felt it was time we had a serious talk and set a specific date for his return to Pakistan to finish the job. Not until then had I grasped the full significance of the problem; he confided to me that he did not plan to go back to Pakistan to continue with the project. It was not only his aversion to going but, he assured me, if he did go he would lose his wife and daughter, and obviously they had a much higher priority. This was quite a blow to me, for I had never thought of such a thing happening.

I was the only other one in the firm with the qualifications to undertake the work and do a good job of it. I should find out as much about the job as I could from Roy and arrange to go over and do my best to finish it on time. However, Roy was not the person to run our office in my place. After consulting with my staff and others whose opinion I valued, we came to the conclusion that it would be a mistake to leave Roy in charge.

The decision to lay off Roy after such a short time with us was probably the hardest decision I ever had to make in the whole of my consulting experience. I have often wondered if I did, in fact, make the right decision, and I still do. It was a human decision, and I do know I would have done a lot better job of it if I had sought God's will on the matter. I would like to have had that decision to make over again on the "guided road." But personal pride and human wisdom prevailed. The job had to be completed or our future in Pakistan would come to a rapid halt, the word would get around, and we would be shut out of other good overseas work, which we had been trying to develop for some time.

I had a loving wife and five loving children but knew that I had to leave them for several months if we were going to make a go of things. The responsibility for the work at the home office was divided in an orderly and logical fashion. So I flew to Pakistan and began eighty-hour work weeks in an effort to do the job well and finish it on time. By making special arrangements with the most qualified people on the Pakistan side, I was able to complete the job on time. The clients were pleased with the results and ready to give us more.

At about the halfway point in the job, when I was confident of getting things done right and on time, I decided I needed a break. One day three of us decided to go wild-hog hunting about ten miles east of the city. We could locate only two guns for the three of us, so we took turns with one of us acting as a brush beater to scare out the game, while the two with guns stationed themselves so as to have the best shot in case one was flushed out. These wild hogs were very dangerous with their long sharp tusks, so we kept close to a climbable tree just in case one came out of the dense brush and turned on us. This was especially important for the man beating with the club. Luck was with us, and I was able to scare out a nice boar, which ran right past one of my friends and was an easy shot. Fortunately, our cook was a Christian and not inhibited by the Muslim custom of not being able to handle or eat pork. We really enjoyed the pork chops and roasts for the better part of a week.

Toward the end of my three-and-a-half-months stay in Lahore the temperature got hotter and hotter until it topped 120 degrees, but it was a dry heat and I was able to stand up to it rather well. It took special precautions to absorb perspiration to make good drawings during such heat, because we had no air conditioning, only electric fans.

Before I left Pakistan, Y. M. Liu met me in East Pakistan and introduced me to Rafical Huq, a middle-aged consultant, whom Roy Welter had already met, who had graduated from the

University of Illinois. We got along fine and soon formed another joint venture, Associated Architects and Engineers, located in Dacca, the capital of East Pakistan, population one and a half million. During the following fifteen years when we worked together we were able to assign several talented men to his staff. On a number of the jobs we did the bulk of the work, if not the most difficult parts, in our Lansing office. Mr. Huq had a large and highly trained office staff so that our relationship and way of working together were efficient and very beneficial to both sides. He was respected for having been trained in the United States, and because we were associated with him we could qualify for some rather important work in his country. For example, we made the two feasibility studies along with the preliminary designs for the storm drainage system for Chittigong, population eight hundred thousand, and then Dacca, with its population now grown to almost two million.

We were obviously in competition with some of the largest and best-known United States consulting firms, who were also the favorites for the work funded by our United States Agency for International Development (USAID) "giveaway" program. I saw one pile of three hundred final plans they had recently completed, but the Pakistan government had rejected them as unaffordable and unbuildable in their country. The work we were employed to do in Chittagong and Dacca was paid for not by the United Sates government but from Pakistan's own funds. And when we were through they had plans which were affordable and could be built in stages, and they were able to fund the construction in stages over the years.

The most interesting and satisfying job Huq and we did together was the eight-thousand-student agricultural university built near Mymensing on the banks of the second-largest river in the country, the Bramaputra. We planned everything except the university buildings themselves, which were contracted to an overseas architect of some renown. Starting from the plain rice fields we transformed about one thousand acres into a very sophisticated university with water, sewer, drainage, streets, and everything else to make a campus. It took a number of years to design and supervise the construction.

During our time there East Pakistan was in two wars, one with India and the other with West Pakistan. East Pakistan finally wound up as the independent country Bangladesh. We found the people there most cooperative and wishing to learn the latest state of the art in engineering, and we shared much of our technical knowledge with them. Although from time to time we assigned full-time people to Bangladesh, I was the one who made frequent trips and coordinated plans with Huq and our clients, then came back and did the same with our Lansing staff members who were assigned to those projects. The final project we undertook and completed in Bangladesh was to design and build a large Indian carp hatchery which turned out two billion fry per year.

Between the two Pakistans we were furnished a lot of adventure. For a small consulting firm we made an important contribution in giving them advanced engineering technology. We also contributed to bringing our two cultures together. The relationship went on to help Mr. Huq's children find the right place for advanced study in the United States and to make them feel more at home here in America. We developed a close working relationship with Mr. Masudul Bari, who for two years ran the big fish hatchery we designed. Later we helped to train him in shrimp culture at our farm in Belize.

During the sixties and into the seventies we were very active in various phases of research and development. Much of this was, in one way or another, related to the processing, treatment, and utilization of municipal refuse. This work included the development of a low-cost vertical two-stage refuse shredder, and we helped the Cobeys of Ohio develop several new refuse shredder-composters. These are still in use and with their latest model, very successful. We worked with Chicago Pump Company on sludge dewatering, refuse moving, and storage devices, and we spent a lot of time with Eimco in the development of high-rate composting machinery.

This later work led us, in stages, to the design and construction of a 300 tpd plant for salvage, shredding, and composting of Houston's municipal waste. This was a contract with one of two private firms to treat and utilize the municipal waste for Houston.

There was little question in everyone's mind that this plant was well done, did not create a nuisance, and was the latest in the technology of that science. Everyone was proud of it except the residential community in which it was built. It was, of course, a part of the city's demand that the plant be built where it was, but we soon learned that the local people would feel "degraded" by having a waste-treatment plant in the backyard of their residential area and were determined to have it removed. Even though the county ruled that the plant was excellent and in no way offensive, politics forced the city to pay our clients the full price of the plant that was built and then caused it to be torn down and sold for salvage. It was a blow to us but cost us only a delay in having our technology become better known and trusted. Obviously we never allowed a plant to be built in the wrong area again.

During 1965-66 we had a chance to build our first incinerator at Bloomington, Indiana, and a large landfill at Sault Ste. Marie, Michigan. A number of smaller jobs helped to feed the hungry staff and keep us going.

During the next year or two we were asked to make first a preliminary and then a final design for a 500 tpd composting plant for Manila, a 60 tpd septic tank waste compost plant for the Miami area, and a preliminary design of a 400 tpd compost plant for St. Louis. We were also called to Boulder, Colorado, to help with the operation of an existing compost plant of the windrow type. Our work with industry also proceeded in the development of new kinds of treatment machinery in the environmental field.

It seemed at last that we had turned the corner.

CHAPTER FIFTEEN

Life Goes On, Work Goes On

Our firm's work with lake restoration and manmade lakes continued. By that time we were doing more in this field than all the other Michigan consultants put together. A natural outgrowth of this kind of work was that the company became more and more innovative. One of the main reasons for improving the condition of a lake was so that the people living around it could make better use of it and enjoy it more. Manmade lakes were made for the same reason and usually increased the value of the surrounding land by a factor of five or even ten.

These concepts grew and grew in our office. Over a period of a year, the idea of the Trans-Michigan Waterway (TMW) was born. We had essentially selected the better, cleaner rivers in Michigan on which to place forty-to-sixty-foot-high dams at about forty-mile intervals and connect them in such a way as to form a continuous clean-water chain of lakes from Lake Michigan on the west side of the state to Lake Huron on the east side of the state. We avoided the rivers which over the years had become polluted. It was easy to see that developers could buy up private low-cost land along this proposed waterway and, as the project was built in stages, make beautiful and valuable subdivisions all along its route.

The concept caught on, and a private corporation was formed, brochures printed, articles published, and a thirty-minute movie made to promote it. A full-time lobbyist was hired, and it was not long before Michigan Senate bill 212 was drawn up to enable the private company to do all the things needed to promote and build the project. The bill included clauses to fully protect property owners from being taken advantage of. The main problem, however, lay with the Michigan Department of Natural Resources, which controlled the rivers and was not about to give up any of those rights to a private company. Even though firms like Consumers Power Company were in favor of the project and had made moderate contributions, progress grew tougher and tougher.

Consumers Power Company had just finished building a giant "peaking" plant on the shore of Lake Michigan where during low electrical-need periods water is pumped up into a reservoir some three hundred feet above the lake. During periods of peak demand the water is released to flow back into the lake to generate much-needed electricity. They had said that this peaking plant was equivalent to a large nuclear generating plant. Even though on the average it uses about 20 percent more electricity than it produces, it produces electricity at the critical times it is needed. Consumers' interest in the TMW was for the same reason. Everywhere we had designed a dam with a large lake above and below, Consumers could build a smaller peaking plant. These would be scattered around the state so the current would not have to be transported nearly as far, thus saving a large investment in the transmission system. They would also recover all the energy from the natural flow of the river as it went over the dam. The state would benefit by increased taxes and from an influx of out-of-state tourists. Furthermore, the whole project would be built without any tax dollars. It took a while, but with the DNR against the project it was just a matter of time before the project was dead.

In the interim a separate corporation formed in Ontario which asked us to lay out a similar plan for Ontario called South-West Waterway Ontario. For a while it looked like their legislature was going to overcome the same kind of problems we had in Michigan, but in the long run their efforts also came to naught. Perhaps the day will come when waterways of this kind will be built in many parts of the United States. They may transport vast volumes of much-needed irrigation water from areas of abundance to areas of drought or places where we have already mined all the geological water from the ground but still need the rich land to raise crops. A good example is the Texas Panhandle, where the groundwater is used extensively and has fallen about one thousand feet in recent years. It will soon be exhausted.

Another example would be to apply many of these principles and divert much of the fresh water entering Hudson Bay from five or six rivers into the Great Lakes. An economic study of each would determine how soon added electric revenues at Niagara Falls would pay out. As agricultural and energy needs grow more pressing, these types of projects will become almost essential.

By 1969 there was a move to tear down the office building we had been using to make room for a large city market. We were also wanting to find a place more to our liking. At that time a real estate friend of mine called my attention to the availability of a one hundred-twenty-year-old German Methodist church and parsonage for sale six blocks north of the state capitol. The beautiful stained glass windows caught my eye, as did the location, price, and many other things about it. After conferring with a close architect friend who had made an old school building into an attractive office for his firm, I decided to run with it if he would act as my architect in the project. Several months later the transformation was complete and we moved into our new and inspiring office. This unique church made into an office was our home for the next five years, until we grew to the point where the walls were virtually bursting and we had also used up all the space of the parsonage next door.

It is hard to say exactly what are the main reasons a consulting firm grows or diminishes from year to year. Likely there are a number of things, with the economy near the top of the list. Reputation, quality of work, and innovation are certainly a part of this process. In our case I would also add the effect our new office had on both ourselves and our clients. It was indeed an inspiration to look at the beautiful stained glass windows day after day. It lifted all our spirits. I would work there frequently after hours to get caught up and got an additional lift by hearing classical music in the background, such as Tchaikovski's Violin Concerto in D.

Fate seemed to smile on us for the first several years in the church-office. We undertook two very satisfying waterways projects: a large marina at South Haven, and helping a unique manufacturer develop interlocking floating marina docks of urethane-filled fiberglass. We were then employed to design a marina using these docks in the Chicago area. The second year we started several large lake-restoration projects including Coldwater Lake and Messenger Chain of Lakes. These were followed by Wolverine and Tyrone Lakes and Wildfowl Bay projects, all in Michigan.

On the industrial side we became involved in helping a new firm called Illinois Waste, Inc. Soon thereafter we spent quite a bit of time with the Waltrip Process, which claimed to accomplish wonders in treating municipal sewage. The process was taken through the throes of a large pilot plant, where it amazed many, even the state health department. Waltrip's company then rushed it into a full-scale demonstration plant at Holly, Michigan, against our recommendation. But there the process floundered when the company reluctantly turned on and off their "black box," which it claimed was the heart of the process, and we revealed that there were grave holes in their claims. Their personnel scattered, and the project fell away, leaving the private investors holding the bag. Had it not been for our objective look at the "science," or lack of science, of the process at Holly, a lot more money would have been lost by the investors. Had the company gone further down the research and development road with us, who knows how much success we would have found. At least expenditures would be much less when experimenting with pilot-size units. During this period we continued to work with Cobey to help them further improve and develop new and better composting machinery.

Three larger projects were brought to us during this same time. One was the detailed design and supervision of construction of over fifty miles of sewer around a very large manmade lake called Sugar Springs, only ten miles from our own development at Blue Lake in northern Michigan. Another was to do the same thing in Burton Township, the largest township next to Flint, Michigan. Over a three-year period we designed and supervised construction of over one hundred miles of sewer, including a number of pump stations. This was done as a joint venture with a Flint consultant-surveyor. Also a large Ingham County storm sewer project kept us jumping to meet deadlines and overcome special problems for such a job.

Our overseas work also was growing. The eight-thousand-student agricultural university in Pakistan continued to involve staff in our home office, and we assigned a young engineer, my son-in-law Art Rowland, accompanied by our daughter Martha, to supervise the construction and design there in Mymensing. Our reputation had spread to India, and I was asked by a private enterprise group to survey six of the largest cities to see about the feasibility of replacing the foul burning rubbish dumps with modern composting facilities. Florence accompanied me on this ten-day Indian project, but instead of seeing a new ugly refuse dump each day she was taken to the best-known tourist sites, including the Taj Mahal. At Puna we were in on a more serious study of a compost project. An Indian professor, Mr. Bopadicka, was constantly in touch with us and trying to push important Indian projects forward. India had an essentially government-controlled business climate, and we never really cracked their resistant shell, although there was a lot of interest and enthusiasm. Lack of money was at the heart of their problem when it came to developing the infrastructure.

In the western hemisphere, San Palo, Brazil, solicited a refuse study from us. Although the private sector was very much alive there, the public sector had no money for the project but was intrigued as to what composting could do for them. I was very much impressed by the many skyscrapers in San Palo, and in addition to the skyline there was a vast growth of industry with smokestacks everywhere.

In the late sixties and early seventies I thought I should look ten years down the road for our firm, find the right people to be its future leaders, bring them in, and train them. The criteria I had in mind were numerous, and such people were not easy to find. If they were as good as I wanted them to be they already would be in a good consulting firm, and if they were not they might never attain the high standards needed. This was a dilemma I grappled with. Essentially I was looking for a very bright eager younger man who had spiritual conviction, leadership and sales ability, as well as a sound technological background in environmental engineering. He must be a respected, honest leader of a firm with a natural feel for business so that the firm would continue to grow and prosper.

One person who appeared to meet these rather severe criteria was Le Young, whom I had met and was impressed with in Lahore, West Pakistan, when I was first there for three and a half months. At the time, he was a talented architect-turned-missionary assisting with the design and supervision of the construction of the mission's buildings. He was near the completion of a beautiful four-hundred-bed hospital. Another member of the mission staff was Dr. Rice, who for a short time had taken over my father's hospital in Suzhou, China, after dad's untimely passing. When Le Young had finished his Pakistan assignment he decided that he needed environmental engineering rather than architecture to be of the highest service to the third world. He therefore returned to the United States for his master's degree in this subject and was now working for a well-known environmental consulting firm in the southern United states. We became reacquainted over an interview and both thought well of his trying out for the job.

Le was with us about three years and contributed a great deal to our firm, to our staff, and to our philosophy and ideology. Le, being also a very creative architect, took a great interest in the four hundred fifty acres of prime subdivision land I was in the process of buying, by Lake Lansing. He eagerly wanted to make a plan for that area to build apartments and condos of concrete with many unique features. However, no income was generated from all the work he and the draftsman were doing on the project. And no matter how hard he tried, he could not get the capital cost of his design in concrete closer than about 20 percent above the conventional "stick" construction everyone was using. I knew that we would not be in a position to do any of the building on speculation ourselves, and no one else in the area wanted to buck the 20 percent odds. I encouraged Le to cut that project back to almost nothing and to become involved in projects waiting to be completed for which clients had funds to pay us. From time to time we would go away by ourselves to discuss the main reason he was there: to continue to train for and perhaps eventually take over the leadership of our firm.

Unfortunately for Le he had serious marital problems since his return from the mission field, which made this transformation more difficult. After many long, friendly, and soul-searching discussions, Le and I came to the conclusion that he would be better suited and happier in a nonprivate enterprise kind of job. We made flexible plans so that this could happen for him, and I would then look for another man to fill the future top leadership job.

I must include here the compelling story of another person who entered and enriched our lives. Hugh Corrough came to us in the summer of 1966 at the recommendation of a close Vanderbilt friend of mine, Dave Braswell, who was a professional counselor in St. Louis. Dave told me a bit about Hugh's background and fantastic accomplishments. He was a chemical engineer who rose through the ranks of industry until as managing director of the Alco Division of the American Locomotive Company he was supervising twenty-five hundred men. The extreme pressure of the labor-management strife took its toll on Hugh, so that about ten years later his alcoholism had caused him to lose everything, even his wife and family. Hugh was now trying hard to put his life back in order. "In my mind he needs a job to fit in with the help he is receiving through Alcoholics Anonymous to be a complete winner," Dave said. "He needs to get away from living with and being dependent on his brother as well. Would you like to give Hugh some kind of job and take him under your wing? He was a tremendous guy and can be again."

During my graduate school days at Harvard I had met one of the three founders of AA, Rev. Sam Shumaker, and knew about the success the twelve-step program had brought to tens of thousands of lives. In fact, I had known several personally. God's power did the changing, and one only needed to fully accept it and keep with the program on a daily basis.

Hugh had hit bottom and was willing to let God work the miracle of change in his life. His friends in AA stuck by him, and so did I, for Hugh was a great guy. Over the next six to eight months I used Hugh to help develop a number of "inventions" which had been dormant. He did a good job pointing up the better ones and culling out the poorer ones and getting industry interested in some of them. In the first six months Hugh had only one "fall off the wagon." From there on he grew in every way. He gave back to his AA friends daily and over the years became one of their best spiritual leaders. Hugh also was an effective leader in our newly formed Bootstrap program (see later chapter 19 "The Saga of Belize". Although it had been a long time since Hugh had done the nitty-gritty design type of engineering work, he was a good associate in our firm and served our clients well for seven years. The high point of his time with us was when Florence and I stood by him as he was remarried to his former wife, Lou. What a thrill!

After Hugh's retirement from the engineering firm at age seventy we still wanted a way to build up his Social Security and retirement fund and at the same time leave the freedom of room at the top for John and Phil, who had joined the firm in July. So Hugh and I formed a new company called Snellco, which operated out of the Snells' home, and Hugh spent all his time running it while I would just confer with him from time to time. The countries in the Middle East were buying all kinds of things on a bid basis, mostly from the United States, including bulldozers, heavy trucks, and cement plants. Hugh knew these things well, and with the aid of a Telex (run by Florence)got quotes from the manufacturers, added on a small commission and expenses, and telexed or wrote in his bid. Most of our bids were close but second and, all in all, we did not make money, but it did keep Hugh busy and gave him the base salary and desired retirement benefits.

Then Hugh had the offer to head the Michigan branch of the National Council on Alcoholism, where he did a superior job for two years. Hugh went the last step and gave up smoking after having been gripped by the habit much of his life. Unfortunately, within months he came down with cancer of the throat, and six months later his life ended. His memory was engraved on the hearts of the hundreds he had helped as a friend. Hugh's life showed us all that, with God's help, it is never too late to get back on your feet and live a victorious life.

In late spring of 1972 I interviewed John O'Malia in our office. He had a responsible position with a well-known Indiana firm, but things were not to his liking there and he was looking for greener pastures with a greater future. Although I was advertising for one individual with top leadership qualities, another highly-placed man in the same firm, Phil (not his real name), accompanied John. Phil's main interest and forte was in the area of client relations and soliciting new work. John, on the other hand, was a project manager with expertise in supervising the production of work which had come in, but he had abilities in client relations as well. Our firm had never really had a well-organized program for client relations, and with our growth and present financial strength it seemed this was a good time to put the right emphasis on this area as well as on production. Growth was dependent on this aspect, and I looked forward to the day when I was not the only or main person to bring in the new work.

So with references checked out, by July we had two new vice presidents and were planning together how to improve and enlarge our firm. Fortunately, we had a good backlog of work in hand, and our financial condition was such that we could absorb two, rather than one, more highly paid men at the same time. John and Phil already had several years of experience working together, and this made it easier. I enjoyed and benefited from our frequent discussions.

Before they had come in July I had contracted to teach a summer course on sewerage at MSU, and this occupied about a third of my time. It was interesting to get back into teaching even for one term. The big difference was that all the students came to class barefooted and in old jeans as was the custom at the time. I had been out of touch!

During the winter and spring of 1972 I had been extremely busy writing eight sections for a new three-volume engineer's environmental handbook, which was equivalent to writing about fifteen technical articles. The work was well worth doing, but the pay just about covered the cost of typing and retyping. The effort did take me away from income-producing jobs. In May I had to make a major technical presentation at the First National Conference on Composting held in Denver.

John O'Malia was assigned to the kind of jobs with which he was very familiar such as the two large sewer jobs and the large storm drain job. He also took on the new sewage treatment lagoon in Webberville. I spent more time on the several lake projects, as yet unfinished, and also on the continuing Illinois Waste Corporation work, the New Hampshire composting job, and the new one on Waltrip's unique method of treating sewage. The Cobey compost machinery design and development also kept me and one draftsman busy.

One of our most interesting jobs in a long time came along during this period and extended over four years. The Ohio Feedlot in South Charleston, Ohio, held twenty thousand head of cattle under roofs and was the largest feedlot east of the Mississippi. The owners, under the leadership of Dr. William Hackett, a very successful and well-known veterinarian, had great plans for the cattle industry and wished to use their facility as a demonstration plant to determine the true value of their unique thinking. The cattle were brought into the feedlot at about four hundred pounds and in about six months were sold at about eight hundred pounds. Half of their consumption was ground corn and other grains and half was corn silage, which took about ten thousand acres to grow in the area. The program, before we became involved, was every four to six months collecting the manure, which had been accumulating on six inches of ground-up wood and bark wastes from a nearby paper mill. This mixture was then used as a fertilizer. The waste products from these twenty thousand head of cattle were close to four hundred tons per day. The management's early thinking had been merely to do a good job of composting these wastes before they were marketed in fifty-pound and one-hundred-pound sacks as an organic fertilizer. After some innovative thinking and research they checked with the Environmental Protection Agency (EPA) to see if it would permit this composting operation in their new plan.

The unique plan was to compost the mixture of manure and ground-up bark and wood with a very high-rate composting method in which the waste was properly stabilized and well pasteurized in about six days. Then it would be used to feed the cattle in place of the corn silage on a pound-for-pound basis. It was a revolutionary concept, and we were privileged to help them with most of the details concerning the high-rate composting. This huge plan involved mechanical turning several times, with air blown up through the material, on a twenty-four hour schedule. Temperatures hovered right around 160 degrees or higher, and odors were no problem whatever. The composting process completely changed the nature of the mixture from a pathogen-infested, bad-smelling mess into a peatlike substance with a faint earthy odor which actually appealed to the taste of the cattle, especially when it was mixed with their normal grains. We helped them obtain almost a precise degree of control of the project after a few weeks of experience. We did have to keep the compost from becoming too high in moisture in the winter months when evaporation rates were down. The process made national news, and the only restriction the EPA seemed to put on the corporation was that the finished cattle were to be sold within the state of Ohio. According to an article in the January 1973 issue of the *EPA Region V Public Reports* the value of the compost was worth forty dollars per ton when used as a feed and twenty-five dollars per ton when used as a fertilizer. The estimated cost of producing the compost was only four dollars per ton. The article went on to tell how the demonstration experiment was planned and monitored by six groups of technical experts, including those in waste handling (in which we were involved), cattle housing, cattle diseases, nutritional value, value of the composted waste to the soil, and the economic aspects of the many facets of the project.

Not long after the group found out how well the process worked and saw that their cattle were growing and even gaining weight faster on this food ration than they had been before, they looked eagerly to a big expansion process. It was rather unusual that cattle in feedlots were raised under roofs and had such fine bedding as the ground-up bark and wood to catch and hold the manure and urine before it could be gathered, composted, and put to such a useful purpose. Most feedlots were in the open and did not use any bedding whatever. The Texas Panhandle had the largest concentration, and Omaha had large feedlots as well. I remember seeing piles of manure in the Texas Panhandle which were four hundred feet wide, forty feet high, and two miles long, and that is a lot of manure—much more than anyone could properly use in the region as a fertilizer. The thought was, however, that if we could compost this waste and use it as about 50 percent of the cattle's own feed, it would certainly bring a revolution to the whole industry, not just to the Ohio feedlot.

Our firm was asked to work with the new corporation formed by the Ohio feedlot people on the best way to compost the Texas manure produced under these new and different conditions, and do it in such a way that it pasteurized the waste and also made it attractive as 50 percent of the cattle-food ingredient.

The Texas waste material scraped up from the feedlot pens was quite different from the material we had been dealing with in Ohio. It was a lot wetter, and instead of having the ground-up bark and wood to absorb the urine, this important liquid fraction either soaked into the ground or was washed away by occasional rains. As much as 10 percent of the product scraped up was sand, clay, or silt, none of which the cattle could tolerate. They seemed to know it was there and would avoid it, but that which they did eat was hard on their teeth as well as their digestive systems. We were able to design, build, and operate for them a plant which would do a good job of composting the gathered manure and even overcome the moisture problems. But the end product from the cattle raised on the open ground was not satisfactory, mainly because of the soil contamination, which at that time could not be separated out from the end product. The big dream of recycling composted cattle manure, urine, and bedding in place of the corn silage part of their feed was dashed. Recent experiments with MBI (1994-95) indicate that removal of sand and other materials from this manure may become quite practical and worth further study and testing as they may apply to the larger problem.

To convert this universally produced type of waste manure into a pathogen-free fertilizer worth about twenty-five dollars per ton for a good profit is quite feasible and should be happening more and more in the future. Its present highest and best use is to place it on the semibarren areas in our agricultural fields, for it is in such places that the raising of green manure to bring up the organic content fails. However, these experiences in Ohio and Texas were far from the end of our innovative use of the composting process and what it can do for humankind, as we shall see in later chapters.

CHAPTER SIXTEEN

Family, Values, and Investments

For some time we had been looking for a home in East Lansing so that our kids would not have to use the bus each day to go back and forth to classes at Michigan State University. We loved the lake, but the inefficiency of the long bus trips loomed large. One day in the fall of 1964 a realtor friend of mine told me about an interesting home that was condemned and due to be torn down the following week. I expressed interest in it.

The house, in a much-sought-after residential area of East Lansing, was built on the edge of a dead lake (now filled in with peat and used as a neighborhood park), and in twenty years this house had settled over twelve inches and somewhat unevenly. To me this was obviously too good a house to tear down. There must be a way to install piles like most of the houses in the area already had. My offer of a thirty-day option to pay only ten thousand dollars, which equaled the price of the lot less two thousand dollars (two thousand dollars was the cost of tearing it down) was accepted. I immediately set about getting a plan for it and checked it with two soils experts, friends of mine. The restoration called for a Detroit contractor to drill eighteen-inch diameter holes twenty feet down to solid ground about every eight feet around the periphery and fill each with concrete and a steel bar one inch in diameter in the center. The top of each pile had a hand-formed reinforced concrete elbow extending under the foundation, so the house sat firmly on the piles and was very stable. In the following thirty two years it did not settle another one-eighth inch.

Our two sons, John and David, were a big help to me in this work and also in replacing the broken under-the-floor hot water heating system with a new peripheral system. After we leased the house for two years to students and then further restored it, we moved in during the fall of 1966. Everyone was pleased except David, who had to transfer from Haslett, where all his friends were, to East Lansing High for his senior year. I don't think he forgave us for the poor timing for several years, but everyone else benefited from the move, and it was much closer for all to attend college.

Each of our children at one time or another worked for Snell Environmental Group (SEG) doing secretarial work, field work, or drafting, usually as summer jobs. It gave them spending money and experience and gave our full-time people a chance to get to know various members in the family. For about twenty-five years my work week averaged 75-80 hours, and the firm was quite successful, but I should be quite open and state that there were other values more important. Although the family came first, I often shortchanged it for my time. The families of the workplace at Michigan State University, the Snell Environmental Group, the Church, and Rotary were all competing for time, energies, and caring.

Our net worth accumulated several times over from investments outside the professional work in the firm—mostly in real estate. As a civil engineer I held special talents and intuition in picking real estate which would accrue in value. Instead of putting our savings in the bank we parceled it out and purchased land contracts over the years. For example, we put together twenty parcels of land totaling 450 acres, just east of Lake Lansing, which twenty years later brought twenty times its original value. This land included two Christmas tree farms which our kids took over and ran as a junior family corporation to help pay all their college expenses. On this project they earned an hourly rates five times the going rates. This work taught them responsibility, the value of money, and how to run a business. The area was wild, beautiful, and inspiring, where herds of deer roamed.

During the children's growing years these 450 acres provided an ideal place to take walks, study nature, and to a lesser degree to hunt. John and Dave had shotguns, and I had taught them to hunt, but it never was a favorite pastime as it had been in my youth. We planted thousands of quality trees and thinned out or eradicated low-grade plants and shrubs to make room for the newcomers.

To have left all the land in its original twenty smaller parcels would have left little or no value or a final fate of fragmentation. In the early 1980s we sold half of the land to the best builder in the area, one who would preserve the natural beauty. The remaining 225 acres and most beautiful of the land went to Ingham County to become part of its 500 acre park with nature trails throughout. Half of our land we had sold to the Nature Conservancy and half we made as a gift, and we are grateful that this beautiful tract of land will be preserved for the enjoyment of posterity. It is now laced with hiking trails used for skiing in the winter.

In 1960 the family's second land investment was four hundred acres of pristine land one hundred miles north of Lansing located in a state game preserve and containing two lakes. We already lived on Lake Lansing which was 450 acres, but that was before it was dredged and vastly improved. We all thought that it would be nice to also have a northern Michigan lot on a beautiful lake where we could build a cottage and get away to enjoy such beauties every other weekend or so. For a week our family of seven stayed with a friend's family of six in their roomy cottage on Houghton Lake. Each day we drove out from there to look for that perfect lake lot. In all, we saw lots on forty lakes but never found quite the right one. We even made a firm offer on the one we liked best, but our offer was turned down. Then toward the end we came across not a lot but two whole lakes and 320 acres of wild forested land. The land had been held by an individual for most of his life, and we were led to it just at the time when he decided he was willing to sell. With the help of the bank and time payments, it was purchased.

One of the lakes, Blue Lake, was seventy feet deep and so clear that we could see to the bottom. This tract of land became the center of our recreational life for most of the family for the next twenty years. We spent our vacations and weekends there, enjoying the beauties of the place while we developed it into what the Department of Natural Resources called the second-best developed lake in Michigan. Blue Lake had ten thousand years' accumulation of marl (fine calcium carbonate deposit) all around the edge, with the embankments dropping off abruptly. By raising the water level eight feet and covering the marl with a foot of sand taken from a nearby hill, we were able to make the lake twice as large, more beautiful, and with the natural beaches it had centuries ago. We also reconstructed the outlet of the lake so that the cold water it discharged came from eight feet down rather than from the surface. With this cold spring water passing on from the deep part of the lake, the top, six to eight feet warmed by the sun, was retained, thereby extending the swimming season several weeks in the spring and the fall. The roads and electric lines were contractor built in stages. The family—mostly Florence and I—with the aid of a chain saw and a brush king, and later an old-model bulldozer, prepared a few lots at a time for sale, and mostly by word of mouth we sold the lots one at a time to a wonderful community of people who have become longtime friends. By means of an association these lot owners maintained the quality of the lake and the whole area. On the advice of our tax consultant, Florence learned to run the business end of the enterprise, drew a small salary, and accumulated a separate social security account, which in our retirement helps with our expenses.

The whole subdivision was built around Blue Lake and included only ninety-three large lots, about half of which were waterfront. The rest of the land was divided into twenty-five wild ranches ranging in size from eight to twenty-five acres, with a number fronting on the second lake and each serviced by an access road. In most cases the parcels were sold with only 10 percent down over a period of several years, with our carrying the mortgages. All in all, not counting paying ourselves for the labor of manual work, we were able over a twenty-five-year period to accumulate a profit before taxes of about $300,000. But mainly we enjoyed every minute of it and acquired a lot of friends, exercise, family values, and an untold amount of inspiration.

Blue Lake was surrounded by twenty sections of State Game Preserve land with beautiful streams and forests. This family investment of Blue Lake did much for everyone in the family, for our enjoyment and learning to further appreciate and love nature. It became a point for many family reunions, bringing up our friends, and playing and working together. It was a fine swimming, canoeing, fishing, and snorkeling lake. It was truly an inspiring place for our lives.

Our two eldest daughters and their families purchased choice ranches for themselves, later selling them at a profit. We kept our cottage until 1986 when the needs for funds in Belize became critical. At that time we gave the cottage to our church who sold it and invested the proceeds in the shrimp farm. We still visit our Blue Lake friends and recently had a marvelous week-long vacation in our old cottage, relaxing and reading and having a reunion with many of our friends.

Another four-hundred-acre investment in northwestern Michigan occurred in the 1960s when we accumulated several parcels of land already in the federal soil-bank program. It was a program where, through government control, farm output and consumption were brought more nearly into balance. After we held the land for about ten years and used the federal payments for not growing anything, the land was free and clear and we sold it at a reasonable profit. The kids helped in spraying the scrub trees and in planting the approved tree types. John and David soon learned the full techniques and took the responsibility to undertake these tasks on their own.

In the mid sixties SEG had done some $25,000 worth of design work for a subdivision for which the developers could not pay, nor could they pay the contractor putting in the roads. Instead of pushing them into bankruptcy, we and the contractor each took as payment a proportional number of rather risky second land contracts based on 15 percent discount. We held sixteen of these. The paper control of these small homes being purchased by people mostly below the poverty line was extensive. Most of the buyers looked at the homes as rental units, and whenever they fell way behind on their payments walked away from them. It then became necessary to fix up the places at our own expense and resell to other people in about the same financial condition. Each of our family members at one time or another contributed, for student-type wages, to the repair of the houses. In about five years our sixteen second land contracts each had turned over at least twice and our files on them increased from half an inch thick to six inches thick. But by this time the value of the houses had increased threefold, and people no longer tried to walk away from them when they had trouble making their payments. Around this time we gave each of our children one or two of the properties to do with as they saw fit. Having learned more about business and the work ethic, they turned their properties into small profits for their own accounts.

In the late 1970s and early 1980s we purchased two apartment complexes totaling about 110 units and a medical center with ten units, plus a 20 percent ownership in a 240 unit apartment complex near Central Michigan University in Mount Pleasant. The latter was poorly managed, lost money, and went under. The other three turned a fair profit and would have returned more had they not been liquidated to help finance the shrimp operation in Belize. Generally, the management was accomplished by others, as I was much too busy with the engineering consulting firm.

Purchase of property in Belize (see Chap 19, "The Saga of Belize"), returns on stocks, liquidation of the stocks to pay the Belize bills, and a loss on oil-well investments represent other financial ups and inevitable downs over the years.

Although having raised five children in no way makes one an expert on the subject, I have some observations which may be worth passing on. First and most important is to marry the right woman, one who will be an ideal wife and mother, and then live happily with her all your life (for us, so far, fifty-seven years). Next in importance is to try your best to be a role model for the children in every way—hard work, strictness, honesty in everything, and exhibiting spiritual qualities in all of life. Finally, it is important to do things for the children and with them and show through all you do that you really love them. One needs to teach them how to work, earn money, and live with others, rather than just give them material things. Each child needs to feel special, and all need to be encouraged to be anything they truly set their minds on being.

It was my privilege to work with our two boys, especially, and show them about how to build almost anything, including carpentry, masonry, plumbing, and electrical things. All had their share of work and fun and the resulting good eating from a large and bountiful garden at Lake Lansing. When John and David were about eight and nine they learned a hard economic lesson— how big was big, and what was a dollar worth?—when they together shoveled two to three inches of snow off part of frozen Lake Lansing with the idea each would earn ten dollars when they had the whole lake clear. They did clear off a nice one-acre area of the lake for skating.

We felt fortunate to be given what I view as an inspired answer to the usual problems teenagers have with their first cars. The engineering company had worn out a panel truck used for surveying, and instead of trading it in for a new one, we purchased it and gave it to the kids for their personal use. The ramshackle truck was in good running order and gave the basic transportation they needed but avoided the "macho" that a fast sports car would have given.

Nature had many valuable lessons to teach all of us throughout our years together. Although each of the children had a hand at hunting—even deer at Blue Lake—it never gripped them. I'll never forget Karen's and Martha's experiences in this. Karen and I tracked down a wounded deer for hours. Martha had one run right by her, and her first shot brought it down in an isolated area. When I found them, she was overcome with emotion for having killed an innocent deer.

Once, when the children were quite young, they were all following along with me. I had a shotgun in hand and a come-apart fiberglass bow over my shoulder. I came up over a ridge, and not over fifty feet away two deer stood feeding. They had not seen me. I put the bow together and sneaked up to the ridge again as all five of the kids watched. I pulled back, took good aim at one of the deer, and let go. In the hurry, I did not have the arrow on the bowstring, and as I shot, the arrow fell to the ground and the deer bounded off into the woods, much to this father's embarrassment.

As the children matured, the lake was often a place where friends were included, and then came the times when dates at home took precedence over the rest of the family weekending at the lake.

Beginning when the children were quite young and going on for a half-dozen years, the whole family got much pleasure attending the travelogues shown at Michigan State University every Saturday night. They enjoyed sitting in the front row, and when certain favorite funny commentators performed, their jokes were retold over and over for several days. Florence and I continued attending concerts and plays of the Lecture-Concert Series. At home we kept the "hi-fi" playing a good selection of mostly classical records and thus were able to pass along to all five children an appreciation of good music.

When we moved to Lake Lansing, television had just become available. It was enjoyed by everyone, and a rather strict viewing-time allowance prevented the wasting of much time. Florence helped with much of the school homework, but Dad usually was brought in for the math and physics problems. All the children had their chores and did them willingly 95 percent of the time. Their partly Scottish father gave them a very generous incidental allowance of twice their age in pennies per week, but they learned to do much better on their own with outside jobs such as delivering papers, cutting grass, working in the library, baby sitting, and running the Christmas tree farm.

All of our children did well in school. Karen, Martha, and John were valedictorians of their classes. We encouraged each to develop a hobby or two of their own choice. Each had a chance to test their tastes with a musical instrument, piano, school band, or church chorus. The family generally attended the newly organized Haslett Community Church as long as we were at Lake Lansing. The much larger People's Church in East Lansing did not have the closely knit family appeal, and our family attendance fell way off. At our lake home the boys and I built onto the double garage a combination club and museum room which was all theirs. Each child also had some interest in sports or exercise. The three girls took up running and various other forms of exercise they integrated into their lives. All rose to the confidence expressed in them that they could be anything they wished to be, and each has risen and developed way above our expectations.

As often happens, the parents are most strict with the eldest, and we and our "Chica" were no exception. She had to be in at 9 PM and then 10; whereas, when it came to David, 1 and 2AM were even tolerated. The girls never seemed to give their mother worries when they were out on dates, for they all had excellent choices of boys. I was especially impressed when Karen's boyfriend Dale came to us and in the good old-fashioned way asked us for her hand. We liked Dale from the start and were delighted to say yes.

As marriage after marriage took place, there came the next stage of our greater family life—grandchildren. Each one was special and a delight to both parents and grandparents. Thus we lived our early family life all over again with many of the benefits and pleasures but without the direct or full responsibilities. Fortunately for us, these last twenty-five years, as the twelve grandchildren have grown, have brought a great deal of pleasure and very few worries. At this writing, five of the twelve are through college or graduate school and hard at work, two still in college, and two in high school.

Following is a list and very brief biographical summary of children, spouses, and grandchildren. It scarcely begins to describe the richness of their lives and experiences and why we are proud of them.

Dorothea ("Chica") Snell, born March 19th, 1942, earned a B.A. and M.A. from Michigan State University in Elementary Education. She is now a full-time fifth grade teacher in Haslett, Michigan, much beloved, and an innovator in integrating disabled students into the classroom. Her marriage to Gerald F. Fenska ended in divorce. On July 20, 1996, Chica's life was made complete as she and Vincent Swift were married. Vince is computer software management consultant for business firms working with Maximus. Chica's three children are Amy Jo Fenska, B.A. in accounting, Michigan State University now applying her accounting in business software; Kimberly Dawn

Fenska, former staff nurse at Sparrow Hospital, Lansing, B.S.N. University of Michigan and now studying for an advanced degree in anesthesiology at Penn State Medical School; Shelley Anne Fenska, enrolled in business at Lansing Community College, and manages an apartment house as well.

Karen Snell, born July 2nd, 1943, earned a B.S.N. and M.A. in Family Studies from Michigan State University. She has been a staff nurse at Ingham Medical Hospital, a public health nurse, and a childbirth educator, and now is an academic advisor in the College of Nursing, MSU. She and her husband Dale J. Dailey, who has had a long engineering career with General Motors, have three children: Aaron James Dailey, B.S. Electrical Engineering, Computer Science, University of Virginia, resides in Boulder, Colorado, and works as a computer programmer; Jennifer ("Alex") Lynn Dailey, B.A. International Relations, Brown University, now working on M.A. in linguistics at the University of Portland; Caleb Alexander Dailey, B.S. Mechanical Engineering, Princeton University, works for General Motors Advanced Engineering in Warren, Michigan, and following an eighteen-month assignment in Hiroshima, Japan, he is enrolled at Massachusetts Institute of Technology on a masters of business administration program plus a master's degree in engineering.

Martha Evelyn Snell, born Dec.11th,1944, B.S. in Social Science, Michigan State University, M.A. Special Education, MSU., Ph.D. Special Education, MSU, now Professor in the Department of Curriculum, Instruction and Special Education in the University of Virginia's Curry School of Education; married to Robert Thomas Rood, Professor of Astronomy, University of Virginia. Their Children are Emilie Catherine Snell-Rood, student at Walton Middle School, and Claire Natalie Snell-Rood, student at B.F. Yancey Elementary School in Esmont, Virginia.

John Raymond Snell,Jr. born Nov.13th, 1948, B.A. Michigan State University, graduate course in energy and conservation, lives in Montpelier, Vermont, heads his own international firm, John Snell & Associates, well known consultants in thermography (the technology of infra-red light) and its uses in industry; married to Elizabeth Parr, B.S. Education, MSU, M.A. Literature & Drama, Vermont College, junior-senior high school language arts teacher. Their children are Andrew Clayton Snell, enrolled in University of North Carolina in Computer Science; Suzannah Kate Snell, seventh grade student in Montpelier, Vermont.

David Moffett Snell, born Dec. 22nd, 1949, B.F.A. Michigan State University; M.F.A. Cranbrook Academy of Art; lives in New Hall, California (Los Angeles area), and after sixteen years rose to vice president of Western Brass and three related corporations and is now the new operations manager of California Metals Exchange (in Los Angeles, a large maker of metal briquettes), married to Janice Eidemiller, who was Department Manager in Sales, Western Brass. Their children are Dustin Moffett Snell, who at age twenty owns a successful computer software company; Joshua Raymond Snell, who attends Bowman High School.

During July 1995 our three generations experienced a high point when we became part of the Moffett reunion in Grinnell, Iowa. Florence and I and all of our children and grandchildren were twenty-four of the fifty-five in attendance. It was a wonderful opportunity for the binding of family ties among the three generations reprresenting nearly all the living members of the Moffett clan.

In a broader sense I consider our larger family to have developed through the various walks of our lives. There were the staff persons in the Civil and Environmental Engineering Department at Michigan State University of which I was chairman, each needing special attention and help to do their best in teaching and research, and the employees and associates of the consulting engineering firm, SEG, many of whom have remained close to us even ten years after my retirement. All these "family" connections were very worthwhile, even though they took valuable time and energy which might have been concentrated on our biological family. "Families" further afield, who were also important and required my time and energy, were our consulting firm's clients without whom we could not have had a firm; the over two hundred members of the Lansing Rotary Club; our churches' families including that of our present church where we have become fully committed to building a strong church; and the family we built in Belize—the Bootstrap Small Farms Program, the new family who built the three-hundred-acre shrimp farm designed to fund the Bootstrap program, and now the persons in Starich, Inc., whom I have helped to become successful. For twenty years we built and enjoyed a Blue Lake family of closely knit nature-oriented families.

An important activity I continue to do for myself, even at my age of over eighty, is a rigorous exercise program three times a week at the health spa, which is an essential part of my living. Flo had been a charter member, and it took me fifteen yours to see the need and value to join and go regularly.

I must say more about my marriage which according to the Bible's words that "a man shall leave his mother and father and take a wife and the two shall become one," has been a Christian marriage. We believe this was part of an inspired plan for the two of us and that each of our five children were God's gift to us and our responsibility to nurture to the best of our ability. Through many years Florence was not only the devoted mother to each of the children, but when I was away on business or exceptionally busy she fulfilled both parents' jobs. Florence has also been my life companion, encourager, and inspiration. She has been the co-pilot of our family life together. She has always been one for me to work for, strive for, and to love, honor, and respect. She has been the needed part of me without which there would have been little or no success. I thank God for the "ultimate gift" I received over fifty-seven years ago and am grateful for every day of our life together. As the children grew older and more mature, Florence was able to travel with me on some of my longer and more interesting international trips. I look back on trips we made together with immense pleasure, whereas many of the others are vague and distant in my memory. These included, among others, trips to Greece (her favorite country), India, Bangladesh, Katmandu, Taiwan, China, Bali, New Zealand and Australia, Bangkok, Japan, Alaska, Belize, Mexico, Puerto Rico, Venezuela, and the Dominican Republic.

`We all know that steel is forged from soft iron with heat and hard hammer blows. And so it is that real character is generated when the ingredients are present, namely hard times and inner determination buoyed up by spiritual strength. The hardest time, perhaps, was the loss of all our $600,000 capital through the faulty shrimp food in the Belize operation. Our financial resources were at the point of rupture, and my inner determination stressed as never before. I needed an extra measure of spiritual strength way beyond that which I was finding at our local church at that time. We needed a miracle and the day-to-day clear direction of the Holy Spirit. This help came through Robert Schuller's and Oral Roberts's books and television programs, which we regularly read and listened to, and later from my visits to conferences at both places. Our accumulation over four years of over $100,000 of state and federal taxes were paid off and our larger Belize financial losses legally formalized as a tax deduction for each shareholder. These two added ingredients were necessary to get our feet back on the ground and our life renewed once again.

Recently an even more important miracle took place in my life, a God-given change in my heart. It came after prayerfully reflecting on my devotional reading of the day by Oral Roberts, "Forgetting the Past." To put it simply, the love in my heart for each of our five children sprung alive. It was not just a mental change in attitude but a spiritual change affecting the very depth of my being. It took this deep change in my heart to overcome the long-term lack of the deep fatherly caring that had been needed by each of our children. It was the gift I needed most for the continuing plan for my life to be free and significant. And as time passes since the spiritual awakening I had for our five biological children, I've learned that this new inner caring needs to be applied to all my relationships. Without this love for others, inspired by the inner spirit, life's greatest satisfaction and happiness cannot be achieved.

CHAPTER SEVENTEEN

Bridge to the Future

By January 1973 John R. Snell Engineers was seventeen years old and regarded as a small but rather successful international consulting firm. During the past thirteen years we had remained at between twenty and thirty personnel with a solid reputation in the environmental field, working in twenty states and over twenty foreign countries. We were able to compete with the big consultants because we understood the needs of the countries in which we operated, had the right contacts, and were cooperative in those countries. At home we became known for our quality of work, for innovative waste treatment methods, and for leadership in research and development. We had also carved out a niche for ourselves in lake restoration, having several times the volume of this type of work of all our competitors combined.

Despite all these positives our long-term future looked bleak. I had just turned sixty, and although I could continue to run this firm successfully for perhaps another eight to ten years, its ultimate fate was sealed unless we brought in some young, high-powered talent and leadership and built up the firm to sustain one hundred to one hundred fifty persons.

Although much, if not most, of our long-term planning for the future was sound, some of it was undoubtedly flawed and brought on stress and internal struggle. But in the end we as a team of builders were stronger and better men and women for the conflicts. In retrospect, one can see that it is difficult for one side to be all right and the other side to be all wrong.

At the beginning of this period I was ready to relinquish certain work and responsibilities to others and knew there was no better alternative. The two newcomers, John and Phil, saw for the first time something worth going all out for instead of being permanent employees in their formerly family-run-and- owned firm. Our financial strength was good. There was a backlog of unfinished work which had more-than-average profit potential. We had a comfortable volume of new work coming in with little or no special effort being exerted to bring it in. Our reputation was good, and we were on the edge of taking on larger and more interesting jobs.

During the period when the three of us first got to know each other we learned to work together smoothly and efficiently. We held many planning meetings, but each one kept busy, as much as possible, on productive work and bringing in more work which would support growth. John started off by taking over the management of several of the larger jobs, especially in the field of wastewater and water treatment. This allowed me to concentrate more on the two areas where my talents and experience would best be used—overseas work and lake restoration. Phil's talents lay in client services not only with existing clients but bringing in new ones. He had many friends in the municipal field, and his sales talents impressed even us as we kidded him for being able to sell snowballs to Eskimos. After a time, Phil expressed strong interest in also handling the financial side of the firm, which gave me a great deal more time for expansion in other areas of our joint endeavor.

Much of the new work was in Indiana, so we decided to open a branch office in Indianapolis and hire Jim Chepules, an experienced, well-rounded engineer, to head it. We then needed to strengthen our Lansing office and added two younger men—each with doctor's degrees in environmental engineering—Ming Cheng and Kurt Guter. Because a number of landscape architecture jobs were available we decided to start a landscape architecture department, first with one and then two men. Usually the landscape or planning jobs led to other municipal work. The next logical step was to add a new client-service man in Indiana, thus allowing Phil more time to spend in Michigan and Ohio. This resulted in the employment of John Silver, who was also exceptional at sales.

Within less than four years our efforts were paying off in Ohio as well, so we rented space in Akron and put an experienced engineer named Bill Bandy in charge and hired a client-service man to help him build the office. This left Phil free to supervise the Indiana and Ohio client-service work and spend more time in Michigan. Also, his work with the financial side of things was consuming much of his time. By then we were getting to be more and more crowded with our bank credit, for our borrowing was at the point where the bank was no longer truly comfortable with our account. Phil had worked out a method of keeping track of the costs and an innovative way of crediting our growth as an asset, which later turned out to be rather optimistic and satisfied only its inventor.

Before too long our Lansing work was cramped by our lack of space in the church office building and we found an excellent building for our needs, four times the size. Members of the new firm were permitted to invest in this building as a partnership, fix it up, and lease it at a fair rental price to the firm. This move was like the molting of a crab, for it gave us the much needed room for not only the immediate growth but for that in the decades to come. It had an inspiring effect on both our staff and our present and future clients and friends. The extra space gave us things we very much needed but could not previously provide: a library, two large drafting rooms, large laboratory space, a large fireproof vault for plans and files, fine office space for everyone including adequate efficient individual space for our engineers, designers, and specialty people. We even had room for workshops, research and development, general storage, and initially room for some of our cars. To top off the new building we installed insulation, air conditioning, and attractive lighting.

Soon after our move to 918 May Street we added several staff members. Among the group was one who came to us just looking for a job. We really didn't need any more employees at that moment, but I interviewed him. He had many excellent qualities, but when he told me he had gone to Harvard, that cinched the matter, and he was hired on the spot. Pratap Rajadhyaksha's native land was India, and he was as hard working and bright as they come. He was especially good with the computer, even on programming new software for many new and helpful items. Pratap's history with the firm continued. He married one of our secretaries, rose in leadership each year, and eventually, in 1988, he and his brother from Ohio would purchase Snell Environmental Group. They integrated it into a group of four firms, each with its own name, specialty, and maintaining its local control. Hiring him was a good move.

During these seven years I averaged over three long trips overseas each year covering many interesting jobs in two dozen countries. By far the greatest amount of work was in Bangladesh, a country in need. For more than a decade the United States Agency for International Development (AID) program shipped into the country enough grain to feed ten million people. Nature had treated the farmers in such a way as to make it difficult for them to feed their own people. During the dry season it was too dry for crops, and during the wet season too wet. Rice was planted in six inches of water and harvested by the use of a boat in twenty feet of water. An important international project was undertaken in Bangladesh about that time which increased by two and a half times the average food production per acre in an area about one hundred miles in diameter. This was done by building a dike around the area. During the wet season the excess water was pumped from within the area to points outside the dikes, and during the dry season the inner core was irrigated. This worked fine and promised, if enlarged, to cut way back on the need of the United States to ship grain to the country. But its bad side effect was that it cut the normal breeding and flow of the Indian carp fry, which for years had been gathered up and bred in each of the farmer's private farm ponds. They needed a very large hatchery to replace this lack of fry, as Indian carp had been a very large protein source for the people. We were given an extensive study contract followed by a final contract to design, supervise the construction, start up the operation, and finally train the staff in this hatchery that produced two billion fry a year. We used Dr. Carl Lagler of the University of Michigan and others as consultants along with our own staff to design and supervise construction.

We made trips to several countries in the Middle East, including Saudi Arabia, Yemen, Libya, Syria, and Jordan. We were treated very well but in one or more cases lost out to the Japanese, because they were in the habit of dealing out money under the table. Corruption was rampant in most of these countries.

Bali, Indonesia, was the site of another large and interesting project financed by the World Bank. The largest Japanese firm, Pacific Consultants, had been contracted to do the job of designing all the site utilities for a twelve-hotel complex to be built on a beautiful beach. The work had been subcontracted to us because of our special knowledge through our Japanese contact and close friend, Sachiho Naito. An Australian groundwater hydrologist had been hired previously and told the World Bank that enough fresh groundwater was available at this site for the sixty-four-hundred-room complex. I strongly doubted the Australian's figures and asked the bank for permission to first check them ourselves and then later to employ a renowned groundwater firm to review them as well. My gut feeling was that there was only a fourth as much water as predicted, which turned out to be correct. After some high-level meetings the project was cut in half. Also to make the water suffice we treated then recycled half the water for nonpotable uses. The project, along with our discovery and alterations, turned out to be a big success and did much to enhance our standing with the World Bank.

Our work in the restoration of lakes and waterways continued to grow, and before I left the firm we had under our belt almost fifty projects, some of considerable magnitude. Typical of the many dredging jobs we designed for shallow and dying lakes was the well-publicized one for Lake Lansing. This 450 acre lake was the only one anywhere near Lansing. Because it had an average depth of less than five feet, people in the area were wanting to have it dredged to a minimum depth of twelve feet, at which depth weed growth would be largely held in check.

Twelve hundred acres of wetland surrounded the lake, most of which the Department of Natural Resources fish division acknowledged had little ecological value. But by the time the project was approved, the federal fish and wildlife agency forced the project to purchase several forty-acre plots of excellent agricultural land, build twenty-foot dikes around them, and use them for the spoil areas for the millions of cubic yards of peat that were dredged out of the lake instead of permitting most of it to be used to recover valuable recreational land from the remaining wetlands in the area. In the end the Lake Lansing dredging project turned around the property values in the whole area, which had been heading downward and now rose on the average ten to twenty times.

We had made and been paid for a number of trips to the Philippines mainly to undertake both preliminary and final designs of large compost plants, but they continued to be short of construction funds. Argentina, on the other hand, finally came through with a compost plant in San Juan in the middle of its wine country. This was a satisfying contact many years after we had been awarded five first prizes and four second prizes in Argentina's international contest for compost designs only to learn that Argentina had been unable to finance them at the time.

Our contact and work through our friend Naito in Japan continued as we were employed to make an extensive study and report for a Japanese firm in the field of composting. We also did a study for a large private firm concerning the feasibility of composting the garbage in six of the largest cities in India, but our client did not have enough political clout to get any of them approved.

Unfortunately, as my days with the firm drew to an end, the leaders carrying it into the future had no special calling to be of service to the third-world countries and, in fact, saw work in these areas as more risky and less profitable than those close to home. Hence, after I left, this overseas work came to a complete halt.

It was also during this period that the EPA supported a demonstration-size project in Crawford County, Ohio, where we studied the value of windrow composting municipal refuse prior to placing it in a standard landfill. We found that precomposting reduced the final volume in the fill by about 50 percent and the strength of the leachate seeping from the landfill by more than 95 percent.

On an income-support basis most of our new growth came from the design of wastewater systems and treatment plants in small to medium-size cities. With the new effort we had placed on sales and client relations the new work brought into the firm increased by several times. Also, having built up our technical design staffs in Lansing, Indiana, and Ohio and having the luxury of moving work from one office to another so as to balance the work load between the design crews improved our efficiency and profitability. Toward the end of this period Marion, Ohio, entrusted us with the design of a major sewage-treatment plant expansion running into several million dollars. Our new highly experienced man in the Indianapolis office and his crew did an excellent job on this and gave us a substantial professional boost.

About halfway through this phase of our expansion we landed a good job with the city of Detroit on a unique method of treatment and disposal of much of its digested sewage sludge. It was called the Fighting Island Project, for it was there that a chemical firm had disposed of a mild yet unsafe waste for years. By experimenting on the pilot-scale basis we were able to show that the premixing of the Detroit sewage sludge with these wastes brought about a neutral safe soil about six feet deep and would enable the city to plant and grow trees in the area and to end a potential hazardous situation.

This Detroit work ended years of our self-insuring our errors and omissions, which up to that time had cost us less than three thousand dollars over a twenty-year period, or an average of only one hundred fifty dollars per year. We had done this by having a program of quality control where everything was checked and double checked. When it came time to sign a contract with Detroit, however, they insisted that we open up a full-blown errors-and-omissions insurance program, which cost us an average of five thousand dollars per year or more from then on. But our losses remained extremely low, and the insurance company prospered.

Our earlier work in designing landfills and dealing with refuse helped to bring on a lot of new work in this field. Several larger cities used us to look ahead to where they should site their new landfills or find alternate methods of disposal. Several large private refuse collection and disposal companies used us in a like manner, and we also supervised the work into the construction phase.

It takes a lot more time and effort to build a consulting firm based on truly democratic principles than it does for one or several owners to build one using tight control. From the beginning I have had a strong interest in the democratic approach. But before John and Phil were brought into the firm there was no consistent program to formulate and expand democratic rules in such a way as to turn out an ideal end product. I was not so interested in building up a strong ultimate ownership in the firm but in building one that was stable, had a good reputation, was profitable, and one that I could ultimately walk away from with all my powers and responsibilities safely turned over to my successors. Then I could wind up with my fair share, and all the time, effort, and money we had put into the firm over the years would pay off in a meaningful way. To do all this correctly also meant that those coming in would make a predetermined advance toward the objective of having full ownership and control. The three of us had no fixed schedule as to how we would go from where we started to where we hoped to be in five to ten years. We wished to build soundly and wind up with a nice-size firm of which we would all be proud. As far as I could tell, none of us had any tricks up our sleeves to take advantage of the others.

After about three years of our joint effort we had added many more people and a lot of debt. In addition to the firm's collateral I personally had signed for the firm to be able to borrow more. This was before the normal expected little differences of opinions came to any real head. But then I began to have some serious perception that all was not right with the inner thinking of one of the other two partners. Fortunately, there were three instead of two of us, and by then we had surrounded ourselves with a second tier of command, each with ideas to contribute and judgments to make for the group.

One of the major things to be decided was whether John was surely the man to take over as president, for which I had hired him, and also when he would have matured enough to shift into that position. It seemed to be the majority opinion that John was the man for the job but that he did need quite a bit of maturing first. Phil, although not a registered engineer, was very bright and aggressive and wanted to see himself in that position. Except for a few of the men Phil had been instrumental in bringing into the firm, most had a strong preference for John. These views were also held by our outside board members and our outside management consultants.

As time passed, John and I realized that Phil had an alternate plan for himself: He would artificially build up the paper value of the corporate shares, then extract himself and a few of his friends from the existing firm into a new one he would form and in so doing leave our present firm in serious financial straits. At the same time he would transfer on paper the real assets of the firm to the new firm based on the formulation he had worked out and was passing around each month to show how well we were doing.

By this means we were also made to look good with the bank. We brought in an outside CPA accounting firm to audit the accounts, but there was still the area beyond its jurisdiction where the value of the corporation was formulated and thus the value of the shares, especially those of Phil and one or two of his close friends. The bank had worked with and trusted me through many years of good experience, but the way Phil presented the figures made it feel insecure about our account. By that time our borrowing had crept up to about three quarters of a million dollars. My real estate and other holdings enabled my personal signature alone to sustain loans up to our current needs.

Early in 1977 it was evident to most of us that to make our mix of personnel work together we would need more than the expertise of the accounting firm to get to the bottom of our problems and help us to solve them. We needed someone who could look into our very depths and see each of us for what we honestly were. So we employed a clinical psychiatrist, Dr. Harold Faith of Grand Rapids, who met with us a number of times both in groups and individually. In about four months he helped each of us see the situation clearly—that Phil needed to be separated from the firm if we were again to achieve harmony and profitability. It was a hard step to take, but the board of directors was unanimous on it except for Phil, of course, and he had no good alternative solution to offer.

On September 28 Phil gave us his letter of resignation. The big question in his mind was then whether he should accept the determination of an independent accounting firm as to what his stock was worth or doggedly hold out for his version of what he thought it should be worth and at the same time do what else he could to take value from our firm for his personal interests. To our surprise he took the low road and the next day gave notice that he was pulling out our whole landscape architecture department, all of whom happened to be his former friends. Phil claimed not only the jobs these people were working on but his right to interfere with our clients and scramble for any of our existing jobs he might be interested in taking.

The battle of the lawyers in the courts took over. We were soon given a temporary restraining order preventing Phil from calling on our clients, but this did not last for many weeks. Court case fell upon court case. It was obvious that the matter would not be settled soon and that both sides would have to dig deeply into their pockets to pay for legal fees. In round figures it was ten years later when the courts forced a settlement on Phil almost identical to what he would have been paid willingly by the firm at the time of the parting.

While many complex questions were brought up and solved in the several back-and-forth suits made in the dispute, we can, without going into detail about them, see the lessons to be learned from the whole experience. It has been pointed out more than once that much of the blame was mine in that I discounted the very negative one of three recommendation letters I had received for Phil at the time of his application for a position in our firm. I should have done due diligence with that party in a follow-up, which I did not do. Also, I should have removed Phil from running our financial affairs much earlier, instead of attempting to reform his thinking while having him continue to make key decisions and thus mold policy. Third, we should have sensed earlier that an impasse was close at hand and employed strong professional help.

The impasse and court cases did much to bring almost all of us a lot closer together, and we added two new valuable men, which we may not have done had the cases not come up. We moved rapidly and brought in an excellent landscape architect who was able to go out and assure each of our clients that their jobs would be handled better with our new staff than they would have been before. We also went to a prominent national consulting firm and hired their number two financial man who had been looking for a way to solve his dilemma for fair advancement. Each of these put us way ahead of where we had been before. It was also quite obvious that one of our client-service men was really Phil's man waiting for the opportune time to move over to Phil's new firm and was in no way loyal to us. He was let go and replaced by a loyal and much more effective man. Dr. Faith, knowing all our players well, continued to work with us and did much to prevent any rifts from forming at this critical time.

We did have another problem, which by comparison was almost insignificant: what to do about John's advancement into first a position of executive vice president and then president. Our staff, board, management consultant, and Dr. Faith all agreed that John needed two to three more years of maturing. We knew that John had lots of talent and he had been doing a very good job of managing the various jobs assigned to him. The problem was what to do in the interim while this desired transformation in him was taking place. It was finally agreed that we should interview for the position and see what was out there. We also had a lot of talent within the firm, but none of the people was just right. We had just absorbed a well-established but small civil firm, Emerson and Porter, and also hired a client-relations man, but none of them met the requirements. Even after our interviews there was some question as to whether we should select the best of those interviewed and give him the place of leadership. By the end of 1978, at which time I was sixty-six years old, the consensus was that we should offer the position of executive vice president to Jim Jackson (not his real name), and after a reasonable time he would take over from me as president. Jim had many of the qualities we were looking for, had a master's degree in business administration, and was a registered engineer, although he was light in the actual experience of consulting engineer. But he had maturity and even a bit of charisma for an engineer.

For all practical purposes, the year 1979 went rather well, with Jim essentially running the day-to-day part of the firm's business. To help Jim take over without his being overwhelmed we added each month one additional responsibility to the overall job, transferred from me to him. The last things I relinquished were overseas work, lake restoration, and research and development. By October 1979 the transfer was complete. Jim took over as president, and I took on the title Chairman of the Board and Specialty Consultant. Also, my salary, as such, stopped, and I went on a ten-year monthly retirement pension of twenty-five hundred dollars per month. I was just sixty-eight. I was rid of the day-to-day frustrations but still deeply involved with the firm. Not only was my personal signature on the $750,000 corporate note, but by that time I had added several substantial personal loans to the corporation as well. We were on a sound financial basis, were making money, and had a strong group up and running toward a secure and prosperous future.

We still had Phil's several lawsuits and our countersuits to deal with, but we were convinced of the rightness of our cause and the fairness with which we had approached each decision. Aside from meetings with the attorneys and their expenses we had all put these controversies involving Phil to one side and were fully concentrated on our forward program of bridging to the future. In fact, we really felt that we had just about arrived there. We had progressed toward becoming a truly democratic firm. Not counting the former shareholders who had pulled out with Phil's group, we had twelve shareholders, with several more waiting to start to buy in. We had a strong board of directors, including Robert Fisher, who had strong banking and legal experience, excellent judgment, and keen insight into personalities. He was able to keep us away from what might have been many petty arguments. Our trusted friend and counselor, Harold Faith, who had brought us through the trying times, met with our people from time to time and helped them to knit together.

Consulting engineering, even when run well and in a profitable manner, is not a get-rich profession as many perceive the medical and legal professions to be, but it is a satisfying endeavor. I found it especially so, for I wanted to help the third world countries. I was also very much interested to improve on the ways things had been done in the past, to push forward the state of the art, so to speak. I also had a strong desire to produce a continuing consulting firm which was democratically run. However, by spreading the ownership across a broad base, it also meant spreading the profits, and a professional firm run in this way was even less profitable for the founder or top man.

I might say that at this point I could look back and see that the road had not always been smooth but the journey well worth it. All in all the Lord had blessed our endeavors in business and given me opportunities from which I had derived great satisfaction. The bridge to the future of the firm was nearing completion, and my new future was just beginning.

CHAPTER EIGHTEEN

Chairman of the Board

The job of bridging to the future, although never complete, was well along. The crisis of having to separate from our group the half-dozen staff members who had been part of the dissension led by Phil was over. They had been replaced by loyal talented engineers and landscape architects, a client-service man, and an experienced financial leader for engineering consultants, Alan Godfrey. We had in place an executive vice president, Jim Jackson, and after nine months of assuming increasing responsibilities he became president in my place.

Our earlier problems involving Phil and his group had been handed over to the lawyers and the court, so we were able to concentrate virtually 100 percent of our time on our professional consulting work. The esprit de corps was at an all-time high. We turned a good profit the second year and paid out $220,000 in bonuses. Salaries averaged $50,000 for key men on the staff. The value of a share dropped from $6.3 to $5.3 when the bonuses were paid, but if they hadn't, taxes would have been much higher. By the second year we had restructured the bank loan with the East Lansing State Bank into two parts: a long-term debt payable at prime plus 2 percent interest with payments made on a monthly basis, and a revolving credit. During the preceding years the company had borrowed several hundred thousand dollars from

Florence and me personally, and the bank insisted on keeping our signature on the notes even after my retirement.

Collection of accounts receivable are always a problem in the consulting field, and ours had crept to about $550,000. We worked out a good plan to pay off more of this Snell debt from four of the largest overdue accounts receivable as they could be collected. This worked out well, and four years after my retirement our loans to the corporation were paid in full.

One of the larger accounts receivable was $120,000 owed us by the government of Bangladesh for our extensive work on the Indian carp hatchery, which was now producing two billion fry per year. Two of our men there had tried hard to make this collection but in vain. The board felt that the whole debt should be written off, as we had been paid $50,000 of it already. Although I had not supervised the work for three years, I was reasonably well acquainted with it and knew the people in Bangladesh. I felt strongly enough about the importance of collecting the debt on this World Bank-financed project that I offered to go over at my own expense, do my best, and if successful take a fair percentage as payment. Fortunately for everyone, I was able to collect almost the entire bill.

My own life and lifestyle changed a great deal as I stepped down from the presidency and took up the new role of chairman of the board and specialty consultant. My average work week for the last twenty years had been seventy to seventy-five hours and now dropped to about fifty-five hours.

For some weeks at a time I would be free to get down to Belize and the work on Bootstrap International. It would be possible to establish an agricultural operation on the land we had purchased. This venture, described in the next chapter, covered roughly the same seven years of my semiretirement from the firm.

First I shall describe the venture of the Snell Environmental Group, lessons learned, and goal accomplishments. The time was not without its hardships, but from these times we often learn the most.

As the retiring founder, I had a special agreement whereby my long years of service with rather low salary were being rewarded with a $25,000 a year annuity for ten years, and I was to contribute fifteen hours per month to the firm, although I at first continued to put in about fifty hours per week. I was pledged not to compete with the firm, and I retained an office and the help of a secretary.

During the first two years I was kept quite busy with five solid wastes projects, a lake project, and two research and development projects. I was also in charge of a preliminary study for sewage collection and disposal for Taipei, Taiwan, and the design of a compost plant for San Juan, Argentina. I enjoyed getting away from the administrative load and working more directly on these various jobs.

Strangely, the Taiwan connection began a chain of events that resulted in the beginning of an extensive shrimp growing project in Belize. Some of the people I was with during my three weeks in Taiwan were also shrimp experts. They later traveled to Belize on their own, became extremely interested in the prospects of growing shrimp there, and with their promise of both technical and financial help persuaded me to start up a shrimp aquafarm (see next chapter).

The two research and development projects the firm assigned to me turned out to be of considerable importance. The first, in the field of biodegradation, was supported by the Environmental Protection Agency. We took sixty of the more important toxic wastes and tested each for the effect high- rate composting would have on the biological breakdown while in close contact. We were amazed to find that over half of the sixty toxic wastes broke down in a week's time, and three quarters in a month's time. Today many research and development firms have learned more about this important field, so that the agencies are gaining confidence, and vast sums of money are being saved in cleaning up many toxic wastes. The state of the art is now moving ahead very rapidly.

To my way of thinking, the second project was even more important. It had to do with a low-cost way to anaerobically stabilize presalvaged, preshredded municipal refuse in large bins wherein 90 percent of the theoretical methane gas was extracted in about three months, and the safe residue could be spread on agricultural fields. It appears that as much as seventy to eighty dollars per ton could be saved by using this method, and that the gas produced over a wide area would be enough to heat half the homes within the areas served. The program is being offered to be shared with other countries on a concurrent basis. China is currently cooperating and considering building a pilot operation (see chapter 19).

During the first years of my retirement, 1980-83, new management concepts were being tried by our new president, but emphasis was still on solid growth. During the first year we nearly acquired another consulting firm, which was in the sunbelt and employed about fifty people. But just as our bid was about to be accepted, a California firm raised its bid 50 percent and took it away from us. We started up a Kentucky corporation and sought work there, but not much came of that. By the third year we opened a Detroit office, for the opportunities had begun to appear there, and our work grew. Work expanded in our branch offices in Akron and Indianapolis, where we had to enlarge our facilities.

We practiced democratic management and ownership. As time passed, more and more of the staff became shareholders, and we gave priority to tenure and quality of work. By this time it was agreed my ownership of about 40 percent would be reduced to 20 percent, which was the amount that John O'Malia owned. Then both of our shares would be reduced equally until they came to 10 percent, which would be the new maximum for senior personnel. Mine would then, by agreement, be reduced to 5 percent, which amount I would be allowed to keep as long as I wished. Except for me, as the founder, all had to sell all of their shares when they left the firm. The value of the shares was calculated after each quarterly audit. In addition to the normal accounting methods used to figure the dollar value of a firm, we gave credit for the value of the backlog of yet uncompleted contracted work on hand. On the average, it cost the firm about 9 percent to secure new work. For an employee to be able to buy stock, there must first be stock available for sale, and that employee had to be approved to buy the stock. He was next allocated the maximum amount he could buy at the level of his professional advancement. Although the stock did not pay dividends, it did generally accrue in value. And by owning it, employees had a share in the control of the company.

Any new president coming in was bound not to have an easy time, especially when he managed by the strict procedures taught him when he took his master's degree in business administration. He was the stranger coming in from the outside and he was dealing with a closely-knit team of professionals who had worked well together for a number of years. He was also bucking the feeling on the part of some that the promotion should have come from within. Jim's management style was markedly different from what the group had been used to during my twenty-five-year presidency. Furthermore, the contrast was made greater by my staying on as chairman of the board and remaining personally to handle several ongoing projects. Jim had won over many of the staff to his methods in the Ohio branch but seemed to have considerable resistance from the Indianapolis branch and the main office in Lansing. By the time Jim came on board, the firm was very fortunate in already having some very talented persons hard at work in finances, personnel, purchasing, and client services. Each of our three offices was headed by a strong and aggressive man who had experience in working with each other and the team as a whole. Shortly after Jim's arrival we recruited an outside board member who had for some years headed a large successful consulting firm specializing in the utilities field, and his wisdom contributed to our board, which strongly supported us.

Despite all of these pluses working for Jim, he was unable to weather the internal storms and strife which often come in a complex situation of this kind. Just three years after he came to us he rather suddenly tendered his resignation.

As chairman of the board I was certainly somewhat to blame, for I had been trying for some time to help mend fences, so to speak, and to lessen the sharply contrasting management methods that were being resisted by the staff. The chemistry between the two of us was not sufficiently compatible for Jim to learn much through me, and finally his frustration came out in attack after attack against me and several of the others. Evidently Jim was not confident that he would succeed, for during those three years he purchased no stock, even though he was authorized to purchase up to the maximum amount allowed (10 percent).

Jim's sudden resignation took us by surprise and put us in a serious dilemma. Either of two of our men could be moved up to the presidency and would have done a good job. John O'Malia was a natural for the job and had been maturing over the last three years. Alan Godfrey, our financial man, had done an excellent job for his previous firm and won the respect of everyone there. His biggest handicap was that he was not an engineer. Although some consulting firms were headed by non-engineers, that practice was the exception. To make either of these two fine men president and chief executive officer also raised the problem as to how long the second man would remain with us and how well the team would operate in the first place. A firm cannot be run well with two heads. But though no one liked this solution we did, in fact, move in that direction, and all were surprised how well it worked despite the skepticism. Alan was made CEO in charge of finance, and John was made president in charge of production and marketing.

The first thing to be done was to define closely these two different areas and see how the overlap was to be handled. The board would keep track by reports from John and Alan as to how they were getting along with their difficult if not impossible assignments of being part of a two-headed firm. A major factor of their success in achieving the impossible was that almost everyone wanted it to work. So despite the fact that there was still a downturn in the consulting field in mid-1984, the firm had made a lot of progress. One difficulty was solved by first deferring 10 percent of the top salaries and then, on advice of our accountant, converting these into salary cuts.

For several years the corporation had partially subsidized the Ohio branch. Then the economy there seemed to turn in our favor and they had an excellent year, whereas the other two branches' income remained low. Feeling their new strength and not liking the new two-headed leadership of the firm, the Ohio employees decided they could do better on their own and approached the board with a general buyout proposal.

About this time Godfrey, Emery, and Seymour resigned, stating philosophical differences as their main reason. This dissension, along with the Ohio branch's feelings, had not been generally known and created something of a crisis. On the plus side we got our firm back to a single head. First the board elected John O'Malia as president and CEO, with Paul Baerman and David Quandt as vice presidents. We then elected Pratap Rajadhyksha as secretary-treasurer and gave him broad responsibilities in the financial field, where he had been learning a lot under Alan. Being extremely bright with the computer he had developed much innovative programming in both accounting and design.

Negotiations with the Ohio group were hard fought but friendly and in a matter of several months completed to the satisfaction of both sides. The corporation gave the Ohio group good credit terms, and we in turn got a good share of the profits they had already earned while they were part of us. The full agreement was complex but fair, and everyone in the long run benefited. By making this move we also averted a number of future problems which might have become serious. Sometimes it is impossible to meld several good people into one team if their personalities are not compatible. Sometimes it is necessary to divide the main firm before the right growth can take place. In retrospect, the Ohio breakaway was inevitably a good thing for both sides. And those who resigned from the two-headed situation found good positions elsewhere.

The buyout changed the firm's financial condition in several favorable ways. We were able to pay off our long-term debt with the bank and put $350,000 in an investment fund. The staff got an 8 percent raise as well as a fair bonus package. We now put more effort into the development of the work in Indiana and Michigan, and the rate of growth in each accelerated. We also took on some larger work, which is important to the prestige and financial well-being of a consulting firm. The nature of the overall consultant work changed somewhat. More emphasis on cleanup of pollution and spills necessitated more laboratory work. We built a large expansion so our lab could accommodate new, faster, rather expensive equipment. Initially this appeared to be premature, but in the long run it worked out very well and probably prevented others from taking our top position in this field. Our work, however, was more on routine testing and little on research, which I liked so much.

John and Pratap made a good leadership team, and their cooperation and distribution of the workload was smooth and efficient. With the training and experience Pratap had under Alan, he grew rapidly and turned out to be more valuable than his teacher. This also left John to the sales and production side of things, in which he excelled. Everyone was at ease again. Another national economic downturn was the only growth-stunting factor.

I was becoming more and more involved in the Belize shrimp project trying to raise money, construct facilities, and operate it efficiently. I had less and less time to think about Snell Environmental Group and how to contribute to its success. This phase of my professional consulting life had become less interesting to me. Until ten years had passed, I by agreement could not compete with SEG, and by then I likely would not wish to do so.

Nearly ten years after Phil had been let go and taken his group out of the firm the courts finally came up with a settlement. This day of final settlement, September 27, 1988, came about seven months after I had left the firm but was something that had loomed in the background those ten years, even though it need never have happened. We were all pleased not only to have the court battles over but were pleased with the decision of the court and the favorable settlement we were given. Certainly Phil and his group would have done far better if they had accepted our early fair offer. But by dragging it out they recovered almost nothing, and the only ones to really gain were the attorneys.

The last important event in my tenure as chairman of the board was its buyout of the firm by an Ohio group headed by V.V. Rajadhyaksha, brother of our own Pratap. The period of negotiation was rather short and friendly, and both sides seemed to be happy about the end product. This Ohio group had already acquired four other consulting firms. By acquiring SEG, they would round out their ability to offer services to their clients and would have a total personnel of about eight hundred persons. The plan was to keep each firm intact with its people, management, and name unchanged yet bring a greater central management efficiency to the group, in part because they were a larger and more diverse group, but also because their top management had a somewhat higher level of knowledge and experience from which to draw.

After several months of negotiation the final buyout agreement was signed on February 12, 1988. We had agreed with our formula that the value of the shares we owned was three dollars each, and this multiplied by 58,000 equaled $174.000, which was the sale price. This was paid with $50,000 down, $40,000 in two annual installments, with a final $44,000 payment. There were all the necessary protective clauses back and forth, and all our shareholders had to vote on the sale. Initially John O'Malia became chairman of the board and chief executive officer, Pratap treasurer, Paul Baerman secretary, and David Quant assistant secretary. They and I constituted the new board of directors.

My resignation as chairman of the board of the Snell Environmental Group in 1985 was an important turning point in my professional life but was just another bend in the road of my life as an engineer. Although it placed less importance on consulting engineering, even this work I loved so much continued. Once a consultant, always a consultant.

The following chapter, The Saga of Belize, tells of my adventures raising shrimp in Belize, which consisted of about one third engineering of the consulting type. Most of that work was with the business and technology problems and in doing something I had never done before.

CHAPTER NINETEEN

The Saga of Belize

The story of Belize began with Bootstrap, International, the foundation started by the Snell Environmental Group in November 1969. That was a successful year financially, and the leaders of the firm wished to express their gratitude by starting something beneficial to humanity, especially to persons in need. Our long-term objective was to help the developing countries of the world where it had already been our privilege to be of service in the engineering field. Now we wanted to do more but close to home.

The program we developed was similar to the Big Brother/Big Sister program, only we concentrated on helping on a one-to-one basis the breadwinner of the family. Except for one paid full-time director, the program was run with dedicated, spiritually minded volunteers from our engineering firm. These volunteers, known as sponsors, generally met about once a week with their assigned "associates" and informally discussed their life problems, especially those related to their jobs. This discussion and sharing, including the application of spiritual values, strengths, and direction, were appreciated by the associates; and in fact, the sponsors gained much from the get-togethers as well.

We worked with, rather than overlapped, existing established agencies and organizations such as Alcoholics Anonymous, churches, and abuse and family counseling agencies. To achieve optimum results it was important to correctly pair off the two people for true compatibility.

Some of our staff members were themselves in AA, and they taught the rest of us an adaptation of the twelve-step program, how to work with it, and how to use it to bring inner strength to those in need.

Everyone was pleased with the program and the many success stories that came with it. We all agreed that to be successful our program required an efficient full-time director to do the hundred and one things that had to be done so that these meetings would take place and accomplish their desired purpose. Our efficiency was about to be enhanced by our use of appropriate literature and tapes and by holding small group meetings to supplement the individual meetings, when we started getting uneasy about running out of money to pay the director who had served us about two years. Unfortunately, by the time the initial grant money ran out, the firm's larger new management decided that because of earnings that year we could not afford to continue such an expensive program and that we should find another which would perhaps do more good, especially for the developing countries but at a fraction of the cost.

Bootstrap then launched a twenty year vegetable seed program. The largest seed company in the United States, Burpee, gave Bootstrap about 70 percent of all its surplus seeds. We picked these up once a year, after they had been returned from the nation's retail stores and brought them to Lansing. Here, with volunteer help, we repackaged the seeds in twenty-four-pound boxes and shipped them all over the world. Most went to church-run groups and some to governments. On several occasions we shipped to where there had been a specific need for food for one reason or another. We shipped an average of five to ten tons per year, and one year twenty tons. Usually the recipient paid for the transportation, but at times we provided that too from our limited funds.

The seed program was launched and led by Dr. Hal Bergan, who before his retirement was in charge of bands for all the Lansing schools. After his death of a heart attack, a retired engineer from the Michigan Department of Transportation, Harvey Kenney, took over.

He served the cause well past the time when his strength was failing, and in early 1993 he also died of a heart attack. During the last year of Harvey's term of service the board decided to turn over this phase of the work to a mission-oriented organization located in Spring Lake, Michigan: International Aid, Inc.

Following the demise of Bootstrap's seed program, only the Belize program remained. Here the emphasis would be to help the little would-be farmer become a successful farmer. We had in mind a peaceful alternative to the forest fires of civil upheaval in Central America.

In 1978, with this Bootstrap concept yet in its early stages of planning, Florence and I visited six locations to find the optimum place to launch the pilot program. We thought that once we were able to make a successful demonstration program we might interest others in spreading the program and its influence on the manifest needs. Although we liked certain benefits of the various places we visited in Crete, Baja California, Guadalajara, Puerto Rico, and the Dominican Republic, we leaned heavily toward Belize as the best location.

Belize could best be described as an ideal vest-pocket democracy of British origin. Its area is about half the size of Michigan, with only about 150,000 population. For every acre of arable land being cultivated in Belize, an additional eight to ten could also be cultivated. Belize would be the least likely Central American country to become Communist. The political climate and the people were friendly, the official language English; and the laws, based on those of the British, were essentially similar to our own. The only drawback was that there was little need or demand for the program in Belize because of the abundance of unused agricultural land. But we felt that we should still be able to run a good demonstration project which could be duplicated almost anywhere.

We traveled twice to Belize to look over two parcels of land, and after these two inspections and rejections of potential sites, a third and great opportunity came. A friend of mine needed some financial help if he was to foreclose on a 8,700 acre parcel of land a Canadian group was buying, but that group had not paid on the mortgage in eight years, and my friend owned half of the mortgage.

It took over $100,000 to foreclose under the Belize law, and Florence and I furnished over 50 percent of the funds. As a result, we acquired 50 percent ownership after all taxes and other monies due were paid. My friend was not as interested in owning the land as in getting his share of the mortgage money and making a profit. So Florence and I struck a deal to buy the whole 8,700 acres of land except for about 250 acres that he wished to retain. The price was large, though we had four years to pay for it in full.

Our plan was to give Bootstrap International about 5,000 acres and keep 3,500 hundred acres privately until some future need came up. Bootstrap sold 2,100 acres to the Caribbean Development Corporation for shares to raise shrimp and kept the rest for its small-farm program.

The overall choice piece of land we had purchased lay along about three miles of the coast of the Caribbean and ran inland about eight miles to the Swasey branch of the Monkey River, the country's second largest. It contained 90 percent of the watershed of the beautiful tidal Sennis River, which had an eight-foot draft and a mouth eight hundred feet wide. Most of the shore was lined with mangrove shrubs and an occasional sandy beach. The land was pristine, with every kind of wild animal present including wild pigs, wild cows, and jaguars. It was located along the Southern Highway, about one third of the way from the southern tip of the country. The weather was tropical, with about one hundred inches of rainfall per year, mostly between July and January. The area was known as Pine Ridge and essentially open, for the last cutting of these tropical pine trees had been about fifty years before. It was kept open by fires, which burned over much of it every one to three years.

When we moved onto the land, there was not a single house or person living on the property. One narrow all-weather gravel road served an eleven-hundred-acre mango farm next door, owned by a retired American doctor who was on the property only a few weeks in the year. Numerous small uninhabited islands abutted the coastline. And about ten miles offshore lay the second-largest barrier reef in the world. Here millions of colorful tropical fish, coral, dolphins, and other marine life abound.

During our first week of visitation and getting acquainted with this tropical paradise, Florence and I stayed forty miles to the north at the Pelican Beach hotel and drove to the property daily in our leased four-wheel- drive land rover. We arranged for the purchase of a 25 x 40 foot house to be moved from Mango Creek village, ten miles to the north, to our property. We also provided for a hand-dug well and a small generator. From then on we could live on site in relative comfort. We could only get away from Lansing a week at a time and needed full-time people to work the farm.. This home overlooked the upper end of our beautiful tidal river. The property was so large that it almost overwhelmed us. We needed to see what would grow and to get an idea of how best to use the land efficiently. Before a small-farms program started, we needed to experiment on what would grow best and work for the project.

The Michigan 4-H recommended a young man for us to hire to live on the property, plant seeds, and see what would grow well. This man had a close friend from Seattle and asked that I hire him as well. They purchased at our expense two large army surplus trucks and a trailer, and the friend brought his own pickup truck towed behind an army truck and most of his earthly possessions in the trailer. Soon after they had settled into the little house and planted a large experimental vegetable garden, a British hippie-type friend joined them, and our man put him on the payroll as well. We employed a small Belizian accounting firm not only to keep track of the expenses but also to pay the men and other expenses. We also arranged for the eldest son of the man who managed the mango farm for the American doctor to work with our crew and show them the practicalities of the land and location. Everything was in place.

After about five months of being away I visited them and expected to see some promising results and recommendations as to what we should do next. Instead, I found the garden 90 percent dead because of flooding. They had failed to put in a main cross-drainage ditch. That meant we had lost a lot of time, because we still didn't know what would and would not grow well in the area. My biggest shock came on my entering the house, where I found them all smoking marijuana. Furthermore, they had burned out the two trucks' engines by running them through extended distances of several feet of water over the road leading to Belize where they unwisely had contracted to truck goods for personal gain.

The youth from Seattle took me aside and confided to me what had been going on. Although he felt he had done wrong, he had followed only under pressure, he said. To make more money the fellows were about to embark on the transport of marijuana which, although plentiful in the country, was strictly illegal. They also had marijuana seeds that they were about to plant.

The situation demanded strong action. I released the 4-H youth and his British friend and put the Seattle fellow on a month's notice so he could bring things into some semblance of order. After this the mango farm manager's son (25 years old) was put in charge of the operation, and our crop planting was to be repeated.

About that time I was approached by a retiring American in the area to buy his fifty-five head of cattle for about $20,000 (U.S.), which I did. There seemed to be ample grazing land, especially along the Sennis River, to support the cattle, and cattle were high on our list of possible good investments for the land.

I kept very busy in Michigan, and another six months passed before I again visited the property. Again my disappointment was great. Of the fifty-five head of cattle, only about five remained. Our Belizian employee said that the jaguars had killed the largest part of our investment. The word was around, however, that they had been shot twice a week and marketed in the city of Punta Gorda(5,000 population) about eighty miles to the south. To add further insult, our accountants had not kept track of our money nor paid the bills. Instead, the younger brother handling our account had diverted about $5,000 of our funds to feed his unquenchable alcohol appetite. After I confronted them with this situation, the other two brothers agreed to take responsibility and make restitution for their brother if I would give them a year to do so. It was, however, two years before they paid in full. Our attorney advised us not to bring charges against either party but instead to learn from each experience.

During this first year and a half I had been trying to find qualified American volunteers to stay on our land and help with our Bootstrap program. But the efforts were in vain largely because of the very bad publicity all of Central America was getting. No one wished to spend much time in this tropical paradise living in a bullet-proof vest. There were safer ways to have a pleasant retirement.

About this time (1980) the second phase of our Belize operation got underway. While still working with the Snell Environmental Group as chairman of the board I accepted a three-week assignment to Taiwan to help with a preliminary plan for the treatment of sewage for its capital city, Taipei. During this visit I met a group of Taiwanese who became very interested in Belize as a potentially ideal place to raise shrimp. At that time Taiwan was raising more shrimp than any other country in the world. Four of the top shrimp growers visited Belize for ten days at their own expense. They made a brief written report to the Belize government that raising shrimp had a lot of potential, and requested permission and encouragement to try these ideas. They would furnish all of the technology and at least 90 percent of the capital. Some of the profits would be a source of funds to support the Bootstrap program for small farmers. Incidentally, at that time Taiwan had a larger per-capita aid program to developing countries than did the United States and was helping several Central American countries in aquaculture..

All seemed to go well with our plan. The Belizian government requested that a full-blown feasibility study be made first—the type of study I was used to making as a consultant. I hired the Taiwanese marine biologist who had come earlier full time for three months to help me with the report. With this report in hand, the government became even more enthusiastic about the possibility of a new aquaculture industry in their country and gave us their full political backing with permission to proceed. The Taiwanese drew up detailed plans for a complete hatchery. I was assigned the task of building the 75 x 120 foot structure with local labor and materials while they purchased and sent a twenty foot long container full of all the needed equipment plus many large fiberglass containers and roofing for the hatchery.

I had just about finished the construction of the $100,000

structure, complete with twenty large concrete tanks, dormitory rooms, and three labs, when I learned the news from Taiwan that the three men who had agreed to take the financial responsibility for the whole project had lost their entire fortunes shipping plane loads of broodstock shrimp from the Philippines to Taiwan in a leased Lear jet. Their first successful shipment was followed by two large loads of shrimp that died en route. The loss was three hundred dollars (US) per shrimp. The situation was so bad that I had to go to Taiwan and put down $8,000 of my own before the valuable and needed contents of the shipping container of equipment and construction materials could be released for shipment to Belize.

The critical decision for me was whether I should walk away from the $100,000 I had spent on the hatchery building or "bite the bullet" and continue the project alone. By this time we had learned that it would not be economically feasible to raise the Taiwan monodon-type shrimp in Belize because the time required to transport the gravid female broodstock that distance was too long for them to stay alive outside their normal habitat. We would now have to go instead with the vannamei-type shrimp, a kind being raised successfully in a number of places in the western hemisphere. After much thought and prayer, we decided to put all our real estate and other assets on the market and raise funds from investor friends and their friends to build the project.

In the meantime, a young Michigan marine biologist who had some experience with shrimp heard about our project and wanted very much to become a part of it. His funds were very limited, but his University of Michigan professor gave him a good recommendation, so we took him on. The first thing he did was to pick a quarrel with the Taiwanese partners and refuse to work with them. Instead, he clandestinely joined with a well-to-do local Belizian businessman and got the government to lease to the two of them about two thousand acres of land it had already promised to lease to us when we had asked permission to start our project. He did this while still in my employ, and I had no choice but to bring our relationship to an end. Soon after this the Taiwanese went broke, so I was really on my own in a venture I knew little about and would never have planned to undertake alone or with my own funds.

By this time we had formed a Belizian corporation, General Shrimp, Ltd., and on the advice of attorneys formed a Michigan corporation called The Caribbean Development Corporation, which was the exclusive owner of the Belize company. While we were waiting for some of our Michigan real estate holdings to be sold we borrowed $250,000 from our United States bank, using our Michigan land as collateral, and proceeded to take bids on the construction of 335 acres of shrimp growout ponds, a large pump station, and inlet and outlet canals. A Cuban-American contractor was the low bidder. He had a lot of construction equipment and was willing to have it shipped to Belize and undertake the construction for less money than the local contractor, who would not have to ship equipment. This contractor was eager to get started in Belize, and we decided to go with him.

At first the contractor made a big splash and moved a lot of earth from the pond bottoms to the area of the dikes, but the shipment of the equipment had put him behind financially, and he started asking for up-front payments to keep ahead of the operation. After some time it was evident that the contractor was very inexperienced in construction and that his equipment was not suited for that kind of earth moving. He got further and further behind in funds and on the planned construction schedule. Finally, we had to exercise our rights under the contract to insist on his continuing the work without further advance payments or we would take over his equipment and complete the construction with our own people. We took the matter to the Belize courts and after some months were awarded damages of $85,000 (US), but unfortunately he was unable to pay anything. Now the Miami banks to whom he owed money for the equipment took possession and sold 90 percent of his equipment on the local market for a rather low price.

During the heat of this crisis we were breaking in a young fisheries man as our Belizian manager. He first came to us with the idea of setting up on our place an operation to grow tropical fish for the wholesale aquarium trade in collaboration with his Miami friend. But upon his arrival he begged me to put him on as acting manager of our shrimp operation while he got his fish-growing program organized. Although this young man had many fine points, he had yet to learn one important aspect of management: not to fight with the people you count on and thereby upset them so they cannot properly function. As things nearly came to a standstill under his poor management, I sat down with him and we agreed that it would be best for all concerned if he found another job and let us move on without him and all the strife. Shortly after he left, he went to New Orleans and in a few weeks came back as president of a new firm to start up a competitive shrimp farm on land we had been leasing from the government for three years.

During that time we had surveyed 2,500 acres and laid out the preliminary design of the shrimp ponds we planned to build as soon as we finalized a suitable joint venture. One of the firms that had talked with us about a joint venture was the one that had hired our man and instructed him to have our lease annulled by one of the few government officials willing to take money for such under-the-table services. Fortunately, before the land could actually be turned over to this company for its use, it went broke, and our friend found himself out on the street again. Although we have been told that there will be no trouble having the leased land returned to us at the appropriate time, the inappropriate loss of it certainly contributed to keeping us out of one of several joint venture prospects and also contributed to our financial problems and ultimate shutdown.

Construction had to proceed. We had purchased three large pumps and the generators to power them; we built the structures to house them using our own local personnel. We also constructed all the concrete intake and outlet structures. The heavy earth-moving work was let to two local contractors on a negotiated unit price basis for one dollar (US) per cubic yard. We completed about 270 acres of growout ponds before shortage of funds curtailed doing the last sixty-five acres until such time as we were able to grow shrimp and then build the ponds on the expected cash flow. Modest projections showed that we should net over $800,000 per year when the 335 acres were fully operational. As each of the growout ponds was completed it was put into operation.

Parallel to the pond construction and operation was the question of the successful operation of the hatchery, which we started operating in 1984, for it was an important part of the whole. Other important parts of the venture were the harvesting, processing, and sale of the shrimp, the purchase of shrimp food, and the feeding. All of these operations took knowledgeable and experienced technical managers, dedicated workers, and good advance planning.

Our three-foot deep ponds varied in size from five to thirty acres. The water pumped from the sea and flowing through inlet canals and inlet control boxes with screens was exchanged about 5-10 percent each day. This kept the water fresh and with ample essential dissolved oxygen, without which the shrimp would die. Twice a day quality feed was distributed around each of the ponds from small motor-driven flatboats. A complex formula determined the ideal amount of daily feed distribution, related to the body size and total mass of body weight in the pond. Since the shrimp generally grew from 3/4 inch (post-larva-5, or PL-5) to about thirty count (thirty shrimp per pound) in twenty weeks, it was important to know the ideal changing daily feeding rate. The initial stocking density of PL-5s was 50-60,000 per acre, and generally about 70 percent survived to maturity.

Harvesting the shrimp from the ponds is an important task and if not done correctly adversely affects both the quality and the quantity. It also requires care to wash the shrimp as they are taken from the ponds in nets or by pumps, after the water is lowered to about 10-15 percent remaining. About two pounds of crushed ice for each pound of shrimp are needed during harvest to maintain their quality.

Processing is the last step which must be performed correctly, or the shrimp lose quality or may even become worthless. Essentially there are three steps: deheading by hand, sizing with an expensive machine, and packing in five-pound boxes and placing these into larger fifty-pound master boxes. While they are still in the five-pound boxes they are exposed to a blast freezer which does the freezing job well and rapidly.

Hard-frozen boxes of shrimp are stored in twenty- or forty-foot long insulated reefers and transported to the distributors, most of whom are in the United States.

There is much detail that the grower must know and be able to do, for it is as easy to lose money raising shrimp as it is to make a profit. There is much satisfaction when each phase is well done and a high-quality product has been shipped.

The essential accomplishment in the hatchery must be first maturation, in which high quality male and female broodstock breed and lay eggs. The second accomplishment is for these eggs to hatch and in about fifteen days grow to be PL-5s and ready to be placed in the growout ponds. To reach this fifteen-day transformation the animals must be fed two kinds of algae in large quantities and also, near the end of the time, imported and rather expensive microscopic-size live brine shrimp.

To accomplish the first maturation operation took a great deal of training and skill and was only accomplished now and then in our hatchery. However, the second operation was rather easily accomplished when we shipped in nauplii (one-day-old shrimp) from a large hatchery in Panama. This lowered the average cost of usable PL-5s from about eight dollars per thousand to about three dollars per thousand, done 98 percent of the time. In fact, we constantly produced more PL-5s than we needed and supplied several other shrimp farms, now starting up in Belize, with their needs. In so doing we were able to pay for part of the overhead of the hatchery.

To employ the necessary number of good people for such an operation, to bring them from the United States, and to settle them happily in a remote country like Belize is to experience various kinds of problems, such as their having inadequate technical skills or inability to manage or get along. At one time or another we encountered all of these in our employees. Over the years we brought in four independent specialty consultants to help our technical people do a better job, and they helped us greatly. At times we had what we considered a truly topflight team, and other times we had grave weaknesses in our group. Another big problem was that I had to be in the States about half of the time to raise money and buy things for the operation. This meant leaving the management of the operation to the second person in command. Our attempts to get good full-time managers were disappointing, to say the least. The operation was too small to support a highly paid person, and when we did bring them in, either their wives suffered from Belizian culture shock and wanted out, or those hired were not quality managers after all.

In an operation of this magnitude and complexity being run by less-than-perfect managers and technical people, one might expect serious problems somewhere, but no one expected one crippling difficulty to show up where it did—in the shrimp-food supply. Initially, all our shrimp food was trucked in from Guatemala City where Ralston Purina has a large mill. Who would suspect difficulties from a name brand with its reputation? But after our first three harvests, it was apparent that we were getting growouts of less than 25 percent of expected international averages. The next well-advertised brand of food we switched to still produced not over 30 percent growout. Finally we switched to the Ziegler brand, and the shrimp grew out at 100 percent of the expected rate in each of our last five ponds. But by then we had spent all of our working capital or operational money, were $150,000 in debt, and had taken a $600,000 loss. The first food not only had produced poor growth but was toxic as well. It was impossible to take the company to court and recover our losses. Others had suffered the same fate and were equally powerless to recover.

Our last hope of financial recovery and paying off our special bridge loans from our investors was to sell the large shrimp crops raised on the good Ziegler food. At this time we had not only a new and untried United States manager but a new untrained, overconfident local ponds manager. In the harvest of our largest pond things went awry, and we lost 80 percent of our $80,000 worth of shrimp. On top of this, two other serious management mistakes lost us considerably more. We were experiencing catastrophe.

This was truly our lowest point. Why, after all we had accomplished and all the problems we had overcome, when we were on the verge of real success, would a series of events bring us to our financial and spiritual knees?

After two days of deliberation and much prayer the answer came to me loud and clear: I was not supposed to remain in this shrimp and Bootstrap work in Belize the rest of my life. I was seventy-eight, and the good Lord had other more important things for me to do with the rest of my life. My stubbornness in trying to overcome all odds and make it work had turned out to be more of a problem instead of part of the answer and had kept God's plan from penetrating our operation.

It was a hard pill to swallow, a hard answer to accept as the Lord's will for me and the enterprises there in Belize, but when I did, it was also clear that we needed to sell the operation and then move on to other things.

We found an interested buyer within two months, but when it came to his finding the money and credit, he couldn't do so and had to let the opportunity go by. By early 1990 we performed our last harvest and ran out of money. We shut down the operation. The second buyer also had a lot of interest and enthusiasm but after some time, about mid-1990, also could not obtain financing. Next, about four months apart, two buyers came along with plenty of credit and money, but each wished us to take much too large a loss. If we had accepted such a loss we would not have been able to pay back all the loans we had made, to say nothing of ever giving anything back to the shareholders.

During these four periods of trying to sell, our Belize bank, where we owed $75,000 (US), demanded that its loan be returned on a rather tight schedule. Three other creditors got tired of waiting and separately went to court and got an injunction to have our property auctioned off bit by bit until enough cash was raised to pay their particular debts plus court and attorney fees. In all four of these cases we were able to intervene in time to save the situation from taking us over the edge into bankruptcy. They were difficult times, and twice we were saved by a matter of less than a day before real trouble would have started. At this writing all the remaining Belize debtors, about twenty-five in all, have been paid on the basis of a uniform negotiated 50 percent of value.

During our first three years of sales effort we had at least a dozen interested potential buyers. In November 1993 the operation was finally sold on an exchange-of-shares basis without an immediate exchange of any cash, but it was only promised as soon as the buyers could spare it. Until our corporations were absorbed, Cherax Hatchery, Inc.,located at Daphne, Alabama, was doing a good job of raising Cherax Lobster for the aquarium trade. There was a lot of hard negotiating between its chief executive officer, Bob Underwood, and myself. With the aid of a Denver lawyer we were able to legalize a detailed and fair agreement. Some months went by while Cherax, Inc. prepared a business plan and toyed with various ways of raising capital. Mainly it was a question of going public right away or finding a large private firm interested in aquaculture. Finally, the latter plan won out.

Their initial investment of $500,000 got things well on their way in Belize but paid none of our debts. Their second investment of 2.5 million dollars enabled them to complete the 335 acres of shrimp ponds and build 80 acres of talapia and lobster ponds using Bootstrap land and fresh water from the Monkey River.

During these last three years I have served the new company, now called Starich, Inc. I have been able to keep them out of a lot of chuckholes, helped to design the new freshwater ponds and pump station, and assisted them in purchasing generators, pumps, and other needed equipment. Recently they have had many successful shrimp harvests and are now formulating what their next expansion moves will be on the 2,500 acres of leased land being made available by Belize. At this point we are all optimistic about the future.

Late in 1996 I assisted STARICH by making a special study as to how they had best treat the wastes from their growing operation.

The Belize saga would have been quite a different story if there had not been a lot of good guys to lend encouragement, positive thoughts, hard work, and hard-earned savings. Often when things were going badly one of these loyal investor friends came along to help turn the situation from negative to positive.

Our General Shrimp Ltd. was the first shrimp company in Belize—the pioneer. Although growth initially was slow and sporadic, a new, well-established, thriving aquaculture industry is now under way in Belize, and it promises to grow and greatly help the economy. Of eight companies trying to grow shrimp in Belize, six are presently successful, two have gone out of business or changed hands. Two, which started out with the untried "intensive" method and failed with that, successfully converted to the well-tested "semi-intensive" method.

The new company, Starich, Inc., has proven itself in the field of semi-intensive shrimp growing and is well on its way to introducing three new products, Cherax Lobster, talapia, and red fish, on the Belize property. Starich has built onto our years of experience and economic base and will be the one, the second generation, to make our original venture a truly sound one. Our initial corporations, General Shrimp, Ltd., and The Caribbean Development Corporation, along with the nonprofit Bootstrap International, which the shrimp company planned to support, have spent fifteen years in Belize and some five million dollars, and brought new technical and management leadership to the country along with the new aquaculture industry.

As Starich moves firmly into success it is anticipated that Bootstrap International should recover perhaps $800,000 from the profits of the venture and before the year 2,000 will seek a new type of nonprofit program in which to invest its time and resources.

Of several of the Bootstrap-sponsored small farms which actually got off to a start in Belize, only two are well on their way to being successful. The original need for such farms is considered to be pretty much behind us, as the political and human rights situations in Central America are now greatly improved.

I do not regret the time or the money I spent on the Belize project. The main thing is that I did what I strongly felt was needed to be done at the time and did not walk away from adversity when it struck, and struck hard. The operation culminated in our spending four very difficult years keeping the whole enterprise from going under, although only the future will tell us the degree of success we have achieved.

In the spring and summer of 1996 the Commonwealth Development Corporation (CDC) took great interest in the operation of Starich and by late August invested two million dollars and loaned another five million. CDC differs from our USAID program in that they try not only to help third world countries but also to make money at the same time. CDC also turned over the operation of four of its other aquaculture projects to Starich, and Starich bought in on each of these a 20 percent financial share. There is a joint plan to build and for Starich to operate cage culture for five thousand tons per year of red fish just off the coast of Belize. Now in early 1997, their plans are already in the construction stage for a large expansion of the Belize operation, both with shrimp on the 2,500 acres of leased land, and with lobster and talapia on the freshwater side, using land purchased from Bootstrap. All this should make Starich one of the largest, if not the largest, aquaculture operations in the world.

The operation should go public about 1999. This will be good news for all of our investors, for their money has been hard at work for a number of years with no way of their withdrawing any of it. The publicly traded shares should be worth a lot more per share than they were several years ago. Bootstrap will then have to choose from its several options as to what worthwhile and not-for-profit projects it will support—a good ending for the saga of Belize.

CHAPTER TWENTY

Full Circle

In November 1994 my brother Fred and I attended the one-hundred-tenth anniversary of my father's hospital in Suzhou, China, which had been declared the oldest teaching hospital in China. We were the invited guests of the new hospital administration. It was a memorial and a nostalgic experience.

The four-day visit in the hospital and many other places in the city of our birth brought back the days of our youth. It was like being lifted to the top of a mountain pass and looking back over the winding road of the sixty years of my adulthood and professional life to when I had last left Suzhou as my home. This panorama, although dimmed somewhat by today's air pollution and by the passage of time, seemed to bring my life together like nothing else could have.

I remembered, as though it were yesterday, the time only a few months before his tragic death from pneumonia when my father and I had discussed what I should do to serve China in the engineering field. Together we decided I would be best prepared by going back to America and taking two to three years of graduate study in sanitary (environmental) engineering. Because I had taken up engineering rather than medicine when I enrolled at Vanderbilt, I now decided to build on my civil engineering training to help the people of China to stay healthy rather than to get well once they were sick. Prevention seemed more important than cure—the basic principle of public health. Although my decision to enter environmental engineering had been made mainly with the idea to serve the Chinese people, history's events had dictated otherwise.

Florence and I visited our hometown Suzhou for one day on a tourist jaunt in 1979, when we toured China for two weeks. At that time it was still a sleepy cobblestoned-streets city of 500,000 and virtually without factories. However, in the past fifteen years two things have pushed Suzhou into the foreground of China's industrial revolution as it grew to over one million. First, it is on the two-thousand-mile-long Grand Canal, now a busy water transportation route; second, it is only fifty miles from Shanghai, the largest city in the world and the busiest city in China. The area between the two cities has rapidly filled through industrial growth.

Our hospital hosts spent the better part of four days with us and showed us not only all the nostalgic things of the past but the phenomenal growth of industry. Large modern six-story apartment houses fill the spaces between the industrial complexes in this area of about twenty square miles, more than doubling the geographical size of the city. It seemed that about a third of the new buildings were still under construction. One thirty-five-story office building stood out. All these are part of China's new program of joint venturing with corporations in much of the free world, from whence the capital has come. We were told that the annual rate of economic growth is about 20 percent, the result of a marriage of low-cost bright, and often skilled labor with international technology and finance.

During much of 1994 I had been looking for the right way to return to China to give to the people from my life's training and experience in environmental engineering. I had wished to give an environmental agency in China the chance to work along with us as we undertook the new research work of Michigan Biotechnical Institute (MBI) this was the rapid and inexpensive extraction of methane gas from municipal refuse before recycling the resistant organic residue to agriculture. My efforts had included correspondence with a well-known university professor in Tianjin and discussions with two skilled scientific men attached to the Chinese consulate in Chicago.

Then I became well acquainted with Forest Meek and his wife, Jean, who lived in Clare, Michigan. They were early retirees from teaching and had recently returned from two years in China teaching spoken English. Their work had met with such success that their lessons had been taped and widely used in China. Also, they were so well liked and respected that they were offered the chance of becoming the United States side of first one and then several joint ventures in industrial projects virtually of their own choosing.

During my November return to China, Forest Meek's partners at Wuhan, the largest city along the Yangtze River, took us in hand, spent three days showing us around, and introduced us to various people. Guo Yue was a brilliant, outgoing twenty-eight-year-old man who headed four international joint ventures, including one manufacturing television sets with sales of almost $80 million the past year. His attractive wife was an executive in the real estate business. Guo had been a rather famous student dissident, but because of his qualities and connections he had remained well respected by the government; hence, they rewarded him by putting him into the joint venture business, and everyone benefited. Among Guo's partners he introduced us to was Liu Ke Ye, chief officer for the Water Conservancy Agency of Hubei Province, a group also tied into several other joint venture programs. Mr. Liu was responsible for the complete irrigation system for the whole province, a very responsible job. He had a close mayor friend, whose city had a rather serious problem with municipal refuse. He took us over to visit that city's officials. It was a two-hour drive each way, with half of the route along an excellent new four-lane limited access expressway. The refuse problems of the city were real, but their lack of organization, energy, and leadership were disappointing. Later he showed us a larger and more alert city.

By the summer of 1977 arrangements for Snell and Meek were made to visit Xiaogan City (pop. 1 million) to plan for a modern refuse treatment and utilization system including making methane gas and use of the residue on the fields.

While in China Fred and I also had enjoyed the exquisite mountain scenery along the Lee River at Guilin, which topped off the whole trip. It was the most beautiful scenery I had ever seen, and we took over seventy pictures. This trip alone was worth the journey to China.

Of greatest interest to Fred and me were the way the Chinese, with a quarter of the world's population, were coping or at least trying to cope with global environmental problems. Pollution of the canals and the air was most evident, and the people were beginning to learn what to do about these problems. Although water coming from the taps looked clean, no one drank it before boiling it. They had grossly compromised their four-thousand-year-old practice of conserving and utilizing every scrap of waste organic or nutrient by placing them on the fields. In their effort to modernize too quickly they had not taken the time to find and initiate a plan nor spent the money required to make this practice safe. This was the area where I felt I could be of help. If the system were complete and properly worked out, it would cost no more and would continue the assurance of fertile fields for the next millennia. It would also help to give the Chinese more time to bring their population into complete control before it becomes top heavy and sinks the nation.

Each family, with few exceptions, had no more than one child, but because of the extended life span of the elderly the population was still growing. I could not help but think that when I was born in 1912 there were only 1.5 billion people in the whole world, but only eighty-six years later (1997) the population will have exceeded six billion and by only fifty-three years later (2050) ten billion.

China is still in the bicycle era, but even now there are grave traffic jams at rush hour in their large cities. Automobiles are encroaching on the field of transportation, and enormous sums are being spent on the construction of modern highways, including thousands of miles of four-lane divided, limited-access highways. The resulting losses of agricultural land, accelerated use of fossil fuels, with resulting pollution, are only to be imagined. Not only is China experiencing this "path of civilization" but most of the rest of the developing world is as well.

The discouraging part of all these observations was that these grave environmental happenings were not part of the pleasant "full-circle" experiences we had been enjoying. Instead, the circles of the environment, and especially the accelerating population growth, were spiraling tangentially out of control, likely never to converge into an acceptable sustainable solution.

If life is to remain meaningful until the circle closes, it is as important to have worthy goals for life's closing chapters as it has been for our professional endeavor. Otherwise there can be no driving purpose along the divine guideposts leading to that final destiny of accomplishment but an aimless coasting to the finish line with little thought of one's final contribution to humanity's betterment. Included in this schedule is a much narrower limit as to what one still has time to accomplish and on which to do well. There must be time enough for life and happiness but not time for too much leisure and idleness, and no time for the negatives of the world.

So it is that I have endeavored to pick the professional projects for these closing years with care. Among all the challenges of the environment perhaps the greatest is the treatment and utilization of solid wastes on agricultural land after extracting its methane gas as useful energy. China is at the head of my list here, but my schedule has had room for Argentina as well, a country where I have long been active. Despite the occasional bickering between the United States and China, I feel sure that we both will take the high road and work together as close friends. In the next several years I see the way opening for me to work with China on a number of its environmental problems, especially the one where the organic and nutrient wastes are properly pretreated and safely and economically returned to agriculture.

A close friend of mine, who has a Ph.D. in environmental engineering, and I are moving in the direction of getting this new technology transplanted into India, and we have already done this in Argentina. In the fall of 1995 I spent considerable time on the problem of how best to dewater, pasteurize, treat, transport, and utilize these wastes in agriculture. The professional contract was with Agua Argentina, S.A., a French company taking over both the water and waste water systems for the city of Buenos Aires. We also worked with two smaller cities on the composting of organic wastes. This study took about four months, including two weeks I spent in Argentina, and it resulted in two thick reports. Fortunately, I had the assistance of two longtime engineer friends in Buenos Aires. They have been urging me to get into a number of other projects, but I have felt quite right to limit my time and energies by turning down new projects.

Another project I have kept alive in my portfolio has to do with the low-cost, rapid anaerobic digestion of presalvaged, preshredded municipal refuse. Our first interest and active work in this project came twelve years ago when the Department of Energy gave the Snell Environmental Group a $50,000 research grant to study the problem. These experiments went very well, and we were able to extract about 90 percent of the theoretical gas in less than three months, whereas in the landfill the average time is fifty to one hundred years, and much of it still is lost. There have been understandable delays in getting the project adequately refunded and taking it on to the pilot-plant scale and then to the demonstration-phase scale. Presently, the bulk of the support is in hand, and the remainder is hopefully close at hand. The resulting system will provide $35 per ton more "tipping fee" just from the methane gas produced, enable cities to pick up yard wastes and salvageables far more efficiently, and practically eliminate the old-style landfills, which most experts now agree will ultimately cause gross pollution for the ground water. To stabilize and spread the organic wastes on the agricultural land alone will be very beneficial to our future food supply and bodily health.

Power-Gen International asked me to present a paper in Dec. '96 in Orlando showing that the countrie's landfills produce enough methane gas to be responsible for global warming equal to that caused by all the carbon dioxide produced by the electrical industry (one (1) cu. ft. of methane gas is equal to thirty (30) cu. ft. of carbon dioxide).

World environmental conferences on Global Warming and related problems took place in Rio, then in Berlin and now in June '97 in New York. The electrical industry is being given the blame because of all their carbon dioxide production. The environmentalists are urging that trillions be spent annually to slow their global warming caused by carbon dioxide production which if it continues might ultimately allow the oceans to rise by as much as 300 feet due to the melting of the polar ice caps. The Orlando paper points out that if this new technology of high rate, low cost methane gas production is widely used and the methane is used to produce electricity from the bulk of municipal solid wastes this then would cut in half the present day pressure on global warming by others and give time for the electrical industry to solve its serious problems. This could be accomplished for less than five percent of the carbon dioxide reduction cost and would also increase the world electric generation by as much as 5-10% using the renewable energy from municipal solid wastes.

Interest has increased since Orlando to the point that my paper presented there has been enlarged and rewritten and will be given in September 97 at the Power Gen International Conference in Singapore.

One of my final professional projects may be to produce a low-cost, high-quality backyard composting bin—a complete package including two how-to-do books (one written by me) and the unique "Chopper-Turner" which I have patented. I hope shortly to turn over this business to others and still have the source of revenue that should enable us to extend our program of helping serve not-for-profit groups to which we feel committed.

The aquaculture project in Belize is rapidly gaining momentum and losing its risk. Whereas two years ago I was spending a lot of time helping the company with many phases of its engineering, it now has an excellent engineer, and I spend much less time giving advice. The new company has now expanded about ten times over and has joined with other larger firms. When they go public and give their investors a chance to recover their investments—likely by the year 1999—we will be able to complete our program of willing our assets to certain selected charities and enlarging family.

Before I close this chapter, "Full Circle," it is only right to point to several circles which were most meaningful in our lives. I look at my wife, Florence, being born in Suzhou, China, a year and a day before I was, as more than a coincidence. She was born a Presbyterian, so I can say with near certainty that it was a predestined happening for both of us, for on December 8, 1939, we were married in Venezuela, and the two were made one. When you feel such unions take place through the bidding of the Holy Spirit you know it is for life and can only turn out in a superior way. Most of what happened in our lives would not have happened without this divine bidding. This important circle is really one of a series of concentric circles, or at least overlapping circles, for us. The circles started with each of our two families saying yes to God and becoming lifelong missionaries in China, with the children of each of these families growing up knowing each other at least in part, first at Shanghai American School and then as we went to various colleges and pursued our individual life professions. The next circle was formed by each of the Snells and the Moffetts having families of their own and these cousins keeping in touch. Then, as we all found out at the Moffett reunion in Grinell, Iowa, in the summer of 1995, many of this next generation of children now had their own grandchildren. Without these continuing family circles life cannot be nearly as rich and interesting.

This chapter would not be complete without another "full circle." Both Florence and I were born into missionary families, both instilled with the desire to be missionaries ourselves. This implanted goal was reborn in each of us as in 1932 and 1936 we attended the national Student Volunteer conferences, first in Buffalo and then in Indianapolis. Each of these conferences brought us not only close to service in the mission field but closer to the hearts of each other. After we were married and were about to return to the United States from Venezuela we had applied and had been accepted to serve in the Presbyterian Mission an Hangzhou University, China. Even though the Japanese War and then World War II prevented us from fulfilling this mission, we have always tried to keep close to the bidding of the Holy Spirit in our year-to-year living.

Now as the circle comes around to its "full" position we have important related items to consume much of our remaining time. This started with my being on the selection committee for the senior pastor for People's Church in East Lansing, Michigan. The task of sixteen months took a great deal of time in the study of 220 applicants and selection of the pastor. I then volunteered to serve for the next three years on the elders board of the church. During the course of this last important "full circle" it became very evident to me and others on the committee that over the past four to five decades there had been a marked decline of most of the mainline churches for one reason or another. Fortunately, there is now a renewed interest in reversing this decline in many of the churches, but as yet no nationwide program to accomplish it. So, in addition to being active with the resurgence of People's Church itself, our goal is to do what we can actively to help in the restoration of the mainline churches of America.

CHAPTER TWENTY-ONE

Believe

Friends have suggested that I include one last chapter wherein I summarize what I see as the keys to effective living and avoiding the downside of life, and what I see as the positive essentials to making life worthwhile. It is like my friend asking me to make a road map from my eighty-four years and erect friendly road signs to guide the way. "Tell us what you can. What should we believe?"

Please do not regard me as a teacher lecturing to his class but rather as one close friend sharing with another his deepest convictions, secrets, and confessions.

I take up this task in all humility, for life is more than engineering and more than body and mind, both of which are understood to a degree by an engineer. First I feel that we must understand and believe that life also has a very strong spiritual side; if we do not we are dealing with unreality.

Here I speak only as an ordinary person with no special education or training. But I do have experience and some resulting convictions, namely, that our planet containing six billion people is in danger of self-destruction and obscurity except for the fact that its Creator has a plan for its salvation. We can learn about that plan and we can have an active part in carrying it out.

Human beings need three things for healthy living: good food, clean water, and pure air. But in this secular age many persons cannot believe in the importance of God's Spirit for our lives. I, however, strongly feel that for a healthy life and a healthy civilization the Spirit is just as important as is air to the life of our bodies.

But first, let us deal briefly with certain physical environmental concerns, each of which, nonetheless, has a distinct spiritual side, for they deal with the very heart of creation itself.

Environmental Concerns

While hundreds of books and thousands of scientific articles have been written on this subject, it is my intention only to touch on it very briefly. The following six categories of environmental concerns are all important to the preservation of our spacecraft Earth. I feel that both the scientific community and the well-read individual would generally agree on these fundamentals. From the scientific studies we can draw certain logical conclusions in which we can believe. The problem, however, is that although we believe, we lack the commitment, stamina, and willingness to sacrifice to accomplish the agreed-upon objectives. In listing these categories I also note their overlapping and interrelatedness.

My first concern is the rapid and uncontrolled growth of the world's population. In 1830 the world's population is estimated to have reached its first one billion. By 1930, or one hundred years later, it had doubled to two billion. By 1998, or sixty-eight years later, the population will have tripled to six billion, and by 2050— in just fifty-two years—it is projected to reach ten billion. Unfortunately, scientists expect the point of no return or worse, "the critical mass," for the population of the world to be about ten billion, at which point we should expect a dire catastrophe. Time is fleeting. We must solve the uncontrolled population growth or endure starvation, suffering, hatred, and the ugliest war beyond our imagination.

The following five added threats to environmental health are important and must be controlled, and while they are secondary to and largely influenced by the population increase, we must deal with each of them in an effective and prompt manner and bear the necessary pain and expense to do so. These five threats are; inadequate control of the consumption of our very limited fossil fuels; unchecked buildup of atmospheric carbon dioxide and methane, and the disastrous global warming which will ultimately follow; inadequate control causing unsafe thinning of our protective ozone layer and the resulting lethal damage to our ecosystem and human health; disregard, through our high use, of energy and other critical resources, and the lack of strict conservation which will result in Western civilization's plight; and our inability to keep up the increase of food production to match the population growth, a multiheaded monster that soon can outgrow our present fears.

Very likely, most of us believe in the basic premises of these six concerns but lack the willingness to make needed sacrifices to correct them, such as money and change of lifestyle. We are on a path of stall and wait until it may be too late, and then we will have condemned our children and our grandchildren to undue pain, hardship, sickness, death by starvation, and a continuing cruel and painful war.

These six environmental concerns may well have a very close relationship to the biblical ten commandments, whose spiritual injunctions parallel the physical implications as to how we must treat the world in which we all live. Obey them by treating God, other people, and nature with love and respect and we will preserve our world and ourselves; disobey them and we face the very worst possible consequences.

War and Peace

Finally, I present another concern as important or more important than the six environmental concerns listed above. In the broadest sense I call it war and peace. The spiritual laws expressed in the ten commandments cover even more closely every phase of both individual and group war or peace.

We all can be thankful that so far we have been spared a global nuclear war. Although it would appear that the Cold War is behind us, we are still a long way from firmly believing that the world will be completely free from mass nuclear terrorism and death. We are still frustrated by the numerous smaller wars around the world. Leaders do their human best to contain them and bring about cease fires and some sort of fragile peace, but we know that the basic causes for war remain in the minds and hearts of the contenders. The seeds of war are widespread—class against class, ethnic wars, religious wars, racial wars, gang wars, and terrorism. We seem never to come closer to solving these kinds of wars between such groups, never able to bring about lasting solutions. We begin to suspect a flaw in our human thinking.

Most important, how can we stop the individual type wars which constantly fill our newspapers, such as break-ins, robberies, family wars, arson, shootings, rapes, and murders? These millions of individual wars perpetuate themselves and are, in fact, the beginnings of bigger wars, and they must be dealt with first. To deal with them we need to determine the basic causes within ourselves and to see what brings our fellow humans to commit any of these crimes—acts grown over time from the hate-breeding seeds of fear, need, and hunger, the seeds of selfishness, greed, impurity, and lack of love.

The Spirit Above and Beyond Human Wisdom

To be sure, beyond our flawed human wisdom is another greater wisdom which we have not adequately sought and followed to give us the right answers. Let us first define what we mean by greater wisdom and what we mean by the Spirit.

I have always been grateful to my father, whom I loved and admired, for passing on to me his deepest secrets for life, often without my realizing what he was doing. Dad said to me on many occasions, "There are two important things in life. One is to be guided by God, and the other is to love our fellow man." These were doubly impressed on my mind and heart, for he was a walking example of them, even up to his early and untimely passing. Dad was a doctor not a minister, yet he understood these two principles of the Spirit from his lifetime of experience and the motivations of his living. He died because he got up from a sick bed to perform emergency surgery on two patients. He sacrificed his own life to save the lives of the patients.

We can often learn more from experience than we can from philosophy or wise words. Take the story of Hugh Corrough, whom I have mentioned in chapter 15. Here was a great executive who, in the ten prime years of his life, was totally defeated by alcohol abuse until life held nothing for him. Modern medical cures failed him, and he was left "on the street." What changed his life completely was the real power within Alcoholics Anonymous (AA). God's Spirit reached into the depth of Hugh's heart and made him different and victorious over his terrible ten-year problem. Yet Hugh was just one of hundreds of thousands of men and women over whom the power of the Spirit acted and helped them overcome their incurable problem to give them new life. The twelve steps of AA and the spiritual power behind it came from the one above, God the Creator of the universe.

Although AA was the first well-known movement of its kind, there now are many outgrowths of it, support groups to help people afflicted with various other kinds of addictions. Further variations have been spawned to fit the needs within our jails. Tens of thousands of hardened criminals, once given up as incurable, are converted by this unseen power of the Spirit, even though they may yet have to live out much of their prison terms. Chuck Colson is founder and leader of Break Point which is very successful in this field.

We do not need to look to addicts or those in jail for examples of how the power of the Spirit of God can change human nature. The churches are full of them, and countless thousands not attending churches are affected as well. Having said this, we also must be honest to admit that among those who profess Christianity there are too many in whom the Spirit of God is not evident, likely because of human weakness.

What are the reasons for loss of spiritual strength? It is certainly not the lack of the power or wisdom at the source—God. Rather, it stems from the many human frailties within us, and I find that I am no exception. It helps, and for many persons is essential, to have strong leaders—men and women of God. Likewise, we need committed people who are willing to place God's will above their own, which is to learn to love as they are taught in the Bible to love.

Good Books and the "Good Book"

Effective mentors inspire and motivate people to do their best. The world today has too few victorious and successful people who make us willing to sacrifice and work very hard to be even a little like them. Too commonly we wish to emulate only those who appear to be financially, educationally, or entertainingly successful, with superficial qualities that often are fleeting or misleading.

I have received much inspiration and guidance from my reading. I could recommend many good books that have influenced my thinking, inner life, and direction of heart. I especially find biography to be one of the best and most interesting teachers, whether the life story of the great or not so great. The bibliography at the end of this chapter is short and generally tilted toward books from which I have learned a great deal. Five are biographies of recent leaders in our Christian faith who, though quite different in their ministries, were, I believe, truly led by God in our modern world. Therefore, everyone can learn much from them: Billy Graham, Frank Buchman, Oral and Richard Roberts, Pat Robertson, and Robert Schuller. Studying their books has helped me to understand many things concerning the Spirit that have been helpful to me in my own endeavors.

Lighter but still inspiring are the books of Og Mandino, including *The Christ Commission*. Also, I have included *Gifted Hands*, by the famous African American heart surgeon from Johns Hopkins University, Ben Carson. Any of the above books will help the reader to believe and begin to know what the power and wisdom of God really is.

Although I have read much in the Bible, I must confess I still only understand it as a novice. However, what I have read in it at various periods in my life has helped me over some very difficult times. During the other times, all of them too long, when the good book gathered dust, my inner spirit wilted. One of the best investments I made in recent years was a large print copy of the Living Bible, by Tyndale Press, a modern translation that is much easier to read and understand. Experience shows me that I do best if I read from a daily devotional book as well as a chapter or more in the Bible. I have learned that this daily exposure to God's Word is very helpful in ordering my mind and spirit and giving me the motivation and direction I need for living.

Some persons refer to the Old Testament as literature, but it is much more than that. It is the story of God's relationship with man from the beginning, and we learn much from these relationships when we read about the historical men and women of the Old Testament, such as Abraham, Moses, David, Solomon, or any one of the prophets. The Jewish people were for centuries God's chosen people, and He had a very special relationship with them. When they believed and obeyed Him, He directed and protected them from all evil, including some very formidable enemies. But when the Jewish people went their own selfish way and disobeyed God, they found the relationship temporarily broken, and often under such circumstances they were overrun by their enemies. The Psalms of David have insight for all of us today and many are also beautiful verse. Two things of special note are frequent, even in the old Testament: the miracles and the frequency with which God converses with not only the prophets and Jewish leaders but also the ordinary people.

To me the real essence of the Bible is found in the New Testament. In a few sentences, it is the story of God giving us His only Son in the form of a human being to dwell among us and teach us and then allowing Him to be crucified on a cross as full atonement for our sins. On the third day God raised Christ from the dead, and after a number of contacts with his disciples and others, He was taken back to be with His Father. He reigns over us, if we are but willing.

The Bible speaks, hundreds of times, of the third member of the Trinity, the Holy Spirit, who is our comforter and our main point of spiritual contact. We can obtain much knowledge and understanding from the New Testament by reading only two books, the Book of John, which is the last-written and most easily understood Gospel, and the Book of Acts, which tells much of the early story of the evangelization of that part of the world and the building of the early churches, mainly by the apostle Paul. The New Testament is full of miracles, and it is very strong on people listening to the Holy Spirit in two-way prayer. One can get much inspiration from listening to Charleston Heston's two videos on the old and new testament narrated in Israel. (see references)

I strongly recommend that we waste little time and learn about the facinating stories in the Bible so that we understand enough for it to become meaningful in our lives. Join a class led by an inspirational person on the Book of John. Or, if you could use a "wake-up call," read with as much understanding as you can muster John chapters 15-17. This has been a very meaningful experience for me. Next, get off by yourself and see if you can believe.

Prayer and Two-Way Prayer

Without God there would be no need for prayer, or for that matter, there would be no prayer. Without prayer God can have little real meaning to us or we to Him. Essentially there are two kinds of prayer. In one kind of prayer we speak to God and tell Him perhaps how we are doing but mainly what we would like Him to do for us. Many of us never go beyond this kind of one-way prayer, and that can become rather superficial and selfish.

There is also two-way prayer, and I believe that is what God has intended our relationship with Him to be. Here we do more than just make our desires known to our Creator; we take planned time to listen and learn what God wants us to do for Him and for others.

I first learned about two-way prayer when I was in graduate school at Harvard and met those in Frank Buchman's movement, Moral Re-Armament. I learned to write down the answers I got and to act on them. I learned, too, that a faint reply filled with static would become much more audible and clear if my life first measured up to the Christian standards of absolute honesty, purity, love, and unselfishness.

These difficult prerequisites took some time to deal with and need my continuing attention. Although many times my adherence to these standards has slipped badly and resulted in poor-quality messages being transmitted to me, the fact that such communication was always available to me has never left my mind, and in this I have always believed.

An early but indelible memory revolved around God giving me the ultimate gift—my wife Florence to be my lifetime partner. This involved two-way prayer. My desire and request was first subjected to firm Christian checking as whether it was His will.

Later in the same year the direction came to me, loud and clear, to spend time with an Austrian visitor to our new American Church in Caracas, which resulted in God becoming real to him and giving him a plan for his life, thus preventing his planned suicide. And then there were the two occasions when I was in uniform serving in North China, and God's direction prevented my being captured by Communists and later on from being shot to death on the road. (These are recounted in detail in earlier chapters.)

There were many more incidents, but life does not have to be one crisis after another. Mine has been made up of the thousands of daily decisions affecting my life and the lives of others, which are important. My only real regret is that there were many times, some for long stretches, in which my discipline of morning meditation and quiet times—or two-way prayer—slipped by the wayside and I was not available. God's soldier was temporarily AWOL.

Experience taught me another important thing: to live this kind of discipline takes not only commitment but also the comradeship and fellowship of those with like commitment. Only in the last two years have I been active with our church's search committee for a new senior pastor. I have learned a great deal about the fellowship of sincere Christians in a common church cause. I have also seen how a less-than-sincere spirituality can weaken that fellowship.

One's belief in two-way prayer is strengthened every time it is tried out and works. I used to have a very sharp tongue and an ability to use it in a devastating way, especially if someone crossed me. Not until I practiced two-way prayer and absolute love with such people did I learn what to do about this enemy-making habit. With God's help and an honest apology it is not hard to make a potential bitter enemy into a long-time friend. And I have had considerable experience in doing just this. One of my more recent experiences was to forgive and ask for forgiveness from a man who had double-crossed me. When we are led to turn enemies into friends by acting before they become real enemies, we avoid the pit of hatred and costly war.

I am still only a simple engineer and lay person unschooled formally in spiritual matters. Nonetheless, my eighty four years of experience have contained lessons that others perhaps will find to be worth further study and verification in their own lives and that they can then pass on to their fellow human beings. Life's journey—indeed, the earth's—is long and hard and its negative prospects awesome. Many causes receiving publicity today are well intentioned and have much appeal and certainly some merit. But my basic questions remain: Is our spaceship Earth, with some six billion people aboard, drifting off into obscurity in a self-destruct fashion, or is there a Creator with a plan looking after it? Can we learn about this plan and have a part in helping it to come about?

Each of us should have the right to be a true optimist, especially if we are willing to study, work, and dedicate ourselves to the divine plan for our individual lives and for our world. But first we must believe.

To believe alone is not enough, though. To be effective, belief must be translated into decision and decision into commitment. Finally, commitment must be translated into both individual and group action designed to greatly improve the way we live together. It must also conserve and care for the numerous gifts bestowed upon us.

To undertake these awesome tasks using only our human thinking would be folly, for it is flawed with prejudice, hate, and greed. We need instead to see and be led by the Creator's wisdom and become proficient at distinguishing the difference between this higher wisdom and our flawed human thinking. This is not an easy task. Perhaps one promising way to begin is to join the movement for establishing small fellowship groups within churches that are dedicated to the remaking of the world one person at a time.

John 20 - The Living Bible

[24] One of the disciples, Thomas, "The Twin," was not there at the time with the others. [25] When they kept telling him, "We have seen the Lord," he replied, "I won't believe it unless I see the nail wounds in his hands—and put my fingers into them—and place my hand into his side." [26] Eight days later the disciples were together again, and this time Thomas was with them. The doors were locked; but suddenly, as before, Jesus was standing among them and greeting them. [27] Then he said to Thomas, "Put you finger into my hands. Put your hand into my side. Don't be faithless any longer. Believe!" [28] "My Lord and my God!" Thomas said. [29] Then Jesus told him, "You believe because you have seen me. But blessed are those who haven't seen me and believe anyway." [30,31] Jesus' disciples saw him do many other miracles besides the ones told about in this book, but these are recorded so that you will believe that he is the Messiah, the Son of God, and that believing in him you will have life.

Bibliography

	The Living Bible (Large Print)	Tyndale House Pub.
Garth Lean	On The Tail of a Comet	Helmers & Howard
Oral Roberts	Expect a Miracle	Thomas Nelson Pub.
Oral Roberts	Oral Roberts Miracle Ministry	O.R. Univ., Tulsa
Richard Roberts	The Joy Of The Lord	O.R. Univ., Tulsa
Billy Graham	The Collected Works of Billy Graham	Int'l Press
Leonard Le Sourd	The Best of Catherine Marshall	Chosen Books
Pat Robertson	The New World Order	Word Publishing
Pat Robertson	The End of The Age	Word Publishing
Robert H Schuller	Prayer: My Soul's Adventure w/God	Harper
Robert A Schuller	What Happens to Good People...	Revell
Bruce Larson	Thirty Days to a New You	Crystal Cathedral Min
Francis MacNutt	Overcome by the Spirit	Chosen Books
Lloyd J. Ogilvie	Greatest Counselor in the World	Servant Publications
Gary Smalley	The Hidden Value of a Man	Focus on the Family
E Glenn Wagner	The Awesome Power of Shared Beliefs	Word Pub.
Norman V Peale	The Power of Positive Thinking	Ct. For Positive Think
T. Willard Hunter	The Spirit of Charles Lindberg	Madison Books
T. Willard Hunter	It Started Right There AA & MRA	Grosvenor Books
J. Lester & P. Spoerri	Rediscovering Freedom	Grosvenor Books
Michael Henderson	All Her Paths Are Peace	Kumarian Press
Ian Mayo-Smith	Poems, Essays & Comments for Everyone	Kumarian Press
Joan W. Anderson	Where Miracles Happen	Guideposts Carmel
Ben Carson	Gifted Hands	Zondervan Pub. House
Og Mandino	The Greatest Salesman in the World	Bantam Books
Og Mandino	Mission Success	Bantam Books
Og Mandino	The Christ Commission	Bantam Books
Daniel J. Boorstin	The Creators	Random House
Hugh Ross	The Creator and the Cosmos	Nav Press
J.C. Polkinghouse	Science & Creation—Search for...	Random House
H. Norman Wright	Quiet Times for Couples	(Family Book Store)
Klaus Brock Muehl	Listening to the God who Speaks	Helmers & Howard
Charleton Heston	2 part video of Bible as told in Isreal	Readers' Digest

To order additional copies of

Toward a Better World

have your credit card ready and call

1-800-917-BOOK

Book price $15.00
Shipping $3.95